dBASE II for Every Business

by

Robert A. Byers

Reston Publishing Company
11480 Sunset Hills Road
Reston, Virginia 22090

ASHTON·TATE
10150 W. Jefferson Boulevard
Culver City, CA 90230
(213) 204-5570

Cover design: D.A. Gray
Cover illustration: D.A. Lee
Production Manager/Designer: Thomas Clark

Editors: Monet Thompson, Marv Lincoln,
Technical Editors: Jim Warner, Steve Kurasch
Publications Director: Jane Mellin

ISBN 0-912677-03-1

TABLE OF CONTENTS

Continued on next page

Continued on next page

ASHTON·TATE

ACKNOWLEDGEMENT

Writing a book is far from being a one-man show. Although the author gets all of the credit, it takes a team and teamwork to produce a book. Quite a few people have worked very hard to produce this one. My thanks to all. In particular, I'd like to thank Monet Thomson who has done the bulk of the editing, Steve Kurasch for his review of the programs, and Marv Lincoln who did his very best to keep me on some kind of schedule. Jane Mellin deserves a great deal of credit for getting the enterprise off on a positive and organized note. Thanks also go to my son Ken, my daughter Lauren, and my very special friend Charlene Ebert for their patience these past few months.

—Robert A. Byers

ASHTON·TATE

ASHTON·TATE

INTRODUCTION

This book is intended for people who want to write programs using dBASE II. In a very real sense it is a sequel to Ashton-Tate's *Everyman's Database Primer*. To gain the most from this book you should have either completed the *Primer* or have some background in dBASE II.

The book is divided into three sections. The three chapters in Section One review dBASE II fundamentals and provide the foundation for the remainder of the book. There are no references back to the Primer or to the dBASE II manual.

The second and largest section consists of seven chapters that describe the application of dBASE II to a series of business problems. We build a foundation for a business software system with a series of programs for customer files, mailing lists and labels, and inventory management. With this foundation we then attack the more dynamic problems associated with sales order entry, order fulfillment, and billing.

The programs in the second section have a dual function. Each solves a simple business problem and all showcase the dBASE II programming language. In so doing, they provide the reader with programming examples. The primary purpose of the programs is to show the reader how to go about writing a dBASE II program to solve a specific problem. The software system itself does not purport to be complete.

The text and programs are illustrated by screens and figures. When it is necessary to break program lines in the text, a block element — ■ — has been placed where the program line is broken. In the programs memory variables have been lowercased so that you can distinguish them from file and field names. In the text, memory variables have been italicized.

Always use the single quote (' apostrophe) or the double quote (") on either side of your character strings in programming. Our typeset material shows closed and open quotes in the text portions, when illustrating programming points. However, you should use the quotes on your computer keyboard when you write your programs. *Never* use the accent mark.

The last section consists of four chapters. It deals with special topics and tricks, and generic discussions of such things as getting the most from the REPORT command and dealing with the date as a data type. The reader should look for tricks in coding in the programs themselves.

The emphasis in the book is really on learning by doing — most of us learn best when we are actually trying to accomplish something. One of the best ways to learn is to look at how someone else has solved a problem, and then to adapt that solution to meet our needs. Our adaptation itself becomes unique and may, in turn, become the model for the next problem solver.

ASHTON·TATE

Section One

Fundamentals of dBASE II

ASHTON·TATE

ASHTON·TATE

Chapter One

DATABASE BASICS

Nearly every business or profession requires some orderly system for the storage and retrieval of information. Gone are the days of mental reckoning; even small, homegrown businesses today can profit from efficient data management systems. Certainly one of the most profitable uses for a microcomputer is database management.

A database is nothing more than a set of data which is organized so that it can be used for some purpose. One familiar example of a database is a telephone directory, a set of data organized so that we can easily find telephone numbers. Another familiar example is the card index system at the library. These databases serve the larger purpose of making the telephone and library systems useable.

Businesses and other organizations have their own kinds of databases: customer files, personnel files, inventories, sales records, tax tables, etc. Schools have student records, class rosters, employee files, inventories, attendance reports. All these databases make it possible to operate a business or organization.

Most databases are set up as tables with rows and columns — a way of organizing information that we have all used and intuitively understand. The telephone directory, for example, is organized in this way.

NAME	ADDRESS	PHONE
Cassidy, B.	2 Sundance Ct., Burbank	398-8923
Day, E. Z.	123 Languid Ln., Glendale	555-1234
Johnson, A.	8931 14th St., Pasadena	799-4309

Until the computer era, all databases were stored on paper in ledgers or filing cabinets. Creating, changing, storing and retrieving data from these paper databases required actual physical manipulation. With computer databases, information is stored as magnetic domains on a disk. Since we can no longer *physically* touch the data using a computer, we need a way of working with it. Our vehicle is a form of computer software — a

Database Management System (DBMS). dBASE II, which we will discuss in this book, is a popular DBMS. Once you have learned the preliminary or basic commands, a database management system allows you to manipulate large amounts of data much more easily than you can with paper databases.

Like most database management systems, dBASE II organizes data in rows and columns. The columns are called *fields*. The rows are called *records*. The column titles are called *fieldnames*. A DBMS is composed of several functional parts as shown in **Figure 1**.

Two or more databases are often used together. For example, suppose we have a database of students and another of teachers, as shown in **Figure 2**. We can find out Tommy Jones' teacher by cross referencing the two database tables on Tommy's room number. When we do this we are relating the information in one table to that in another. This is a simple concept that we use all the time.

A database management system that uses data organized as rows and columns and that allows us to relate (cross reference) data from separate database tables is called a *relational* system. dBASE II is a relational database management system.

In a sense, a database management system is a little like a stock boy in a supermarket: it takes care of all of the routine chores associated with storing, maintaining, deleting, changing and retrieving data. Three "languages" are normally provided to allow you to "talk" to this versatile worker.

- The data definition language provides you with a capability to *create and change the structure* of a database. In a relational system like dBASE II, the structure consists of the fieldnames, the size of each field (fieldwidth), and the kind of data to be stored in each field (fieldtype).
- The data manipulation language allows you to *alter the contents* of the database. Adding, editing, and deleting records are the province of the DML.
- The query language provides the ability to *locate and retrieve data* for your own purposes or to interface the system to an applications program.
- The report writer provides a standard capability to extract data from the database to produce either printed or screen displays.

In dBASE II the three "language" elements and the report writer are combined into an integrated package called the "Applications Development Language" (ADL). Most people just call it dBASE II. To get started in dBASE II you need to learn a little terminology.

dBASE II Basic Terminology

When you are ready to begin entering your data into the computer, you will need to set up a file. You do so by giving your file a name, establishing the record structure, and telling the computer the type and width of each field. dBASE II has built-in prompts to assist you in creating your file.

Database Names

dBASE II databases are stored on disk as disk files. Each file has a unique name called a filename. Since dBASE II must work through the computer's operating system when storing or retrieving database information, it must conform to the operating system's rules for filenames. Fortunately for users, most major operating systems have compatible rules for filenames.

Filenames may have *eight* or fewer characters. They must begin with a letter and cannot have embedded blank spaces.

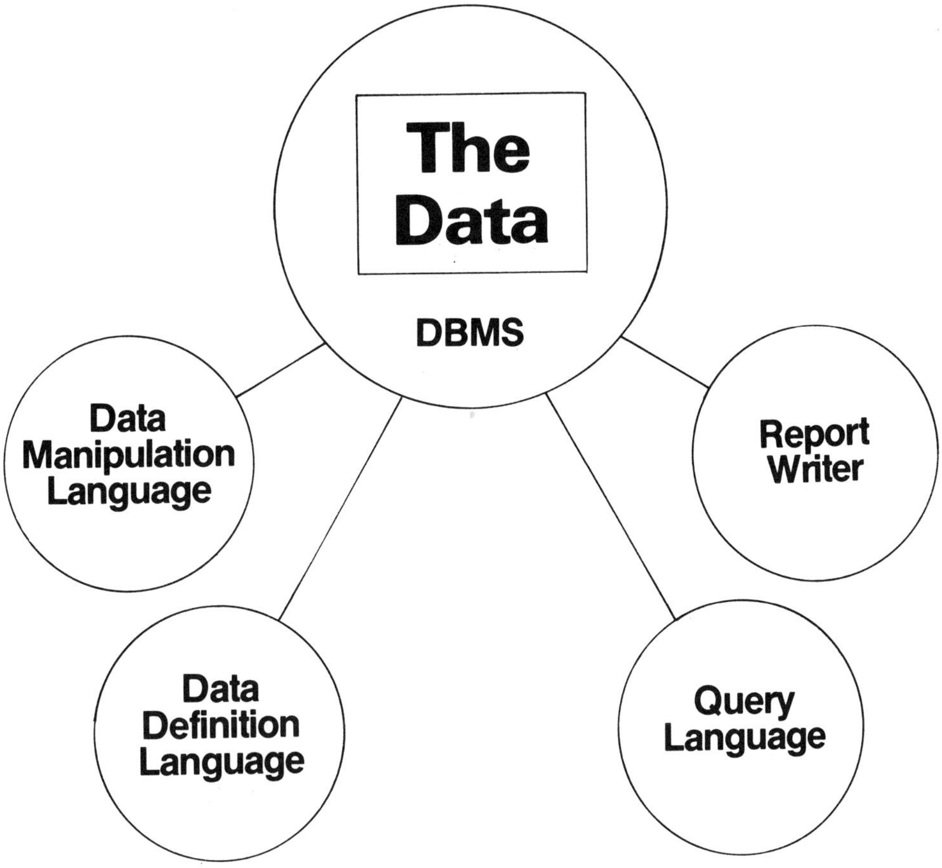

Figure 1. Pictorial diagram of DBMS

Student's Name	Room	Grade
Aardvark, Angela	13	1
Beaver, Eager	26	1
Codfish, Calvin	15	2
Jones, Tommy	20	3

Teacher's Name	Room	Grade
Brown, Will	25	1
Newton, Mary	16	2
Plato, Peter	13	1
"	"	"
"	"	"

Figure 2. Relational Database Example

Good file names:	DATASET1 DATABASE ALPHA
Bad file names:	12A1 DATA SET

To go back to our phone book example, we might name such a file "PHONEBK."

Fieldnames

The rules for fieldnames (column titles) are similar to those for filenames. A fieldname may have *ten* or fewer letters and numbers. It must begin with a letter and may not contain embedded blank spaces. In our phone book example, the fieldnames would be "name," "address," and "phone."

Fieldtype

The fieldtype determines the kind of data that may be stored in a field. There are three fieldtypes: character, numeric, and logical.

Character fields may contain anything that can be entered from the keyboard: letters, numbers, blanks, and symbols. A telephone number could be a character field because there is no need to do arithmetic with it.

Numeric fields may contain numbers, a decimal point, and a minus sign. Numbers can be either integer or decimal. Numeric fields are used when arithmetic is to be done on a field.

Logical fields may contain either T and F or Y and N (true or false, yes or no). They are used for those fields where the stored value can be only one of two possibilities. For example, with our PHONEBK file, we could set up a field named "current." Then if we asked the computer if the number was current, we could retrieve data from that field as Y or N (current or not current), depending on which had been entered for that record.

Fieldwidth

The fieldwidth is simply the number of equivalent typewriter spaces in the column. The fieldwidth of a Logical field is always one. Otherwise, setting up fieldwidth is a matter of estimating the widest you think a field will need to be.

Basic Command Vocabulary

One of the advantages of dBASE II is that you can make profitable use of it without really knowing very much about it. dBASE II is a command-oriented DBMS. This means you must tell it what you want it to do. When you are ready to work with your file, you can work with it interactively from the keyboard — performing all of the basic database functions — using only a very limited vocabulary. The basic command vocabulary consists of only 20 words.

CREATE	SORT	DELETE
USE	INDEX	RECALL
APPEND	LOCATE	PACK
DISPLAY	FIND	REPORT
LIST	EDIT	QUIT
SUM	COUNT	COPY
FOR	REPLACE	

These command words do just what each implies. To get a better feel for how they are used and what they actually do, we will create a database that contains the data shown in **Figure 3**. This sample database contains only five records, but it

PART NAME	QTY	MIN STOCK	UNIT PRICE
HAMMER, 16 OZ CLAW	6	6	10.88
WRENCH, 5/8 BOX	4	6	4.29
WRENCH, 3/4 BOX	8	5	6.19
HAMMER, 10 OZ BALL	5	3	8.15
PLIERS, 8 IN GAS	11	5	3.89

Figure 3. Sample database

is adequate to demonstrate the use of the basic vocabulary. All of the database operations are the same whether we have five records or 50,000.

The Operating System

Your microcomputer database management system is a program which runs under the microcomputer's operating system. It follows rules which are dictated by the operating system, such as the structure of database names (filenames). It works in conjunction with the operating system, and in most cases isolates you from the peculiarities of a particular system.

dBASE II works with the following microcomputer operating systems:

CP/M®
CP/M-86™
PC DOS™
MS DOS™
TRSDOS™
CONCURRENT CP/M

For the most part, while you are using dBASE II, you will not be aware of any differences between these operating systems. There are a few differences, however, of which you will need to be aware. Whenever we encounter an area where operating system differences affect dBASE II we will point them out.

Using dBASE II

In all of the above operating systems, the operating system prompt will appear at the far left side of your video terminal and will look like:

A>

To use dBASE II, first type in the characters DBASE after the operating system prompt.

A>DBASE

Then press <RETURN> (or ENTER, etc., depending on your computer). This causes the program DBASE.COM to be loaded into your computer's memory. When dBASE II has been loaded the screen will display:

PLEASE ENTER THE DATE OR RETURN
■ FOR NONE
(MM/DD/YY):

After the date has been entered, the screen displays (for version 2.4, for example) :

*** dBASE II Ver 2.4 26 Mar 1983

The "period" under the asterisks is called a dot prompt. It is dBASE II's way of telling you that it is ready to accept commands.

To get dBASE II to do something useful we first need a database. To create a database with dBASE II we type the word CREATE after a dot prompt; the computer will respond by asking for a filename. The dialogue with dBASE II that defines our database is shown in **Screen 1**. The B: which precedes the filename SAMPLE indicates to dBASE II that the file is to be stored on the B disk drive.

First we have to set our file structure. Each of the fields of the database is defined by entering the fieldname, the fieldtype, and the fieldwidth — each separated by commas with no spaces. Fieldtype is designated by a C for character, N for numeric, and L for logical. (Note that we only entered a decimal in Field 4, PRICE.) dBASE II

```
 . CREATE

ENTER FILENAME: B:SAMPLE

ENTER RECORD STRUCTURE AS FOLLOWS:
 FIELD    NAME,TYPE,WIDTH,DECIMAL PLACES
 001      PARTNAME,C,20
 002      QTY,N,3
 003      MINSTOCK,N,3
 004      PRICE,N,7,2
 005
INPUT DATA NOW? Y
```

Screen 1. Example of creating a database

assumes there are no decimals unless otherwise instructed.

We indicate that we have finished defining fields by entering <RETURN> when prompted to enter a field. In this case we enter <RETURN> when prompted for the definition of Field 5.

In the example we have indicated that we want to enter the data immediately. As soon as the Y is entered after "INPUT DATA NOW?" the screen will clear and you will be presented with the display shown in **Screen 2**.

The cursor, which we will indicate with a " ^ ", is positioned for you to enter the partname. To enter data you need only type in the data as desired. The cursor will only move within the areas on the screen delimited by the colons, which is the width you established when you set up the file. Pressing the <RETURN> key instead of entering the partname will terminate the data entry process and return you to the dBASE II command level (i.e. a dot prompt). If you should make an error while entering the data you can move the cursor around on the screen by using the control key in conjunction with the E, S, D, and X keys. The control key is used like the shift key. Pressing Control while pressing the E key will move the cursor one field toward the top of the screen. Control X will move the cursor one field toward the bottom of the screen. Control S will move the cursor one character position left, and Control D will move the cursor one character position right.

When the data entry process associated with CREATE is terminated, the database file is closed. At this point you are no longer using any database. To use an existing database, type USE followed by the disk drive identifier and a filename.

```
. USE B: SAMPLE
```

The USE command closes any file that you may have been using and opens the file you have named. In this case you have opened the file SAMPLE located on the B disk drive.

To add additional records to an existing database, use the command APPEND.

```
. APPEND
```

APPEND presents you with a display identical to that shown in Screen 2 except that the record number will be that of the record you are adding.

DISPLAY and LIST allow you to look at records in the database. LIST displays all of the records in the database in use. This is demonstrated in **Screen 3**. The numbers in the far left column are the database record numbers. DISPLAY ALL produces a result similar to that of LIST except the resulting display pauses after every 15 records.

The DISPLAY command displays the current record. In this case the database is positioned to the last record because of the use of LIST. DISPLAY is illustrated by **Screen 4**.

LIST, DISPLAY and many other commands can be enhanced or made more specific as shown in **Screen 5**. In the two examples shown in this screen, we have limited the display to those records which met a specified condition. In the first, we look at only those records where the content of the field PARTNAME begins with HAMMER. Note that HAMMER is enclosed by apostrophes. The apostrophe in this case is called a DELIMITER. In the second example we are comparing the contents of two fields QTY and MINSTOCK. The display shows only the record where the content of the field QTY is less than the content of the field MINSTOCK.

We can also show only selected fields by naming the fields to be displayed. This technique can be combined with the last example; see **Screen 6**.

Note that in this example we also displayed the results of an operation done on two fields. We have multiplied (*) the contents of the field QTY by the

```
RECORD #00001
PARTNAME  :^                        :
QTY       :   :
MINSTOCK  :   :
PRICE     :        :
```

Screen 2. Example of standard data entry screen

```
. LIST

00001  HAMMER, 16 OZ CLAW      6    6     10.88
00002  WRENCH, 5/8 BOX         4    6      4.29
00003  WRENCH, 3/4 BOX         8    5      6.19
00004  HAMMER, 10 OZ BALL      5    3      8.15
00005  PLIERS, 8 IN GAS       11    5      3.89
```

Screen 3. Listing of contents of sample database

```
. DISPLAY
00005  PLIERS, 8 IN GAS        11    5     3.89
```

Screen 4. Example of the DISPLAY command

```
  . DISPLAY FOR PARTNAME='HAMMER'
00001  HAMMER, 16 OZ CLAW       6    6     10.88
00004  HAMMER, 10 OZ BALL       5    3      8.15

  . DISPLAY FOR QTY<MINSTOCK
00002  WRENCH, 5/8 BOX          4    6      4.29
```

Screen 5. Example of the DISPLAY FOR command

```
. DISPLAY ALL PARTNAME,QTY,UNITPRICE,QTY*UNITPRICE
00001   HAMMER, 16 OZ CLAW        6    10.88       65.28
00002   WRENCH, 5/8 BOX           4     4.29       17.16
00003   WRENCH, 3/4 BOX           8     6.19       49.52
00004   HAMMER, 10 OZ BALL        5     8.15       40.75
00005   PLIERS, 8 IN GAS         11     3.89       42.79
```

Screen 6. Example of selective field display

contents of the field UNITPRICE and displayed the result in the right column.

Note also that the records are displayed in the order they were entered. If you wish to have the records in a database file rearranged in some order — whether alphabetical or numeric — you can do so with the commands SORT and INDEX.

An alphabetical sort on the field PARTNAME is shown in **Screen 7**. Sorting creates a new database file, which in this case we have named INVENTRY and located on disk B. Note that the items are now in alphabetical order by part name and that the record numbers for each part are different than they were in our original database SAMPLE.

An alternative method for sorting the data is shown in **Screen 8**. This technique is called INDEXING. Indexing creates a new file called an INDEX file, but maintains a relationship between items we are interested in and the record number. Note that in this example the part names also appear in alphabetical order, yet the record numbers are the same as in the original file SAMPLE.

When you are working with a file and cannot remember the name of a field, you can use DISPLAY STRUCTURE, as shown in **Screen 9**, to give you the database fieldnames. Note that DISPLAY STRUCTURE also shows you the number of records, the last time you changed the database (if you entered the date as asked or if you have an IBM PC), and the total number of bytes in a record. You should note that the total number of bytes may be one more than the sum of the bytes for each field in order to allow for the delete asterisk. This can become significant if you have a large number of records or are copying records onto another disk.

The SUM command will add the contents of a numeric field or an expression involving fields as shown in **Screen 10**. SUM can also be used with a condition such as SUM FOR PARTNAME = 'WRENCH'.

COUNT will count the number of records which meet a specified condition. This is illustrated by **Screen 11**.

COPY will copy all or part of a database to another database. This is illustrated by **Screen 12**. COPY becomes an important command when you want to revise the field structure of a file without losing any of the records in the file.

The REPORT command provides a powerful method for preparing formal formatted reports on the contents of the database. An example of REPORT is shown in **Figure 4**. A report is prepared by answering a series of simple questions. The report preparation is shown in **Screen 13**. A report can be directed to a printer by simply typing REPORT TO PRINT. The REPORT command will be covered in more detail in Section III.

Editing a record requires either that you know the record number of the record you wish to edit or that you are positioned at the record already. You can determine the record number by using the DISPLAY command or you can use the LOCATE or FIND commands. The FIND command can only be used with an indexed database. These two commands are illustrated in **Screen 14**.

Note that the LOCATE command returned with the record number of the desired record. The database is then positioned to Record 5. Had the record not been located, the computer's response would have been END OF FILE ENCOUNTERED. The FIND command returned with a simple dot prompt. This indicates that the record was found and the database is properly positioned. Had the record not been found the response would have been NO FIND. In both cases we can edit the record by using the dBASE II command EDIT A, which allows us to edit the current record. If you do know the number of a record, you can just say EDIT and the number. EDIT 3, for example, would cause dBASE II to edit Record 3.

EDIT invokes a screen display which is identical

```
  . SORT ON PARTNAME TO B:INVENTRY
SORT COMPLETE
  . USE INVENTRY
  . LIST
00001  HAMMER, 10 OZ BALL      5    3     8.15
00002  HAMMER, 16 OZ CLAW      6    6    10.88
00003  PLIERS, 8 IN GAS       11    5     3.89
00004  WRENCH, 3/4 BOX         8    5     6.19
00005  WRENCH, 5/8 BOX         4    6     4.29
```

Screen 7. Example of sorting on a field — PARTNAME

```
  . USE B:SAMPLE
  . INDEX ON PARTNAME TO INVENTRY
00005 RECORDS INDEXED
  . LIST
00004  HAMMER, 10 OZ BALL      5    3     8.15
00001  HAMMER, 16 OZ CLAW      6    6    10.88
00005  PLIERS, 8 IN GAS       11    5     3.89
00003  WRENCH, 3/4 BOX         8    5     6.19
00002  WRENCH, 5/8 BOX         4    6     4.29
```

Screen 8. Example of indexing a database

```
 . DISP STRU
STRUCTURE FOR FILE:  B:SAMPLE .DBF
NUMBER OF RECORDS:   00005
DATE OF LAST UPDATE: 05/10/83
PRIMARY USE DATABASE
FLD       NAME       TYPE WIDTH   DEC
001      PARTNAME      C    020
002      QTY           N    003
003      MINSTOCK      N    003
004      UNITPRICE     N    007    002
** TOTAL **               00034
```

Screen 9. Example of DISPLAY STRUCTURE

```
. SUM QTY*UNITPRICE
215.50

. SUM QTY
34
```

Screen 10. Example of the SUM command

```
  . COUNT FOR PARTNAME='WRENCH'
COUNT = 00002
```

Screen 11. Example of COUNT command

```
  .COPY FIELD PARTNAME,UNITPRICE TO TEMPFILE
00005 RECORDS COPIED.
```

Screen 12. Example of COPY command

```
PAGE NO. 00001
05/10/83

                         SAMPLE DATABASE REPORT


      PART NAME        QTY MIN    UNIT PRICE STOCKVALUE
                           STOCK

HAMMER, 10 OZ BALL      5     3         8.15      40.75
HAMMER, 16 OZ CLAW      6     6        10.88      65.28
PLIERS, 8 IN GAS       11     5         3.89      42.79
WRENCH, 3/4 BOX         8     5         6.19      49.52
WRENCH, 5/8 BOX         4     6         4.29      17.16
** TOTAL **
                       34                        215.50
```

Figure 4. Example of a dBASEII report

```
 . REPORT
ENTER REPORT FORM NAME: B:SAMPLE
ENTER OPTIONS, M=LEFT MARGIN, L=LINES/PAGE. W=PAGE WIDTH
PAGE HEADING? (Y/N) Y
ENTER PAGE HEADING: SAMPLE DATABASE REPORT
DOUBLE SPACE REPORT? (Y/N) N
ARE TOTALS REQUIRED? (Y/N) Y
SUBTOTALS IN REPORT? (Y/N) N
SUMMARY REPORT ONLY? (Y/N) N
COL      WIDTH,CONTENTS
001      20,PARTNAME
ENTER HEADING: PART NAME
002      3 QTY
ENTER HEADING: QTY
ARE TOTALS REQUIRED? (Y/N) Y
003      5,MINSTOCK
ENTER HEADING: MIN  STOCK
ARE TOTALS REQUIRED? (Y/N) N
004      10,UNITPRICE
ENTER HEADING: UNIT PRICE
ARE TOTALS REQUIRED? (Y/N) N
005      10.QTY*UNITPRICE
ENTER HEADING: STOCKVALUE
ARE TOTALS REQUIRED? (Y/N) Y
006
```

Screen 13. Example of report preparation

```
   . LOCATE FOR PARTNAME='PLIERS'
RECORD: 00005

   . FIND PLIERS
   .
```

Screen 14. Example of locating a record

to APPEND. The cursor can be moved about on the screen by use of the Control Keys as described above. In addition, we can move backward a record at a time by use of Control R or forward a record at a time by use of Control C. Control W terminates the EDIT process.

Another command from our basic vocabulary that will change the contents of our sample database is REPLACE. REPLACE can change the contents of a single record, all the records, or some of the records based on a condition. To illustrate, suppose that we want to increase the unit price (UNITPRICE) of wrenches by 10 percent. The process for doing this is shown in **Screen 15**.

Deleting records is a two step process. The DELETE command marks a record for deletion, then PACK actually removes the record. If you change your mind, you can "unmark" a record with the command RECALL. These three commands are demonstrated in **Screen 16**.

When you are finished with dBASE II, typing QUIT after a dot prompt will close all open files and return you to the operating system as shown in **Screen 17**.

dBASE II as a Programming Language

As we have seen in this quick overview of the basic dBASE II vocabulary, the individual commands are simple and powerful. The technical term for these commands is *Non-Procedural*. Conventional programming languages such as BASIC, PL/I, FORTRAN, and COBOL are *Procedural*; that is, you have to provide a sequence of instructions (a program) to accomplish the results that we have achieved with simple one-line commands.

dBASE II has both procedural and non-procedural features. It is a structured language similar in some ways to the "modern" languages PL/I and Pascal. At the same time it has many of the "teaching" features of BASIC. It is an interpreter, in that we can set up pieces or sections of our program from the keyboard to test our methodology. This ability to accept commands from the keyboard makes dBASE II particularly easy to learn.

Some experts have estimated that between 50 and 80 percent of traditional programs are devoted to the tasks of storing and managing data, preparing reports, and handling screens. In dBASE II much of this is already done for you, reducing the programming task in dBASE II down to about 20 percent. dBASE II also provides an enormous array of tools for you to work with while programming.

What, then, are the disadvantages? There are two. First of all, dBASE II does not handle higher math, only business math (through Version 2.4). If the transcendental functions are important to you, dBASE II may not meet your needs.

A second disadvantage is that dBASE II is slow when compared to FORTRAN and PL/1. This is part of the tradeoff you have to make: you trade speed for power and ease of use. Speed is of extreme importance in the traditional large computer world where operations costs can average as high as 56 cents per CPU second. In the micro world, reduced speed can be irritating at times, but is of little importance. Also, speed is relative. Adding two numbers together can take about 7 milliseconds in dBASE II. By many standards, that's pretty slow. On the other hand, it seems virtually instantaneous to the computer user.

All in all, for the computer beginner, dBASE II is a terrific first language. Much of the dog work of programming is already done for you: the DBMS part of the language takes care of managing data files, screen handling is simple and direct, and the report writer will produce much of the needed paper output —so you can concentrate on learning those things which will allow you to produce a

```
  . REPLACE UNITPRICE WITH UNITPRICE*1.1 FOR PARTNAME='WRENCH'
00002 REPLACEMENTS

  . DISPLAY FOR PARTNAME='WRENCH'
00004  WRENCH, 3/4 BOX        8    5     6.80
00005  WRENCH, 5/8 BOX        4    6     4.71
```

Screen 15. Example of REPLACE command

```
   . DELETE FOR PARTNAME='HAMMER'
00002 DELETION(S)

    RECALL FOR PARTNAME='HAMMER, 16 OZ'
00001 RECALL(S)

   . PACK
PACK COMPLETE, 00004 RECORDS COPIED
REINDEXING INDEX FILE - B:INVENTRY.NDX
00004 RECORDS INDEXED
```

Screen 16. Example of record deletion

```
  . QUIT
*** END RUN     dBASE II     ***

A>
```

Screen 17. Getting out of dBASE II

specialized application. You can learn a little at a time and still produce a significantly useful result at any point. Sooner or later, you'll learn how to use dBASE II's tools to make the computer really perform for you. With programming, you get better results more quickly and with less effort.

Let's face it: The whole idea is to have the computer really help us in our daily business, not just to produce neat computer programs. dBASE II can improve your productivity even if you are an experienced computer professional. Since time is money, this improvement in productivity is money in your pocket. Even if recoding to a faster language becomes necessary, you can still use dBASE II as a design language. Most design languages are really syntax checkers — you can use dBASE II to test the logic. Design and testing are the major time-consuming elements in programming. Coding (especially recoding) is of relatively little consequence.

In Chapter Two, we will look at beginning programming.

A Short History of dBASE II

dBASE II's legacy dates back to the mid-1960's and a management information system called RETRIEVE, which was marketed by Tymshare Corporation. The Jet Propulsion Laboratory in Pasadena, Calif., used RETRIEVE until the late 1960's, when it purchased three UNIVAC 1108 computers. Jeb Long, a new programmer at JPL, was assigned the task of writing a program which would perform the same functions as RETRIEVE. The new file management system Long developed was called JPLDIS. This system continued to evolve over the next several years and is still used on many UNIVAC 1100 class computers.

In the late 1970's, Wayne Ratliff, who worked at JPL under a contract with Martin Marietta, became interested in microcomputers. Ratliff was a friend of Jeb's, and began to develop a system which, for the user, was very much like JPLDIS. The story goes that Wayne developed the initial version of his micro database system to help him win at football pools! Wayne marketed this micro version of JPLDIS himself, under the name VULCAN.

Though VULCAN rapidly evolved to the point where it had its own personality and character, customer sales did not follow: by 1980 there were only about 60 customers of VULCAN. Then an entrepreneur named George Tate entered the scene after seeing an ad for VULCAN in a computer publication. Soon VULCAN got a new name — dBASE II — and a new company, Ashton-Tate, was formed to market it. The rest is history.

ASHTON·TATE

Chapter Two

BEGINNING TO PROGRAM

If you're new to programming, you will find that it's not really difficult — "even a grown-up can learn to do it."

To give you the idea, let's suppose that we have a database called SCHOOL consisting of information on elementary school students. For the rest of this chapter we are going to discuss programs that count the students. If you are already familiar with the fundamentals of programming with dBASE II, you can skip the rest of this chapter and go on to Chapter Three.

Of course, one method of counting the students grade by grade is directly from the keyboard, as in **Screen 1**.

Or, we could write a simple dBASE II program like **Program 1**.

There isn't any practical difference between typing commands one at a time from the keyboard and typing them into a program.

dBASE II programs are called COMMAND FILES. To write a program, you simply type the commands into the computer using a word processor such as WordStar® or the dBASE II tool provided for just this purpose — MODIFY COMMAND.

When we use MODIFY COMMAND, the computer will ask us for a program name which must adhere to the standard rules for filenames. MODIFY COMMAND will add the characters .PRG (for IBM PC type computers) or .CMD (for CP/M computers) to the end of the filename. These characters indicate to dBASE II that the file is a program.

Once the filename has been entered, the screen will clear and the cursor will be positioned at the top. You can then type in the commands one line at a time as shown in Program 1. CANCEL indicates the end of the program.

When you finish typing in the commands, press Control-W to save the file on the disk.

Another way to write programs is to use a word processing program. Most word processors have a special mode for writing programs. In WordStar this is the "non-document" mode — Option N. Strange things can happen if you accidentally

```
. USE SCHOOL
. COUNT FOR GRADE='1'
78
. COUNT FOR GRADE='2'
81
. COUNT FOR GRADE='3'
79
. COUNT FOR GRADE='4'
74
. COUNT FOR GRADE='5'
80
. COUNT FOR GRADE='6'
81
```

Screen 1. Example of dBASE II COUNT command

```
USE SCHOOL
COUNT FOR GRADE='1'
COUNT FOR GRADE='2'
COUNT FOR GRADE='3'
COUNT FOR GRADE='4'
COUNT FOR GRADE='5'
COUNT FOR GRADE='6'
CANCEL
```

Program 1. Example of simple counting program: COUNTER

```
SET ECHO ON
USE SCHOOL
COUNT FOR GRADE='1'
COUNT FOR GRADE='2'
COUNT FOR GRADE='3'
COUNT FOR GRADE='4'
COUNT FOR GRADE='5'
COUNT FOR GRADE='6'
SET ECHO OFF
CANCEL
```

Program 2. Example of simple counting program: COUNTER, commands displayed

write a program using the normal document mode — Option D. If you suspect that you have written a program using the document mode, you can copy your program back to itself using PIP with the Z option. If you use a different word processor, consult your user's manual to be sure that you are using the proper mode.

How do we get dBASE II to run a program? This is accomplished by using the command DO followed by the program's filename. We can run the program named COUNTER by typing DO COUNTER after a dot prompt.

When our program has finished, ***DO CANCELLED appears on the screen and dBASE II returns to its keyboard mode. The dot prompt appears on the line following the ***DO CANCELLED. The computer execution of our sample program would look like **Screen 2**.

In its normal keyboard mode dBASE II conducts a two-way dialogue with you. You type in a command, it prints out its response. Both the command and the response are visible on the screen. However, when a program is run, the commands are not normally displayed — only the responses are.

If you want to combine command and response, use the SET ECHO ON/OFF command. SET ECHO ON allows us to see the commands exactly as we've written them in the program.

Program 2 will generate **Screen 3**.

At this point we are going to digress from our development of programming examples and briefly discuss the syntax of dBASE II commands.

dBASE II Command Structure

Commands must be entered in the proper syntax. Each dBASE II command begins with a verb (the basic command). Many commands can also have modifiers to tailor the command to meet some particular need. For example:

DISPLAY [scope] [<exp list>] [FOR >exp>]
■ [OFF]

This is the syntax of the DISPLAY command. The square brackets indicate that the enclosed item is optional. When DISPLAY is used without any modifiers, it displays only the current record in the database.

SCOPE is the amount of the database the command applies to. If not specified, the scope defaults to the current record or ALL (the entire database). Permitted syntax for scope is either ALL or NEXT n, where n is a number. If the optional FOR clause is used the scope always defaults to ALL unless you restrict the scope by using NEXT n.

<exp list> allows you to specify what you want displayed. Each command that allows you to specify the <exp list> defaults to either all or nothing. You can specify FIELDNAMES, *memvars* (see below), operations on fields and memvars, and text enclosed by delimiters. An example of an <exp list> is:

NAME, ROOM, GRADE, SCORE*100,
■ 'student data'

FOR <exp> allows you to specify which records the command logically applies to. The expression involves a comparison of the contents of one or more fields. An example of an expression to be used in a FOR clause is:

FOR GRADE = '6' .AND. ROOM = '11'

There are two comparisons in the example. The contents of the field GRADE are compared with '6'

```
. DO COUNTER
78
81
79
74
80
81
*** DO CANCELLED
```

Screen 2. Execution of COUNTER program

```
COUNT FOR GRADE='1'
  78
COUNT FOR GRADE='2'
  81
COUNT FOR GRADE='3'
  79
COUNT FOR GRADE='4'
  74
COUNT FOR GRADE='5'
  80
COUNT FOR GRADE='6'
  81
*** DO CANCELLED ***
```

Screen 3. Response of modified counter program

and the contents of the field ROOM are compared with '11'.

.AND. is one of three dBASE II "logical operators": .AND., .OR. and .NOT.. Logical operators always begin and end with a period.

OFF inhibits the normal display of the record number at the beginning of each record.

Another example of syntax is given by:

STORE <exp> TO <*memvar*>

Here we have no optional parts; you supply the items within the brackets. The expression is the item that you want to have stored.

Up to 64 MEMVARS (memory variables) can be stored in memory. Memory variables are one or more characters stored in a specific location in memory, which we can find and bring back when needed. The rules for memory variables are the same as for fieldnames; memory variables can be as large as 254 bytes; and they can be character, logical, or numeric. STORE 25 TO *number* is an example of the syntax.

Use of MEMVARS

Program 2 showed us how to display commands on the screen with SET ECHO ON. To do the reverse and inhibit dBASE II's normal display of responses, use SET TALK OFF. Then, if we want a more polished screen display in counting our students, we can use memory variables to temporarily store the response to each count command. If we do this we can display the content of the variables with descriptive text.

In order to distinguish memory variables from field and file names in the programs, we have used lower case type to indicate memory variables. In the text, memory variables will be italicized.

When TALK is off, data will be displayed only through the use of one of the display commands. The OFF following the command DISPLAY prevents dBASE II from displaying the record number of the current record. In this program, we have stored the results of each counting operation into a memory variable, which then displays the text enclosed by the delimiters. **Program 3** would generate **Screen 4**.

Each time we have counted the students in a grade we had to "read" our entire database. In each program we have read the database six times — once for each grade. If a database is large, reading it can take some time, depending on its size and the particular computer system being used.

Suppose we have a 160,000 byte database and a computer system that reads the database at 1600 characters a second. Counting the students in a grade takes 100 seconds. Counting the students in all six grades takes ten minutes.

Whether ten minutes is good or bad depends a lot on how often one wants to count kids. If it's only once or twice, we'll accept the ten minutes and let it go at that. But, if we want a class count more often, we will want the result much faster.

One way to achieve this is by not reading the database as often. Suppose that our database has been indexed on the grade. In that case we can use **Program 4**.

This program produces the same result as Program 3: Screen 4. All the records for each grade are grouped together. The FIND 1 command positions the database to the first record belonging to grade 1. Since all of the records belonging to a grade are grouped together we can use the WHILE clause instead of the FOR clause in a command. (WHILE can be used with any dBASE II command that FOR can be used with, except LOCATE). WHILE starts with the current record and processes only as long as the content of the database matches the WHILE condition. By counting in this way, we process each student's record one time

```
SET TALK OFF
USE SCHOOL
COUNT FOR GRADE='1' TO grade1
COUNT FOR GRADE='2' TO grade2
COUNT FOR GRADE='3' TO grade3
COUNT FOR GRADE='4' TO grade4
COUNT FOR GRADE='5' TO grade5
COUNT FOR GRADE='6' TO grade6
DISPLAY OFF '# IN GRADE 1', grade1
DISPLAY OFF '# IN GRADE 2', grade2
DISPLAY OFF '# IN GRADE 3', grade3
DISPLAY OFF '# IN GRADE 4', grade4
DISPLAY OFF '# IN GRADE 5', grade5
DISPLAY OFF '# IN GRADE 6', grade6
SET TALK ON
CANCEL
```

Program 3. Example of simple counting program

```
SET TALK OFF
USE SCHOOL INDEX GRADE
FIND 1
COUNT WHILE GRADE='1' TO grade1
COUNT WHILE GRADE='2' TO grade2
COUNT WHILE GRADE='3' TO grade3
COUNT WHILE GRADE='4' TO grade4
COUNT WHILE GRADE='5' TO grade5
COUNT WHILE GRADE='6' TO grade6
DISPLAY OFF '# IN GRADE 1', grade1
DISPLAY OFF '# IN GRADE 2', grade2
DISPLAY OFF '# IN GRADE 3', grade3
DISPLAY OFF '# IN GRADE 4', grade4
DISPLAY OFF '# IN GRADE 5', grade5
DISPLAY OFF '# IN GRADE 6', grade6
SET TALK ON
CANCEL
```

Program 4. Counting from indexed database file

```
  . DO COUNTER
# IN GRADE 1        78
# IN GRADE 2        81
# IN GRADE 3        79
# IN GRADE 4        74
# IN GRADE 5        80
# IN GRADE 6        81
 *** DO CANCELLED
```

Screen 4. Example of dBASE II COUNT command

as opposed to six times, or about six times faster than the earlier programs.

When we use an indexed file as in Program 4, each operation will be slower than if the file were not indexed because we access the records in a "logical" sequence. This sequence is different than the physical arrangement of the records on the disk, necessitating more movement of the disk head.

There are two basic kinds of database access in dBASE II: sequential and direct. In *sequential access* we leaf through the database a record at a time. Most of the high-level commands in dBASE II (LIST, COUNT, SUM, etc.) operate sequentially. *Direct access* allows us to go directly to any record — provided we know which record we want to go to.

Our first programs in this chapter were non-procedural. We simply told the computer what we wanted and it figured out how to do it. As we have progressed we have become more concerned with *how* we do things, and our programs have become much more procedural. Our next example of counting kids will be entirely procedural. The basic tools are DO WHILE/ENDDO and IF/ENDIF. Though most programming in dBASE II will use a combination of procedural and non-procedural elements, **Program 5** is entirely procedural. To truly customize what we want to do, we will nearly always need to be procedural.

When we use the constructs DO WHILE/ENDDO and IF/ENDIF, the commands in between will be executed whenever the expressions following DO WHILE and IF are true. Note that the program does not require any special ordering of the database records. The end result of Program 5 is identical to that of Programs 3 and 4 (Screen 4). Program 5 is also substantially faster than Program 3.

Program 5 examines every record in the database one record at a time. Depending on the content of the GRADE field, the content of one of six memory variables is increased by one. We advance one record (sequentially) and repeat the process until we come to the end of the database. When we have examined every record, we display our results.

In this program we need to initialize our variables *grade1* through *grade6*. You cannot add 1 to *grade1* until *grade1* exists. To exist, it must have a value.

The expression used with DO WHILE is .NOT. EOF (end of file). EOF is a dBASE II function which means end of file.

The expression used with IF compares the content of the field GRADE with the grade of interest. In the context of this program COUNT FOR GRADE = '1' is roughly equivalent to:

```
DO WHILE .NOT.EOF
   IF GRADE = '1'
      STORE grade1 + TO grade1
   ENDIF
   SKIP
ENDDO
DISPLAY OFF grade1
```

In this program we also elected to use the ? command in place of DISPLAY OFF. The ? is used to display fields, memory variables, expressions, and text. ? can be used even when there is no database in use. This is not true with the DISPLAY command.

Writing programs is a matter of putting commands together to solve problems. Once you have learned the commands, you can easily put them together to solve simple problems. We will see later in this book that complicated problems usually can be solved by considering them as several simple problems. Difficulties encountered in programming solutions to complex problems usually have little to do with the complexity of programming, but rather with our grasp of the problem itself.

```
SET TALK OFF
USE SCHOOL
STORE 0 TO grade1,grade2,grade3,grade4,grade5,grade6
DO WHILE .NOT. EOF

IF GRADE='1'
 STORE GRADE1+1 TO grade1
ENDIF
IF GRADE='2'
 STORE GRADE2+1 TO grade2
ENDIF
IF GRADE='3'
 STORE GRADE3+1 TO grade3
ENDIF
IF GRADE='4'
 STORE GRADE4+1 TO grade4
ENDIF
IF GRADE='5'
 STORE GRADE5+1 TO grade5
ENDIF
IF GRADE='6'
 STORE GRADE6+1 TO grade6
ENDIF

SKIP

ENDDO
? '# IN GRADE 1', grade1
? '# IN GRADE 2', grade2
? '# IN GRADE 3', grade3
? '# IN GRADE 4', grade4
? '# IN GRADE 5', grade5
? '# IN GRADE 6', grade6
SET TALK ON
CANCEL
```

Program 5. A procedural approach to the counting problem.

Quite often there will be any number of possible programming solutions to a problem. The approach selected is often a matter of personal choice. Other factors governing the selection of an approach might be the number of times we will use the program, who the program is for, and the need for program speed.

New programmers should not worry about writing "elegant" programs. There is no "better" program than one that solves a problem. One of the best ways to learn to program is through trial and error.

Chapter Three

THE TOOLS

In this chapter we will briefly describe the "toolkit" that can be used to program in dBASE II. This toolkit is particularly rich for most business applications because of the ability of the dBASE II language to manipulate character data. This ability is dBASE II's greatest strength as a language; its weakness is an inability to handle higher math. Fortunately, most business problems are handled with the four basic math functions — addition, subtraction, multiplication, and division.

The discussion of each of the tools is cursory. We are not trying to replace the dBASE II manual, which is the place to look if you want more information regarding any of the tools.

The most basic of the tools are the database files and the query language. In Chapter One, we briefly discussed database files and part of the query language. The query or command language provides the ability to locate and retrieve data and interface the system to applications programs. This is the language we will use for programming.

In addition to the database files, dBASE II uses several kinds of disk files:

DATABASE	(.DBF) FILES
INDEX	(.NDX) FILES
COMMAND	(.CMD) FILES
PROGRAM	(.PRG) FILES
REPORT FORM	(.FRM) FILES
FORMAT	(.FMT) FILES
TEXT	(.TXT) FILES
MEMORY	(.MEM) FILES

The Files

Database (.DBF) Files

Databases consist of one or more database files. A database file stores data in records and fields. Each record is automatically assigned a record number.

Database files can have up to 65,535 records or 8,388,480 bytes. The file size limit comes from CP/M 80 and can reasonably be expected to be increased in the future. Each record can contain up to 32 fields or 1000 bytes. A field can contain up to 254 bytes.

Index (.NDX) Files

Index files allow us to use the data in a database in a different order than the physical order of the database records. Index files translate between a key (data of interest to us such as a name) and the database record number.

The key is limited to 100 characters. A key can be part of a field or can comprise several fields. To index a school roster by class we would use:

INDEX ON GRADE + ROOM + STUDENT TO class

where grade, room and student are fields in the database.

Up to seven index files can be used simultaneously with a database file. The first file named controls the access to the database. All the index files will be kept updated when changes are made to the database.

Command (.CMD) and Program (.PRG) Files

Command and program files are both dBASE II programs. The difference is in the file identifier. On PC-type machines, dBASE II identifies programs with .PRG. On computers using CP/M 80 it identifies programs with .CMD.

The creation and use of these files is the essential purpose of this book.

Report Form (.FRM) Files

These files are created and used by the REPORT command. They contain the information needed to prepare reports. Form files can be edited using a word processor or the dBASE II command MODIFY COMMAND.

If MODIFY COMMAND is used, care must be taken to include the file identifier .FRM with the filename. If you do not, dBASE II will assume the filename refers to a command file.

MODIFY COMMAND <filename> .FRM

Format (.FMT) Files

These are special files that create custom screen forms for data entry. These files may be created with MODIFY COMMAND. If MODIFY COMMAND is used, care must be taken to include the file identifier .FMT with the filename to avoid confusing the file with a command file.

MODIFY COMMAND <filename>.FMT

Text (.TXT) Files

Text files are pure ASCII files and contain only the printable ASCII characters. They can be "read into" a dBASE II database as a special form of the command APPEND. They can be created from a database by a special form of the command COPY.

They can also be used to "record" dBASE II processing, either from the keyboard in the query mode or from dBASE II programs.

Memory (.MEM) Files

These files are used to save dBASE II memory variables as a disk file. The files are created by the command SAVE and read back into memory by the command RESTORE.

The Language

The query language is composed of commands, functions and operators. The commands are verbs such as COUNT and DISPLAY that can be tailored to your uses, as discussed in Chapter Two.

Functions are special tools that can be used in conjunction with commands. For example, the EOF (end-of-file) function allows you to test for an end-of-file condition in a program.

Operators allow you to perform arithmetic and logical operations. The + sign is an example of an arithmetic operator. The .AND. is an example of a logical operator.

The commands can be grouped into a number of functional categories. A command can belong to more than one of these functional categories:

CREATING DATABASES
USING DATABASES
CHANGING DATABASES
SORTING AND INDEXING
EXTRACTING INFORMATION
DISPLAYING INFORMATION
PRINTING
POSITIONING
DATA ENTRY COMMANDS
PROGRAMMING SUPPORT
MEMORY VARIABLES
GENERAL FILE OPERATIONS
SPECIAL FUNCTION COMMANDS
dBASE II PARAMETER CONTROLS

Creating Databases

The following commands can be used to create new database files:

CREATE COPY JOIN SORT TOTAL

Only CREATE can originate a completely new database. The remaining four commands create database files that are based on already existing databases.

Using Databases

Only two commands allow you to use a database file directly:

USE and SELECT

USE EXAMPLE, for instance, closes the database file in use and opens the file EXAMPLE.

We are allowed to use two database files at a time. These are referred to as the primary and secondary files.

```
SELECT PRIMARY
USE EXAMPLE1
SELECT SECONDARY
USE EXAMPLE2
```

This sequence opens the files EXAMPLE1 and EXAMPLE2 and identifies them as the primary and secondary files. While using the files we can switch back and forth between them with SELECT PRIMARY and SELECT SECONDARY.

Changing Databases

There are two ways we can change a database: we can change the form of the file or we can change the content of existing records.

COMMANDS TO CHANGE FORM

MODIFY STRUCTURE	DELETE
APPEND	RECALL
INSERT	PACK

MODIFY STRUCTURE — Allows redefinition of existing file structure. Changes the fieldnames, fieldtypes, and fieldsizes. MODIFY STRUCTURE erases all records.

APPEND — Adds records to the end of the database.

INSERT — Inserts a record inside the database.

DELETE — Marks a record for deletion.

RECALL — Removes the record deletion mark (undeletes).

PACK — Removes all records marked for deletion and renumbers all remaining records.

COMMANDS TO CHANGE CONTENT

BROWSE — Full-screen editing of 19 records at a time. Particularly good for updating columns.

CHANGE — Provides capability to change contents of a named set of fields.

EDIT — Full-screen editing of a single record at a time.

READ — Full-screen editing; used with the GET command to "edit" either fields or memory variables.

REPLACE — Direct replacement of field content.

Sorting and Indexing

Commands that are used to sort and index database files are:

SORT INDEX REINDEX

SORT ON <fieldname> creates a copy of the database where the records in a new database are in alphabetical or numeric order for the named field.

INDEX ON <expression> creates a file that relates the dBASE II record numbers to the expression. A database used with an index file appears to be sorted by the expression. Index files are used in conjunction with database files. Indexing is faster than sorting.

REINDEX reindexes any index files in use.

Extracting and Displaying Information

The following commands are used to extract and display data:

DISPLAY	SET FORMAT TO
LIST	READ
?	EDIT
??	BROWSE
@ row,col SAY	SUM
USING	COUNT
@ row,col GET	REPORT
PICTURE	SET HEADING TO

DISPLAY — Used to display all or part of a database record.

LIST — Used to display all or part of the database records.

? — Displays fields, memory variables, expressions, text. Used alone will display a blank line.

?? — Same as the question mark except the double question mark does not issue either a carriage return or a line feed. Used where you want to display an item at the current position of the cursor or the printhead.

@ row,col SAY — Displays items beginning at the named row and column. More than one item can be displayed with a SAY by concatenating (or joining) the items. Can be used with the USING clause. USING provides a mask to help customize the display.

@ row,col GET — Displays a single field or memory variable at the named row and column.

SET FORMAT TO — Used with the EDIT, APPEND, INSERT and READ commands to create a display using a FORMAT FILE.

READ — Used to call the display from a FORMAT FILE and for full screen editing with the GET command.

EDIT — Full screen display of a single record.

BROWSE — Full screen display of 19 records. As much of a record as will fit on one line of the screen is displayed.

SUM — Sums contents of up to five expressions. Can be used with NEXT, FOR and WHILE clauses.

COUNT — Counts database records; can be used with NEXT, FOR and WHILE clauses.

REPORT — Prepares standardized reports on the content of a database. Can be used with FOR, WHILE, and NEXT clauses.

SET HEADING TO — Used with REPORT command to display special information on the first line of the report.

Printing

Special commands are provided to route data to the printer. These commands are:

SET PRINT ON/OFF
SET FORMAT TO PRINT/SCREEN
SET MARGIN TO
REPORT TO PRINT
SET HEADING TO
EJECT

Positioning Commands

The following commands are used to position the database:

FIND
LOCATE
CONTINUE
GOTO or GO
SKIP

FIND — Positions the database to the first location of a specified key field. Uses an INDEX file to perform the positioning.

LOCATE — Positions the database to first location of the specified parameter. Does the positioning by use of a sequential file search.

CONTINUE — Positions to the next occurrence of parameter specified.

GOTO — Positions the database to the specified record number. This is a direct address positioning.

SKIP — Moves forward or backward the number of records specified with the skip. This is relative addressing.

Data Entry Commands

Commands that are normally used for data entry are:

APPEND	CHANGE	SET FORMAT TO
INSERT	EDIT	INPUT
BROWSE	READ	ACCEPT

APPEND — Adds records to the end of the database.

INSERT — Adds a record to the middle of the database.

BROWSE — Provides the ability to do full screen editing on up to 19 records at a time.

CHANGE — Allows you to change the contents of selected fields.

EDIT — Provides full screen editing for a data record.

READ — Used with the SET FORMAT TO and @ x,y GET commands for full screen data entry into memory variables and fields.

SET FORMAT TO — Calls up special screens to be used with the APPEND, EDIT, and READ commands.

INPUT — Provides a capability to prompt a user to enter numeric and logical data into a memory variable.

ACCEPT — Provides a capability to prompt a user to enter character data into a memory variable.

Programming Support

A few commands are included in the language primarily as programming tools. These particular commands allow us to use the remaining commands more effectively.

DO	LOOP
DO CASE/ENDCASE	WAIT
DO WHILE ../ENDDO	NOTE or *
RETURN	CANCEL
IF/ELSE/ENDIF	MODIFY COMMAND

DO — Used to "call" a dBASE II program.

DO CASE/ENDCASE — Provides a means to select from among a set of choices.

DO WHILE/ENDDO — Provides a means to repeat a number of commands as often as is necessary.

RETURN — Terminates the program in use. Takes you to next higher level program.

IF/ELSE/ENDIF — Provides a means to select options.

LOOP — Takes you back to the DO WHILE .. command. Used to "escape" from a processing path. Closest command in dBASE II to the GOTO command of FORTRAN or BASIC.

NOTE or * — Provides the ability to add comment lines to the program.

CANCEL — Terminates programs in use. Returns user to the keyboard.

MODIFY COMMAND — Invokes a simple text editor for the purpose of writing or changing program files.

Memory Variables

Some of the dBASE II commands can store data as dBASE II memory variables. Others are designed to deal only with memory variables.

STORE	SUM	INPUT	SAVE	WAIT
COUNT	ACCEPT	RELEASE	RESTORE	

STORE — Stores an item to memory.

COUNT...TO — Stores the result of the counting command in memory.

SUM...TO — Stores the results of summing operation to memory variables.

INPUT — Stores keyboard input of numeric or logical data to a memory variable.

ACCEPT — Stores keyboard input of character data to a memory variable.

RELEASE — "Erases" memory variables.

SAVE — Saves memory variables to a disk file.

RESTORE — Reads a disk file of previously saved memory variables back into memory.

WAIT — Used to "pause" the program. Can be used to enter a single character into memory.

General File Operations

A few commands are utilities to provide information about files or to work with files as opposed to records.

DISPLAY FILES ON	DELETE FILE
DISPLAY STATUS	RENAME
DISPLAY STRUCTURE	RESET
SET ALTERNATE ON/OFF	
SET ALTERNATE TO	

DISPLAY FILES ON — Displays disk directory.

DISPLAY STATUS — Displays database files in use, index files used with the databases, what the indexed files are indexed on (index keys), and the status of dBASE II processing parameters.

DISPLAY STRUCTURE — Displays the structure of the database file in use.

SET ALTERNATE ON/*OFF* — Allows you to route data displayed on screen or sent to printer to a disk file.

SET ALTERNATE TO [<file>] — Allows you to create a .TXT file for saving screen/printer output to disk.

DELETE FILE — Allows you to delete a named file.

RENAME — Allows you to rename a file.

RESET — Allows you to change disks — CP/M 80.

Special Function Commands

QUIT	MODIFY COMMAND
REMARK	WAIT
TEXT/ENDTEXT	LOAD
PEEK	CALL
POKE	

QUIT — Takes you out of dBASE II.

REMARK — Display of one line of text without delimiters.

TEXT/ENDTEXT — Display of a block of text without delimiters.

PEEK — Displays content of named memory location.

POKE — Writes to named memory location.

MODIFY COMMAND — Creates or changes any ASCII files by writing directly to those files from the keyboard.

WAIT — Inserts a "pause" in the program.

LOAD — Loads a named assembly program into memory areas not used by dBASE II.

CALL — Calls a previously loaded assembly program.

dBASE II Parameter Controls

There are a number of dBASE II processing parameters that can be controlled by the user. Parameters take two forms: SET...TO or SET...ON/OFF. The SET...TO parameters are not invoked unless the user takes a specific action. The SET...ON/OFF parameters are pre-set in dBASE II. The pre-set or "default" value is underlined in the description below.

SET CALL TO
SET CARRY ON/OFF
SET COLON ON/OFF
SET COLOR TO
SET CONFIRM ON/OFF
SET CONSOLE ON/OFF
SET DATE TO
SET DEBUG ON/OFF
SET DEFAULT TO
SET DELETE ON/OFF
SET ECHO ON/OFF
SET EJECT ON/OFF
SET ESCAPE ON/OFF
SET Fn TO
SET FORMAT TO
SET HEADING TO
SET INDEX TO
SET INTENSITY ON/OFF
SET LINKAGE ON/OFF
SET MARGIN TO
SET PRINT ON/OFF
SET RAW ON/OFF
SET SCREEN ON/OFF
SET STEP ON/OFF
SET TALK ON/OFF

SET CALL TO — Provides a means of selecting between several loaded assembly programs.

SET CARRY ON/OFF — Writes content of last entered record into new record during APPEND. Useful when there is little change from record to record.

SET COLON ON/OFF — dBASE II normally displays a colon at each end of a field or variable in full screen entry.

SET COLOR TO — Sets screen attributes (16-bit computers).

SET CONFIRM ON/OFF — Normal operation is to move automatically to the next item in full screen entry. CONFIRM requires a <RETURN> to advance an item.

SET CONSOLE ON/OFF — Stops display of data (including keyboard entry) on the terminal.

SET DATE TO — Allows internal setting of system date.

SET DEBUG ON/OFF — Routes command lines and control lines from SET STEP ON to a printer. Used when debugging programs with full screen operations.

SET DEFAULT TO — Allows setting of default disk drive which is different than the logged drive.

SET DELETE ON/OFF — Hides deleted records from dBASE II.

SET ECHO ON/OFF — Displays command lines from programs.

SET EJECT ON/OFF — Prevents dBASE II from ejecting a page when beginning a new report.

SET ESCAPE ON/OFF — You can normally escape from a program or a command by pressing the escape key. Provides an override to prevent that from happening.

SET Fn TO — Provides the ability to change the function key assignments (IBM PC only).

SET FORMAT TO — Allows selection between format files, the CRT, and printer for commands using the @ x,y SAY and GET commands.

SET HEADING TO — Allows entry of a heading line with the REPORT command.

SET INDEX TO — Allows selection of index files.

SET INTENSITY ON/OFF — Normal full screen operations are at either full and half intensity or normal and reverse video. Sets everything to standard video during full screen operation.

SET LINKAGE ON/OFF — Ties two database files together (based on record numbers) for display and reporting purposes.

SET MARGIN TO — Sets the left print margin.

SET PRINT ON/OFF — Turns the printer on and off.

SET RAW ON/OFF — Stored information is

packed. Normal display of fields places space between the fields for the viewer's convenience.

SET SCREEN ON/OFF — Enables and disables full screen operations.

SET STEP ON/OFF — Allows you to step through a program one command line at a time.

SET TALK ON/OFF — Toggles normal dBASE II response to commands on and off.

Arithmetic Functions

dBASE II provides the capability to perform the four basic arithmetic functions: adding, subtracting, multiplying, and dividing. The standard arithmetic operators recognized by dBASE II are:

+	addition
−	subtraction
*	multiplication
/	division
( )	parentheses for grouping
<	less than
>	greater than
=	equal
#	not equal
< >	not equal
< =	less than or equal
> =	greater than or equal
INT(X)	integer of x

Logical Operations

dBASE II also provides the capability to use the standard logical operators:

( )	parentheses for grouping
.NOT.	Boolean not
.AND.	Boolean and
.OR.	Boolean or

To illustrate the use of a Boolean operator, consider the following command:

```
DISPLAY FOR ROOM = "3"
■ .AND.GRADE = "5"
```

This command would display all the records in the database where the content of the field ROOM was 3 and the content of the field GRADE was 5.

String Operations

dBASE II is particularly good at string operations. The functions and operators used for string operations are:

+	string concatenation (joining) "alpha" + "bet" = "alphabet"
-	string concatenation with blanks inserted on right "alpha "-"bet" = "alphabet "
$	substring operator "alphabet" = memvar $(memvar,3,2) = "ph"
@	string search operator @("ph",memvar) = 3
LEN	string length LEN(memvar) = 8
TRIM	trims trailing blank spaces "alphabet " = memvar TRIM(memvar) = "alphabet"
!	upper case function !(memvar) = "ALPHABET"
VAL	converts a string to a number, stops at first letter "12B13" = numvar VAL(numvar) = 12
STR	converts a number to a string 123.6 = numvar STR(numvar,8,2) = " 123.60"

Other Functions

A number of other functions are provided as tools for special situations. The list below shows some sample commands using these functions.

#	record number
	STORE # TO place
	IF # = 27
*	deleted record
	COUNT FOR *
	DISPLAY FOR *

As of the current edition of dBASE II, deleted records cannot be copied or used in a report prepared by the REPORT command.

EOF — end of file

```
DO WHILE .NOT. EOF
IF EOF
```

TYPE— data type

U — undefined — doesn't exist
C — Character
N — Numeric
L — Logical

```
IF .NOT. TYPE('memvar') = 'U'
```

FILE— test for file existence

```
IF FILE ('MENU.CMD')
```

CHR — Character. Allows you to store and transmit the nonprintable ASCII control codes. CHR is used mainly to create special effects on the CRT or the printer. Substantial examples are given in Chapter Fourteen. CHR(10) issues a line feed and CHR(13) issues a carriage return. CHR uses the decimal value associated with a character.

```
STORE 'ALPHA' + CHR(10) + CHR(13) TO X
? CHR(27) + CHR(49) + 'HI'
```

RANK — This is a convenience function provided for cases when you want to use a CHR function but you don't have an ASCII conversion table available. The RANK function will tell you what decimal number is associated with a printable ASCII character.

```
STORE RANK('E') TO CONTROL
? RANK('E')
? CHR(RANK('E'))
```

& — macro substitution allows use of the contents of a variable in limited circumstances.

```
STORE 'SCHOOL.DBF' TO memvar
```

(USE *memvar* is not permitted — there is no file named memvar.)

USE *&memvar* is the same as USE SCHOOL.

This function is used where dBASE II would not normally expect a memory variable and would normally take what had been typed literally. (Note: RunTime™ does not allow an "&" as the first character on a line).

This has been a very brief overview of the tools that we will be working with in dBASE II. To recap, our tools are:

The Files
The Language

The language consists of commands, functions, and operators. Functions and operators are used with the commands in order to specify what we want dBASE II to do. All of these can be put together in an enormous number of ways. For an overview of dBASE II functions, operators and commands, see Appendices A, B, and C.

Section Two

Setting Up a Business System

ASHTON·TATE

ASHTON·TATE

Chapter Four

A BUSINESS EXAMPLE

Many of us learn to program because we have a specific task we want the computer to do. Often, we don't have enough time to pursue a traditional academic approach and study program theory. We have something we need to do — and we need to do it now. So we learn programming by looking at programs that others have written and seeing how the programming tools are used within the fabric of a real example. It's a natural way to learn.

To help you learn programming in dBASE II we are going to develop a set of hypothetical business applications. This will allow us to demonstrate the language in a practical context. Most of the dBASE II programming tools will be used at least once; of course, some tools will be used over and over again. Basic patterns for the structure of dBASE II programs will become apparent. You should try to look at the examples on two levels: as a solution to the apparent business problem, and as a solution for a generic problem.

For the next several chapters we will pretend to be a book distributor. Our business is buying books from publishers and reselling them to book stores. To help us run our business more efficiently we are going to purchase a microcomputer and dBASE II. Since the hardware we need — i.e., the disk system required — will depend on the size of the databases with their associated indexes and program files, we will design our software first and then purchase the required hardware.

Much of the day-to-day activity of our business has to do with record keeping. To assist us, we will design our software system to provide help in the following areas:

- Customer Record Keeping
- Mailing Lists and Labels
- Inventory Management
- Sales Order Entry
- Order Fulfillment and Invoicing
- Accounts Receivable

There are two ways to go about writing a program that will do what we want. The first is to write a single large, complex program that will do everything. Generally speaking, this is a *bad* idea. The second method is a modular system comprised of several small, simple programs to address each business function (see **Figure 1**). Each module is a separate program that does one part of the total job. Through this modular approach we can build our system one program at a time, with the added advantage of being able to change a program or add a program with relative ease.

To tie all of the individual programs together into one coherent package we will use a *menu system*. Here, we use one program to display a list of other programs that can be selected from the "menu." A diagram of a menu system is shown as **Figure 2**.

If we have a lot of selections we can choose to have a super-menu or "menu of menus." This is the approach that we will use for our book distributor's software system. Our menu system is shown as **Figure 3**.

The diagram of our menu system (Figure 3) looks a lot like an organizational chart. All of the submenus belong to the Main Menu — a hierarchical system. It is the simplest of the various possible menu schemes.

The purpose of each menu is to display a list of choices and provide a means for us to select one of the choices. Most of the choices provided by **Program 1** — our Main Menu — are also menus. Each of these second-level menus has, in turn, a list of things that can be done from that menu.

For example, if Menu 2, the Customer File Menu, is selected, we will be presented with a list of the functions that can be performed from that menu. When an item is chosen, we are actually "calling" a program to perform the task — such as adding new records to a customer database.

A hierarchical menu system does not allow you to go directly from a program in the Customer File Menu to one in the Sales Order Menu. When we finish using a program we are automatically returned to the menu from which the program was selected. To select a program from another menu we must return first to the Main Menu, select the menu that contains the program we want, and then select the desired program from the submenu.

The advantage of using a menu system is obvious — it provides a way of "remembering" which program, out of all of the programs on the disk, is the particular one that we want to use. It also indirectly "documents" the software system. We can use a menu system to do pretty complicated stuff with almost no training. The principal disadvantage is that you can only do what is on the menu.

About Programs

If you write a program (sometimes called a command file) in dBASE II using a 16-bit computer such as the IBM PC, dBASE II will automatically append .PRG to your program's filename. If you're using an 8-bit computer running on CP/M, dBASE II will append .CMD. We will append .CMD/.PRG to the names of our programs.

If we are in the operating system we can load dBASE II and "run" our menu program MENU with one command. Type DBASE MENU after the operating system prompt.

```
A> DBASE MENU
```

To "call" the program MENU.CMD/.PRG from within dBASE II you simply type DO MENU after a dot prompt:

```
. DO MENU
```

Both of these examples have assumed that the

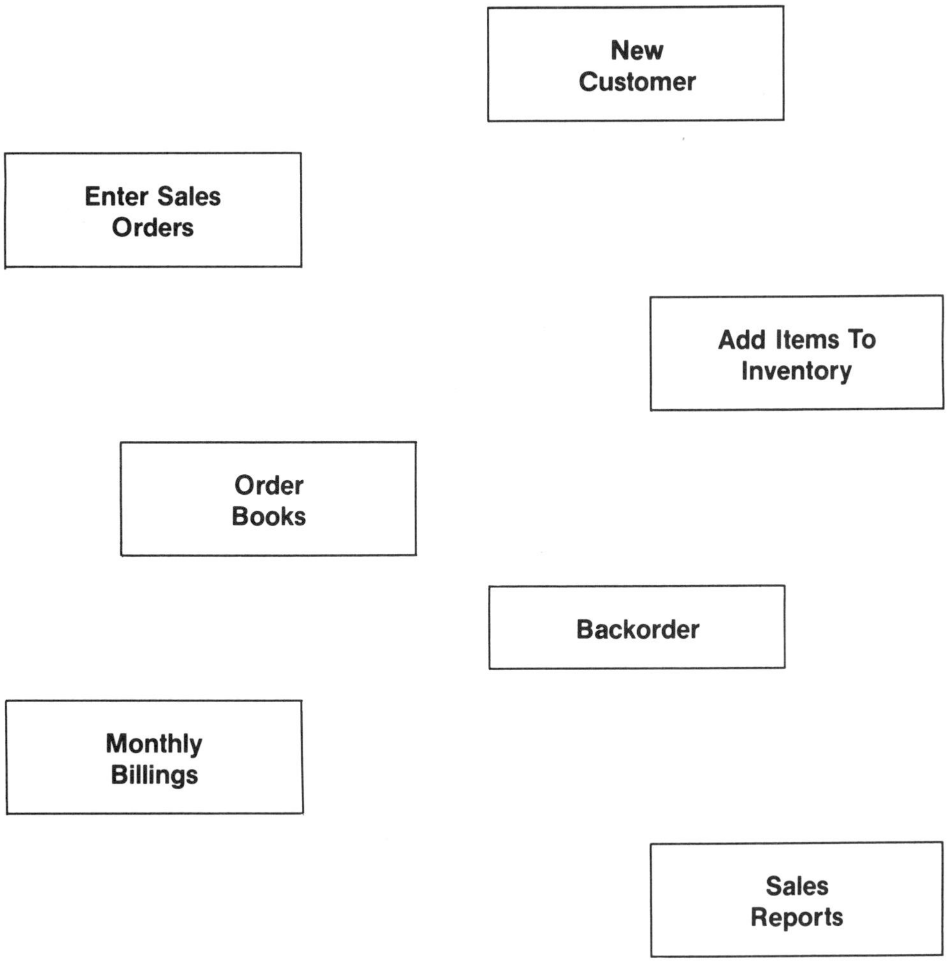

Figure 1. Each Box Represents a Function

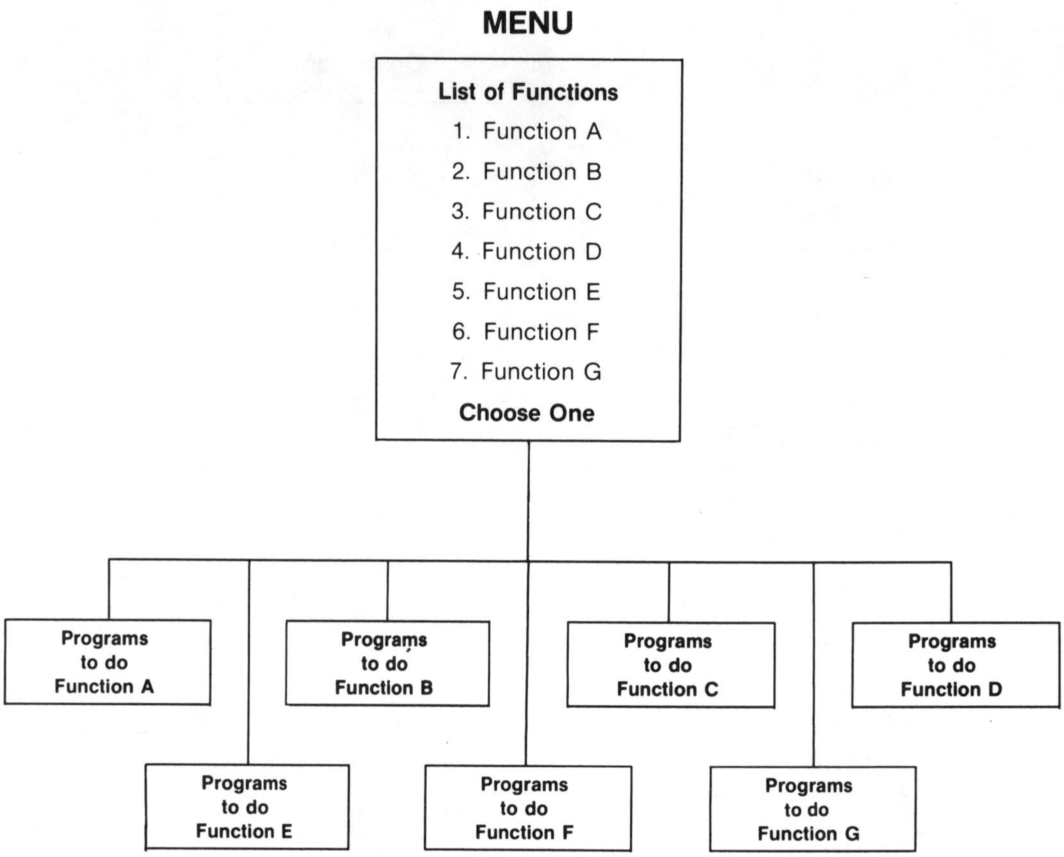

Figure 2. Diagram of Menu System

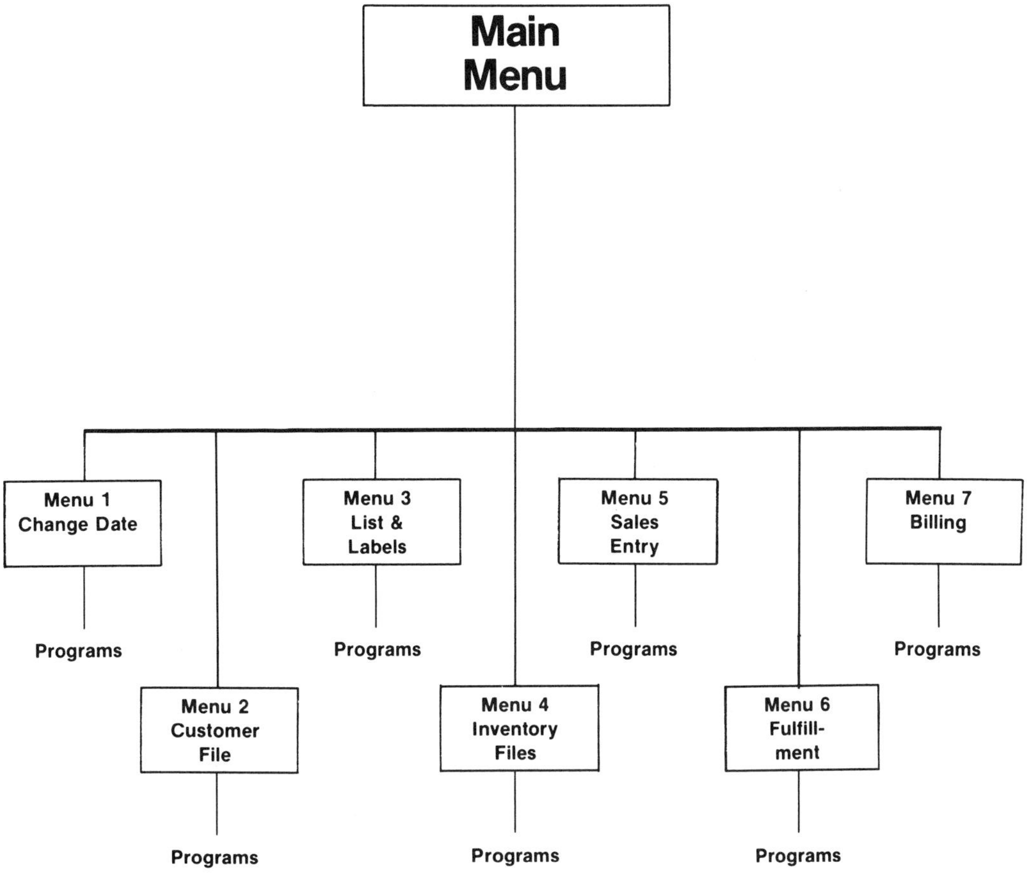

Figure 3. Hierarchical Menu System

```
BOB'S BETTER BOOKS

    10 Jun 1982

1 - Change the Date
2 - Customer File
3 - Mailing Lists and Labels
4 - Inventory
5 - Sales Orders
6 - Invoices
7 - Accounts Receivable


0 - Finished

: :  Pick One
```

Screen 1. Screen display for main menu

program MENU is on the logged disk drive. We will assume in our business example that all of the programs, databases and indexes reside on disk drive B and that disk drive B is big enough to hold all of them. If not on the B drive, you must identify the disk drive the program is on (DO C: MENU).

For the most part, programs written in dBASE II can be used directly on either 16-bit or 8-bit machines. There are very few differences, although the language is a little richer for the IBM PC type machines. We will try to point out the few places where there are differences.

A program need not end in .PRG or .CMD. One might, for example, want to have two versions of a menu program. One is the version for operational use, the other is a new version that is being developed. We can call the new version MENU.NEW. To run the new version we use:

```
. DO MENU.NEW
```

We are going to name the programs of our business software systematically. The programs to be selected from MENU will be named MENU followed by their item number. As an example, Item 1, Change the Date, becomes MENU1.CMD/.PRG. Programs that are selected from a submenu such as MENU3 will be similarly named: MENU3-1, MENU3-2, etc. This gives us a ready means of keeping track of the programs.

We will develop the sections of our business system in the order they appear on the Main Menu. This allows us to do the simplest items first. Also, we will need both the customer file and the inventory file before we can develop the sales order entry system.

When we write programs, or have them written for us, we must begin with a clear idea of what we want the programs to do. Only then can we customize the software to our exact needs. The time spent in development is justified by the increased efficiency (for people) that our programs provide.

The Program

Now, let's begin the actual programming of the Main Menu and the submenus. When we bring up our Main Menu program we want the screen to appear like **Screen 1**.

We have considered our needs, and are reasonably certain that we've set up the Main Menu to encompass all of them. We've also decided how we want the display for the Main Menu to look. So we begin by developing a program to provide this display as well as the means to select items from the display. Our program to do this is shown as **Program 1** — the Main Menu program.

```
SET TALK OFF
```

When we enter the program our first action is to SET TALK OFF. This inhibits dBASE II's normal conversational mode. With TALK OFF nothing will be displayed on the screen unless we take some direct action to cause the display. Of course, error messages from both dBASE II and the operating system will continue to be displayed if and when errors occur.

```
SET DEFAULT TO B
```

SET DEFAULT allows us to place all of our programs and databases on a disk drive other than the logged drive without having to identify the drive at the time each file is called. This command makes the named drive appear to be the "logged drive" for operations within dBASE II.

The SET command, by the way, controls a host of dBASE II processing parameters besides TALK and DEFAULT. The status of these parameters, and status information on the database and index

```
* Program .....:MENU.CMD (or MENU.PRG)
* Notes .......:This program is the Main Menu.

SET TALK OFF
SET DEFAULT TO B
RESTORE FROM Date ADDITIVE
SET DATE TO &mdate

DO WHILE T
   ERASE
   @  5,30 SAY "BOB'S BETTER BOOKS"
   @  7,32 SAY cdate
   @ 10,25 SAY '1 - Change the Date'
   @ 11,25 SAY '2 - Customer File'
   @ 12,25 SAY '3 - Mailing Lists and Labels'
   @ 13,25 SAY '4 - Inventory'
   @ 14,25 SAY '5 - Sales Orders'
   @ 15,25 SAY '6 - Invoices'
   @ 16.25 SAY '7 - Accounts Receivable'

   @ 19,25 SAY '0 - Finished '
   @ 21,29 SAY 'Pick One'

   STORE ' ' TO choice
   @ 21,24 GET choice
   READ NOUPDATE

   IF choice = '0'
      QUIT
   ENDIF

   IF choice $'1234567'
      STORE 'MENU'+choice TO selection
      DO &selection
   ENDIF
ENDDO
```

Program 1. MENU.CMD/.PRG The main menu program

files selected, can be displayed with the command DISPLAY STATUS.

RESTORE FROM DATE

This command "restores" dBASE II memory variables that have previously been saved on disk. DATE is the name of the disk file. This file will appear on a disk directory as DATE.MEM. The programs in the business example will make use of two date variables, *mdate* and *cdate*. If an *mdate* is 10/11/82, the *cdate* would be 11 OCT 82.

Before we can use the menu program we must first create these memory variables and SAVE them to the file DATE.MEM. We can do this with:

```
STORE '10/11/82' TO mdate
STORE '11 OCT 82' TO cdate
SAVE ALL LIKE ?date TO B:DATE
```

From now on, our system will take care of the process of changing and saving the date by means of Menu Item 1. This menu selection calls a program (Program 5 in Chapter 12) whose function is to change, validate, and save these two date variables.

The Main Menu program was written to work on either 8- or 16-bit machines. With a 16-bit computer such as the IBM PC, we could take advantage of the fact that dBASE II "reads" the PC's system clock. This is not true of CP/M 80 computers.

SET DATE TO &mdate

This replaces the dBASE II system date [DATE( )] with the contents of the variable *mdate*. The ampersand identifies *mdate* as a memory variable and permits its use in a command line.

The system date is used to update the database header when a change is made to a database record. It is also used in dBASE II reports. We will use it extensively throughout our business example. (The general subject of dates is discussed at length in Chapter 12).

DO WHILE T

This causes the commands between DO WHILE T and the command ENDDO to be repeated as long as the expression following DO WHILE is true. T stands for True. The command we used creates a loop and literally means DO FOREVER.

On each pass through the loop the program clears the screen, displays the menu, and waits for an item to be selected. If an item selected is not valid, the program takes us to the top of the loop where it starts all over again.

ERASE

The ERASE command clears the screen.

@ 5,30 SAY "BOB'S BETTER BOOKS"

Text, expressions, memory variables, and fields can be displayed with the SAY command.

The @ row,col SAY is used to display the expression following the word SAY on the screen. The information is displayed on the listed row, beginning on the listed column. In dBASE II the screen is numbered from the top down. The top row is Row 0. It is not recommended that you use Row 0. Columns are numbered from left to right. The first column is Column 0. It is also not recommended that you use Column 0.

Either a pair of apostrophes or a pair of quotes may be used as delimiters. The same delimiter must be used on each end.

This example uses quotes because of the embedded apostrophe in "BOB'S." Some computers have both the apostrophe (') and the accent mark (`) on the keyboard. The accent mark *cannot* be used as a delimiter!

```
@ 7,33 SAY cdate
```

Displays the content of the memory variable *cdate* on Row 7 beginning with Column 33.

```
STORE ' ' TO choice
```

Stores a blank space to memory variable *choice*. It creates the variable if it does not already exist. A variable must exist before it can be used. Once a variable has been created you must take overt action to get rid of it.

```
@ 21,24 GET choice
```

Displays the variable *choice* on the screen on Row 21, Column 24. Only memory variables and database fields can be displayed with GET.

```
READ NOUPDATE
```

Places the cursor at the beginning of the first item displayed with the GET command, in this case the variable *choice*. This allows you to type directly into the variable from the keyboard. Only printable characters can actually be entered into the variable from the keyboard. dBASE II may act on control characters but filters them and prevents their actually becoming a part of the variable.

The READ command will cause the program to pause at this point until the user enters something from the keyboard.

The word NOUPDATE prevents any index files in use from being updated. On the first pass through the menu we have no indexes in use. This may not be true on subsequent passes. If the variable being "read" with READ should change, dBASE II checks each index file in use to be sure that an index key has not been changed. This doesn't take long — but it can be noticeable. It is good practice to use the NOUPDATE whenever you are not changing an index key.

READ stores our choice to the memory variable *choice*.

```
IF choice = '0'
  QUIT
ENDIF
```

The IF command is sometimes referred to as a switch. It executes the commands between IF and ENDIF, when the expression following the word IF is True. The expression in this example is *choice* = '0'. If the variable *choice* contains a 0 we want to QUIT — one of the more important dBASE II commands. When we QUIT, dBASE II takes care of all of its housekeeping: writes and clears its internal buffers, closes all open files, and then exits to the operating system.

Note that the zero is contained within delimiters. This is because our variable *choice* is a character string; entering a number doesn't change the variable type. A number can be either a character or a number, and we need to tell the computer which it is.

```
IF choice $ '1234567'
  STORE 'MENU' + choice TO selection
  DO &selection
ENDIF
```

This switch illustrates several dBASE II tricks, and replaces 21 lines of conventional dBASE II programming code. In our menu system we had seven possible choices, Items 1 through 7, named MENU1, MENU2, etc. These tricks work because we used this structure in naming our programs. We couldn't have pulled them off if we had named these programs JOE, FRED, etc.

Normally one would have an IF/ENDIF for each of the menu possibilities. There would be a whole sequence of IF's, each of which would look like:

```
IF choice = '1'
   DO MENU1
ENDIF
.
.
.
.
.
IF choice = '7'
   DO MENU7
ENDIF
```

The program would examine each IF sequentially until a condition was satisfied. Then the commands inside the IF/ENDIF would be executed. When finished, the program would continue to check the IF's until the ENDDO was reached.

The first trick we use is the substring operator — the $. The command line now reads, "if choice is contained in the character string marked by the delimiters." Not only does this replace a series of switches, it also replaces a possibly long string of logical ORs. We could have written:

```
IF choice $ '1234567'
```

as:

```
IF choice = '1' .OR. choice = '2' .OR. choice
= '3' ...etc.
```

These two accomplish exactly the same result. Which do you like?

Our next trick is to concatenate or join the character string MENU with the contents of the variable *choice* to get our SELECTION. When we use the + sign between character strings we glue the two strings together. Kids often like to say 2 + 2 is 22. They're close; '2' + '2' is '22'. Maybe that's why they do so well with computers.

If our choice had been Item 1 — Change the Date — the variable *selection* would contain the character string MENU1. We tell the computer to execute the program by:

```
DO &selection
```

The ampersand tells dBASE II to use the *contents* of the variable *selection*. DO *selection* has meaning only if there is a program named SELECTION. If *selection* contains MENU1,

```
DO &selection = DO MENU1
```

This is a good example of using string operations to cut down on the amount of vertical code. dBASE II is an interpreter and must "read" all of the vertical code. We improve the speed of the program by minimizing the amount of vertical code. Even though the execution of the desired selection is slightly slower, the overall program speed is faster. In this particular example the relative speed is of no consequence; this will not always be the case. However, we don't want to dwell on the aspect of speed. One of the criticisms of professional programmers is their over-emphasis on speed. Nevertheless, you should pay attention to writing your program in such a way that the execution speed is consistent with your needs whenever it is possible to do so.

The order of the two IF/ENDIF switches in the program is important. The IF choice = '0' switch is placed first because we are also going to use '0' as a way of returning to the Main Menu. The program will return at the ENDIF following DO &*selection*, and if IF *choice* = 0 were to follow, the program would QUIT. That's not what we wanted. You can see why we need to have a structured way to move from the submenus to the Main Menu. (The problem of moving between menus is usually handled by the DO CASE command for just this reason.)

Our introductory program accomplishes a lot in a small program. It outlines our software system, displays what we want displayed, provides a means for us to select from among the options on the display, and rejects any selection which is not on the menu. It can be easily added to, when necessary, and it will run on any computer that has dBASE II.

Chapter Five

THE CUSTOMER FILE

The customer file is a basic element of many business systems. In this file we store essential information such as name, address, phone number and customer ID number. Our customer database file is named CUSTOMER.

Since the customer file is used by other programs, such as Sales Orders and Accounts Receivable, it is important to reliably link customer records within a business system. The customer's name is not necessarily unique. (Consider, for example, the name "Acme Hardware.") We provide this identifier by assigning each customer a unique number. We have chosen to enter this customer number (CUSTID) as a character field since we normally do not perform arithmetic with it.

In this chapter we will use the Customer File (MENU 2 from our Main Menu) to demonstrate programs that add, change, and delete records from a database. The programs will be MENU 2-1.CMD/.PRG, MENU 2-2.CMD/.PRG, and MENU 2-3.CMD/.PRG, respectively. We could do all of these things without a program, but we use a program because it allows us to do more than simply APPEND, EDIT or DELETE, as we shall see.

With CUSTOMER.DBF three index files are to be used and maintained (see **Figure 1**). The customer identification number index CUSTID.NDX is primarily intended to link CUSTOMER.DBF records to records in other databases. The customer name index allows access to the records in a way that is convenient for us. The ZIP index arranges the records alphabetically by zip code, and is intended for use by a mailing program. Note that in our system the computer assigns the record numbers and the entry date; there is no provision for changing these.

A database does not need to have records already entered in order to have an index file, and, in fact, it's quicker to set up an index *before* records are entered.

Since we plan to do more than one thing with the customer file, we will construct a menu to al-

DESCRIPTION	FIELDNAME	FIELDTYPE	FIELDWIDTH
CUSTOMER NAME	NAME	C	30
ATTENTION	ATTN	C	30
STREET ADDRESS	ADDRESS	C	25
CITY	CITY	C	20
STATE	STATE	C	2
ZIP CODE	ZIP	C	5
TELEPHONE NUMBER	PHONE	C	14
CUSTOMER SINCE	DATE	C	8
CUSTOMER ID NUMBER	CUSTID	C	6

RECORD SIZE .....141 BYTES

```
FILE TO BE INDEXED ON:  CUSTID      TO CUSTID
                        NAME        TO CUSTOMER
                        ZIP+NAME    TO ZIP
```

Figure 1. Customer database plan

low us to select from our choices. The display created by this menu program is shown as **Screen 1**. The menu program, MENU 2.CMD/.PRG, is shown as **Program 1**.

Description of the Menu Program

The very first thing that we should do in any program is to dedicate a few lines that briefly state what the program is and when it was written or changed. The asterisk at the beginning of the line is the same as the command NOTE. dBASE II ignores lines beginning with either * or NOTE. It's normally a good idea to make notes throughout your program to describe what you are doing and why — particularly if you do anything tricky. In our examples we will not normally show comments since we are describing the program anyway.

SET TALK OFF inhibits dBASE II's normal conversational mode — only what we direct is displayed. We then open the customer file with USE CUSTOMER and position the database to the last record entered with GO BOTTOM. The reason we are doing this is so that we can determine the last customer ID number. We will need this number later if we add a new customer to our database.

At this point we must deal with the case where there are no records in the database. If there are none, the database will be positioned to Record 0. We test whether or not we have records in the database with:

```
IF #>0
```

(The # is used in dBASE II as a symbol for the record number. It is also used for "not equal to.")

If we have records (remember, we are at the last record), we store the content of the field CUSTID to a memory variable *mcustid*. (It is *not* a good idea to have the same name for a memory variable and a field.) In addition, we create a character string *lastentry* composed of the customer ID, the customer's name and address. (Don't forget to leave spaces enclosed in delimiters in order to separate these fields). These two variables, *mcustid* and *lastentry*, will be used in the program to add records.

If there are no records in the database, we store 100000 to *mcustid*. This means that our first customer will be numbered 100001. Note that we also create a memory variable, *lastentry*, with a blank. This is because we want to display the variable in our program to add records. dBASE II will respond to a non-existent variable with a SYNTAX ERROR message.

DBASE II allows us to have 16 open files. A DO loop counts as an open file. When we enter this DO loop we will have used five of our 16 files. We will be opening three index files and an additional program for a total of nine. These nine files are:

1. MENU.CMD/.PRG (from Chapter 4)
2. DO WHILE (in MENU.CMD/.PRG)
3. MENU2.CMD/.PRG (customer file menu program)
4. DO WHILE (in MENU2.CMD/.PRG)
5. CUSTOMER.DBF (in MENU2.CMD /.PRG)
6. MENU 2-1.CMD/.PRG (add records)
7. CUSTID.NDX
8. CUSTOMER.NDX
9. ZIP.NDX

We still have a lot of files left, but file utilization is something to keep in mind.

In this menu we have elected to use DO CASE to select our program choice. DO CASE is similar to IF except that only one of the cases can be honored

```
BOB'S BETTER BOOKS

  CUSTOMER  MENU

    10 JUN 1982

  1 - Add Records
  2 - Edit Records
  3 - Delete Records
  0 - GO BACK TO THE MAIN MENU


  : :- PICK ONE
```

Screen 1. Screen display for customer menu

```
* Program .....:MENU2.CMD (or MENU2.PRG)
* Notes .......:This program is the Customer File Menu.

USE Customer
GO BOTTOM

IF #>0
   STORE VAL(CUSTID) TO mcustid
   STORE CUSTID+'  '+NAME+' '+ADDRESS TO lastentry
ELSE
   STORE '  ' TO lastentry
   STORE 100000 TO mcustid
ENDIF

DO WHILE T

   STORE ' ' TO choice
   ERASE
   @  2,30 SAY "BOB'S BETTER BOOKS"
   @  4,32 SAY 'CUSTOMER  MENU'
   @  6,34 SAY cdate
   @  8,25 SAY '1 - Add Customer Records'
   @  9,25 SAY '2 - Edit Customer Records'
   @ 10,25 SAY '3 - Delete Customer Records'
   @ 14,25 SAY '0 - GO BACK TO THE MAIN MENU'
   @ 17,25 SAY '  - PICK ONE'
   @ 17,24 GET choice
   READ NOUPDATE

   DO CASE
      CASE choice='1'
         DO Menu2-1
      CASE choice='2'
         DO Menu2-2
      CASE choice='3'
         DO Menu2-3
      CASE choice='0'
         RELEASE mcustid,lastentry
         RETURN
   ENDCASE
ENDDO
```

Program 1. MENU2.CMD/.PRG Customer file menu program

on each pass through the loop.

Note that we have again used NOUPDATE with the READ command.

Before we return to the Main Menu we RELEASE the memory variables *mcustid* and *lastentry*. They have no further value for us and we might need the space later. It is good practice to release variables each time you leave a program.

Menu Item 1 Adding Records (MENU 2-1.CMD/.PRG)

What do we want our program to do? We use a program for adding records, rather than the command APPEND, because we want the program to do a number of other things in addition to simply adding records.

We want the program to check and see if our "new" record is already in the database. It is generally not a good idea to have multiple records for the same customer. Since having two customers with the same name isn't out of the question, we don't want the computer to prohibit the entry, we just want it to show us enough of the duplicate(s) to allow us to decide whether or not to enter the new record.

We also want the program to assign and enter the customer number, and to enter the date into the DATE field.

Since it's easy to lose track of where you are when adding records, we also want the program to keep track of the last customer entered and display that information on the screen.

How do we build the program? Our first step is to select the index files to be used with the database CUSTOMER. In this program we'll use all three indexes: CUSTID, NAME, and ZIP. The first index in the list is the one that we will actually be working with. The other two are used to keep the files properly updated.

In this example we will use a slightly different version of DO WHILE. First we store a logical True to a memory variable named *addrec* (for "add records"). As long as *addrec* is true the loop will continue to repeat.

Immediately inside of the loop, the screen is erased and 30 blank spaces (the exact size of the field NAME) are stored to a memory variable *mname*. We display the memory variable *lastentry* on the bottom line of the screen and prompt the user to enter the new customer's name.

At this point there are two possibilities: either we entered a name or we didn't. If we didn't, we want to terminate the program and return to the menu. So, we test for a blank field. If the field is blank we store False to *addrec*. The LOOP command takes you back to the DO WHILE. Since *addrec* is now False the program automatically jumps to the ENDDO. We release all of the variables created in the program and return to the menu.

Some people consider the use of LOOP to be poor programming practice in a structured language such as dBASE II. We use LOOP in these examples because it is easily identifiable and helps us understand what is going on. In MENU 2-1.CMD/.PRG, we would need a number of embedded IF/ELSE commands to accomplish the same result.

If a name was entered we discard any trailing blanks and store the name to the new variable *trimname*. The ! function converts the expression to upper case characters. We want to always insure that all of the data stored in our example databases will be in upper case. We may know the two characters "A" and "a" are equivalent, but the computer does not. Since the computer is not good at judging context, all comparisons should be in upper case. STORE ! ('abc') TO *alpha* would store ABC in *alpha*.

The TRIM function discards the trailing blanks.

```
* Program .....:MENU2-1.CMD (or MENU2-1.PRG)
* Notes .......:This program adds records to the Customer File.

SET INDEX TO Customer,Custid,Zip
STORE T TO addrec
DO WHILE addrec
   ERASE
   STORE '                                  ' TO mname
   @ 23,1 SAY 'LAST ENTRY '+lastentry
   @ 21,1 SAY "ENTER THE NEW CUSTOMER'S NAME" GET mname
   READ NOUPDATE

   IF mname = '
      STORE F TO addrec
      LOOP
   ENDIF

   STORE !(TRIM(mname)) TO trimname
   FIND &trimname
   STORE F TO oktoadd

   IF #>0
      ERASE
      @ 1,1 SAY 'RECORDS WHICH MATCH CANDIDATE NAME'
      DISPLAY OFF NAME,ADDRESS WHILE NAME = trimname
      INPUT "ADD THE NAME ANYWAY (Y/N)?" TO oktoadd
   ENDIF

   IF #=0 .OR. oktoadd
      APPEND BLANK
      STORE mcustid+1 TO mcustid
      SET FORMAT TO Menu2-1
      READ NOUPDATE
      REPLACE NAME WITH trimname,DATE WITH DATE(),;
              CUSTID WITH STR(mcustid,6)
      SET FORMAT TO SCREEN
      STORE CUSTID+'  '+NAME+' '+ ADDRESS TO lastentry
   ENDIF
ENDDO

RELEASE addrec,mname.oktoadd,trimname
RETURN
```

Program 2. MENU2-1.CMD/.PRG Adds records to the customer file

We use it to maximize our chance of finding any possible duplicate records. Suppose that we had a record called SMITH INC. and we had entered SMITH into *mname*. If we searched using *mname* we would not recognize SMITH INC. as being a possible duplicate. Why? Because we would be doing a comparison on the entire 30 characters. INC. is not the same as four blank spaces. With TRIM we would do the comparison only on the first five characters (the size of SMITH).

FIND &*trimname* means find the record matching the contents of the memory variable *trimname*.

At this point we again have two possibilities. We either found a possible duplicate record or we didn't. If we found one the record number will be greater than zero. If we didn't, the record number will be zero.

If we think we have a duplicate we clear the screen and display the NAME and ADDRESS of possible duplicates. The INPUT command allows us to query the user as to whether or not to enter the record. We used INPUT because it will be displayed on the first line on the screen below the last item displayed. We don't know beforehand where that will be. INPUT can be used to enter either logical values or numbers.

If we didn't find a duplicate or the user decided to enter the item anyway, we add a blank record to the database and add 1 to the number stored in *mcustid*. This is the customer number for our new customer. Now we SET FORMAT TO MENU2-1. This activates the format file MENU2-1.FMT shown in **Figure 2**. When the READ NOUPDATE command is issued we get the screen display shown in **Screen 2**. Note that the "NAME", "DATE", and "CUSTOMER ID" are displayed but cannot be changed.

Why did we use NOUPDATE when we have in fact entered data that affects the index files? Because on the very next line we will use the REPLACE command. REPLACE causes the indexes to update and there isn't any point in doing it twice.

Menu Item 2 Editing Records (MENU2-2.CMD/.PRG)

What do we want our program to do? We want to be able to enter either the customer's name or identification number, and have the computer select the correct record for us to edit. As long as we don't have a customer name that begins with a number larger than 100,000, this is easy to do.

If we enter a non-existent name or number, we want to be told that we've made an error and be allowed to change our entry.

If there is more than one record in the database with the same customer name we want those customer names and addresses displayed. And we want some means of selecting which (or none) of those displayed we want to edit.

We want a placeholder, so that if we're distracted between records we know exactly where we are. All or part of the last record edited should remain on the screen when we select the next record to edit.

How do we build the program? When we enter our program, the first step is to store 30 blank spaces — the size of the field NAME — to the memory variable *mname*. Then we're prompted to enter either the customer's name or number. Note that again we use the NOUPDATE option.

Again there are two possibilities to consider. We either enter something or we don't. If we do not enter anything we want to return to the menu.

If we enter a name or a number we want the computer to figure out which it was. This is bush league artificial intelligence. Our scheme for selecting between the two possibilities relies on no customer having a name beginning with a number

```
* Program ......:MENU2-1.FMT
* Notes ........:This is the format screen for adding records to the
* .............:customer file.

@  3,28 SAY "BOB'S BETTER BOOKS"
@  6,1  SAY 'CUSTOMER NAME   : '+mname
@  6,50 SAY 'CUSTOMER NUMBER: '+STR(mcustid,6)
@  8,1  SAY 'STREET ADDRESS ' GET ADDRESS PICTURE;
'!!!!!!!!!!!!!!!!!!!!!!!!!!'
@ 10,1  SAY 'CITY.......... ' GET CITY PICTURE '!!!!!!!!!!!!!!!!!!!!'
@ 10,50 SAY 'STATE ' GET STATE PICTURE '!!'
@ 12,1  SAY 'ZIP CODE...... ' GET ZIP PICTURE '99999'
@  8,50 SAY 'CUSTOMER SINCE :'+DATE()
@ 14,1  SAY 'TELEPHONE..... ' GET PHONE PICTURE '(999)-999-9999'
@ 16,1  SAY 'ATTENTION..... ' GET ATTN PICTURE;
'!!!!!!!!!!!!!!!!!!!!!!!!!!!!!!!'
```

Figure 2. MENU2-1.FMT. Format file for adding customer records

```
                  BOB'S BETTER BOOKS
CUSTOMER  NAME  :TEDIOUS TECHNICAL TOMES  CUSTOMER  NUMBER: 120213
STREET ADDRESS :                       :  CUSTOMER SINCE: 01/22/51
CITY           :                   :      STATE :  :
ZIP CODE       :        :
TELEPHONE      :(   )-   -  :
ATTENTION      :                          :
```

Screen 2. Screen display for adding customer records

```
* Program .....:MENU2-2.CMD (or MENU2-2.PRG)
* Notes .......:This program edits the Customer File records.

STORE T TO editrec
ERASE
DO WHILE editrec
   STORE '                                        ' TO mname
   @ 21,1 SAY "ENTER THE CUSTOMER'S NAME OR CUSTOMER NUMBER" GET mname
   READ NOUPDATE

   IF MNAME='                                        '
      STORE F TO editrec
      LOOP
   ENDIF

   IF VAL(mname)>100000
      SET INDEX TO Custid,Customer,Zip
      STORE $(mname,1,6) TO findcust
   ELSE
      SET INDEX TO Customer,Custid,Zip
      STORE !(TRIM(mname)) TO findcust
   ENDIF
   FIND &findcust

   IF #=0
      @ 22,1 SAY findcust+' IS NOT IN THE DATABASE'
      LOOP
   ENDIF
   @ 22,0

   IF #>0
      STORE # TO placemark

      IF .NOT. CUSTID = findcust
         SKIP

         IF NAME = findcust .AND. .NOT. EOF
            ERASE
            @ 1,1 SAY 'MULTIPLE RECORDS FOR '+findcust
            SKIP -1
            DISPLAY NAME,ADDRESS WHILE NAME = findcust
            INPUT 'ENTER NUMBER FROM LEFT COLUMN - 0 TO ABORT' TO placemark
         ENDIF  for case name = findcust
      ENDIF  for case where we selected by customer name
```

Program 3. MENU2-2.CMD/.PRG Edits customer records *Continued on next page*

Continued from the previous page

```
        IF placemark>0
           GO placemark
           SET FORMAT TO Menu2-2
           READ
           CLEAR GETS
           SET FORMAT TO SCREEN
        ENDIF  for valid record number
     ENDIF    for case where we found the record
  ENDDO
  RELEASE editrec,mname.placemark,findcust
  RETURN
```

Program 3. MENU2-2.CMD/.PRG Edits customer records

greater than 100,000. We use the VAL function to test *mname*. If VAL(*mname*) is more than 100,000 then the entry is a customer number. Otherwise it's a customer name. The VAL function terminates with the first character that is not a number or a blank space; for instance, VAL(10B16) is 10.

The results of the VAL test allow us to choose the order of the index files. It also tells us how to handle the variable. If it's a customer ID, we store the first six characters of *mname* to a new variable, *findcust*. Otherwise, we want to store the contents of *mname* — with all the trailing blank spaces removed and as upper case characters — to *findcust*.

The ! function converts to upper case. The TRIM function discards the trailing blank spaces in a variable. We combined the two into a single operation, as we did with the program for adding records.

We either find the desired record, or we don't. If we don't find the record we display a message on Line 22 that tells us what we looked for. Then we loop back to the beginning and try it again. (The reason for the display is to help the user diagnose the reason the computer did not find the desired record.)

If the record is found, the program has to consider two possibilities: name or number. If the entry is a name, we need to test for multiple records. We first check to see if it's a name by comparing *findcust* to the CUSTID. They can't match if *findcust* is a name. So, if there's no match, we then test for multiple records. There is no test for multiple records if we have entered a number because each customer ID number is unique. In either case we store the record number of the record we found to a variable *placemark*.

To test for multiple records we skip to the next record. Now we compare the contents of *findcust* to the contents of NAME. Note that we also test for the end-of-file. If we had hit the end-of-file we would still be at the same place we were before the skip and *findcust* would be equal to NAME.

If there are multiple records, we erase the screen and display the RECORD NUMBER, NAME, and ADDRESS. The prompt to enter the number from the left column is really saying: enter the record number. We do provide for an out: enter a zero, a non-existent record number.

Test for a valid record number with IF *placemark* > 0. If we pass the test then GO *placemark*. GO *placemark* means go to the record number stored in *placemark*.

The screen display used for editing the record is shown in **Screen 3**. The format file to create that display is shown in **Figure 3**. Note that here we do a straight READ. This means that if we change anything in the database, there is a slight delay while the three index files are updated.

We leave the display on the screen when we prompt the user to enter the next customer name or number. This is our placeholder. To prevent the user from moving the cursor to one of the field display areas we use CLEAR GETS. This "cancels" the READ operation for fields and variables input before the CLEAR GETS command.

Menu Item 3 Deleting Records (MENU 2-3.CMD/.PRG)

Deleting records is serious business. Once a record is gone, it's gone.

For this reason, deleting records is a two-step operation. DELETE marks a record for deletion and PACK actually removes it. When we use PACK all of the records after the deleted record are renumbered (the dBASE II record numbers are reassigned) and the index files are re-indexed. This is a time-consuming operation on a large database. It's usually a good idea to delete several records at a time, if possible at a quiet time of the day.

```
                       BOB'S BETTER BOOKS
CUSTOMER NAME  :TEDIOUS TECHNICAL TOMES      :  CUSTOMER NUMBER:  120213
STREET ADDRESS :2123  MONTMORENCY PLACE :        CUSTOMER SINCE :  01/22/51
CITY.......... :CITY OF INDUSTRY  :              STATE  :CA:
ZIP CODE...... :91232:
TELEPHONE..... :(213)-521-6578:
ATTENTION..... :GEOFFREY D. MARTINDALE III    :
```

Screen 3. Screen display for editing customer records

```
* Program .....:MENU2-2.FMT
* Notes .......:This program is the format file for changing Customer
               :records.

@  3,28 SAY "BOB'S BETTER BOOKS"
@  6,1  SAY 'CUSTOMER NAME  ' GET NAME PICTURE;
'!!!!!!!!!!!!!!!!!!!!!!!!!!!!!!'
@  6,50 SAY 'CUSTOMER NUMBER: '+CUSTID
@  8,1  SAY 'STREET ADDRESS ' GET ADDRESS PICTURE;
'!!!!!!!!!!!!!!!!!!!!!!!!!'
@ 10,1  SAY 'CITY.......... ' GET CITY PICTURE '!!!!!!!!!!!!!!!!!!!!'
@ 10,50 SAY 'STATE ' GET STATE PICTURE '!!'
@ 12,1  SAY 'ZIP CODE...... ' GET ZIP PICTURE '99999'
@  8,50 SAY 'CUSTOMER SINCE :'+DATE
@ 14,1  SAY 'TELEPHONE..... ' GET PHONE PICTURE '(999)-999-9999'
@ 16,1  SAY 'ATTENTION..... ' GET ATTN PICTURE;
'!!!!!!!!!!!!!!!!!!!!!!!!!!!!!!'
```

Figure 3. MENU2-2.FMT. Format file for changing customer records

```
* Program .....:MENU2-3.CMD (or MENU2-3.PRG)
* Notes .......:This program deletes records from the Customer file.

SET INDEX TO Customer,Custid,Zip
STORE T TO delerec
STORE F TO drec,query2
ERASE

DO WHILE delerec
   STORE '                                  ' TO mname
   @ 21,1 SAY 'ENTER THE NAME TO BE DELETED' GET mname
   READ NOUPDATE

   IF mname = '
      STORE F TO delerec
      LOOP
   ENDIF
   STORE !(mname) TO mname
   FIND &mname

   IF #=0
      ERASE
      @ 22,1 SAY TRIM(mname)+' IS NOT IN THE DATABASE'
      LOOP
   ENDIF
   @ 22,0

   IF #>0
      STORE # TO placemark
      SKIP

      IF NAME=mname .AND..NOT. EOF
         ERASE
         @ 1,1 SAY 'MULTIPLE RECORDS FOR '+mname
         SKIP -1
         DISPLAY NAME,ADDRESS WHILE NAME=mname
         SKIP -1
         STORE # TO stop
         STORE T TO test
         DO WHILE test
         INPUT 'ENTER NUMBER FROM LEFT COLUMN - 0 TO ABORT' TO placemark
           IF placemark=0 .OR. (placemark>=start .AND. placemark<=stop)
              STORE F TO test
           ENDIF
         ENDDO
      ENDIF
```

Program 4. MENU2-3.CMD/.PRG Deletes customer records

Continued on next page

Continued from the previous page

```
         IF placemark > 0
            GO placemark
            SET FORMAT TO Menu2-3
            READ
            SET FORMAT TO SCREEN
            INPUT 'DELETE THIS RECORD (Y/N)?' TO query

            IF query
               DELETE
               STORE T TO drec
            ELSE
               RECALL
            ENDIF
         ENDIF
      ENDIF
   ENDDO

   IF drec
      ERASE
      DISPLAY OFF NAME,ADDRESS FOR *
      INPUT 'FINISH DELETING THESE RECORDS Y/N? ' TO query2

      IF query2
         PACK
      ENDIF
   ENDIF
   RELEASE editrec,mname,placemark,drec,query
   RETURN
```

Program 4. MENU2-3.CMD/.PRG Deletes customer records

```
* Program .....:MENU2-3.FMT
* Notes .......:This program is the format file for deleting Customer
               ;records.

@  3,28 SAY "BOB'S BETTER BOOKS"
@  6,1  SAY 'CUSTOMER NAME   : '+NAME
@  6,50 SAY 'CUSTOMER NUMBER: '+CUSTID
@  8,1  SAY 'STREET ADDRESS : '+ADDRESS
@ 10,1  SAY 'CITY.......... : '+CITY
@ 10,50 SAY 'STATE : '+STATE
@ 12,1  SAY 'ZIP CODE...... : '+ZIP
@  8,50 SAY 'CUSTOMER SINCE : '+DATE
@ 14,1  SAY 'TELEPHONE..... : '+PHONE
@ 16,1  SAY 'ATTENTION..... : '+ATTN
```

Figure 4. MENU2-3.FMT Format file for deleting customer records

When we request a record for deletion we want the record displayed. We want to be asked if we really want to delete it. We also want to be able to RECALL a record. RECALL removes the deletion mark.

Once we've positioned the database to the record we want to delete, we display the record using the format file shown in **Figure 4**. We ask the operator if this record is to be deleted. The answer is stored to the variable *query*. If *query* is true, we mark the record for deletion and we store a T to the variable *drec*.

When we have identified all of the records to be deleted, we leave the DO loop. If *drec* is true we display the name and address from each record marked for deletion. Then again we ask if the user really wants these records deleted. If s/he does, we remove all of these records with PACK. Otherwise we remove the deletion marks with RECALL ALL.

ASHTON·TATE

Chapter Six

LISTS AND LABELS

One of the more popular uses of a database system is to print out mailing lists and mailing labels. Typically, mailing lists are customer files, geared toward mailing monthly statements, advertisements, form letters, or whatever. Since the Post Office has a fondness for customers who sort by zip code, the database used for mailing must at least be indexed by zip code. A further refinement is to index the mailing list alphabetically by zip code, as in Chapter Five; that is, the zip codes are in order and the names for each zip code are in alphabetical order.

We will use Menu 3, the third item on our Main Menu, to generate a number of programs to print lists or labels from our customer file.

In **Program 1** we have used the $ to identify a row number relative to another row. In the first line we established Row 2 as the base row. We want the second displayed line to be two lines below the first (on Row 4). $ + 2 then displays in double space; $ + 1 is in single space. If we were to insert a line into the display, we would not need to renumber the row numbers. The same idea can be applied to the column position.

Note that choices 1 and 3 both select the program MENU3-1, which prints the customer list alphabetically or by customer ID. This is not indicated on the display.

Menu Item 1 Printing Mailing Lists Alphabetically or by Customer Number (MENU3-1.CMD/.PRG)

We want an alphabetical listing of all of the customers in our customer file, as in **Figure 1**. The program to prepare the report is shown as **Program 2**. Menu Item 3, printing the list by customer numbers, is done exactly as Menu Item 1, so both utilize Program 2.

Some customers in our list do not have entries for the ATTN field; consequently, some entries have three lines and some have four. We do not want a blank line printed between the customer

```
                    BOB'S BETTER BOOKS

                   MAILING MENU PROGRAM

                       10 OCT 1983

   1 - Print the list alphabetically
   2 - Print the list alphabetically by zip code
   3 - Print the list by customer number
   4 - Select and print items from list
   5 - Print single-column mailing labels
   6 - Print multi-column mailing labels
   0 - Get out of this menu system

 : :   PICK ONE
```

Screen 1. Screen display for mailing menu

```
* Program .....:MENU3.CMD (or MENU3.PRG)
* Notes .......:This program is the Mailing Menu program.

USE Customer
DO WHILE T
   STORE ' ' TO choice
   ERASE
   @   2,30 SAY "BOB'S BETTER BOOKS"
   @ $+2,29 SAY 'MAILING Menu PROGRAM'
   @ $+2,32 SAY cdate
   @ $+2,16 SAY '1 - Print the list alphabetically'
   @ $+1,16 SAY '2 - Print the list alphabetically by zip code'
   @ $+1,16 SAY '3 - Print the list by customer number'
   @ $+1,16 SAY '4 - Select and print items from list'
   @ $+1,16 SAY '5 - Print single-column mailing labels'
   @ $+1,16 SAY '6 - Print multi-column mailing labels'
   @ $+1,16 SAY '0.  Get out of this menu system'
   @ $+2,20 SAY 'PICK ONE'
   @ $,15 GET choice
   READ NOUPDATE

   DO CASE
      CASE choice='1'
         DO Menu3-1
      CASE choice='2'
         DO Menu3-2
      CASE choice='3'
         DO Menu3-1
      CASE choice='4'
         DO Menu3-4
      CASE choice='5'
         DO Menu3-5
      CASE choice='6'
         DO Menu3-6
      CASE choice='0'
         RETURN
   ENDCASE
ENDDO
```

Program 1. MENU3.CMD/.PRG Mailing menu program

```
                     MAILING LIST PRINTOUT AS OF 10/15/82

102003               AARDVARKS ABACUS                          (213) 555-5555
                     123 ANTEATER AVE
                     BEVERLY HILLS, CA          91222

.....                   ........                ...            ......

100001               TEDIOUS TECHNICAL TOMES                   (213) 521-6578
                     GEOFFREY D. MARTINDALE III
                     2123 MONTMORENCY PLACE
                     CITY OF INDUSTRY, CA       91232
```

Figure 1. Format of printed list

```
* Program .....:MENU3-1.CMD (or MENU3-1.PRG)
* Notes .......:This program prints customer lists either alphabetically or
* .............:by customer ID.

ERASE
IF choice = '1'
   SET INDEX TO Customer
ELSE
   SET INDEX TO Custid
ENDIF
GO TOP
SET FORMAT TO PRINT
SET MARGIN TO 15
STORE 0 TO page
STORE 'MAILING LIST PRINTOUT AS OF '+cdate TO pagetitle

DO WHILE .NOT. EOF
   @ 6,25 SAY pagetitle
   STORE 8 TO line

   DO WHILE line<55 .AND. .NOT. EOF
      @ line,1  SAY CUSTID
      @ line,15 SAY NAME
      @ line,50 SAY PHONE

      IF .NOT. ATTN = '
         STORE line+1 TO line
         @ line,15 SAY ATTN
      ENDIF
      @ line+1,15 SAY ADDRESS
      @ line+2,15 SAY TRIM(CITY)+', '+STATE
      @ line+2,42 SAY ZIP
      STORE line+4 TO line
      SKIP
   ENDDO
   STORE page+1 TO page
   @ 62,40 SAY STR(page,3)
   EJECT
ENDDO

SET FORMAT TO SCREEN
SET MARGIN TO 0
RELEASE page,pagetitle,line
```

Program 2. MENU3-1.CMD/.PRG Print list alphabetically or by customer number

name and the address. If you glance at **Program 2**, you will see that there is a line (IF .NOT. ATTN = '   ') which allows for an entry if one is needed.

The @ x,y SAY command can be used to print by using SET FORMAT TO PRINT. We have to be a little careful when we use this technique. Items must be printed sequentially on each line and each line must be printed in sequence on a page. If you are printing a 30-character field beginning on Column 1, you must not begin the next item on that line before Column 31. If a command is given to print at an "earlier" position on the page than the current position of the print head, the printer will seem to go berserk. It *will* go to the commanded position, but on the next page. Though the @ command can make formatting pages very easy, it cannot back up the printer. If you make a mistake inside of a DO loop, you'll waste a lot of paper in a hurry.

Note that after the index had been selected we used the command GO TOP. This positions the database to the first record indicated by the index file (the first logical record).

SET FORMAT TO PRINT will cause the displays from the @ x,y SAY commands to be routed to the printer. They will *not* appear on the screen.

In this example we have a DO loop inside of a DO loop. The outer loop, DO WHILE .NOT. EOF, runs until we reach the end-of-file mark.

When we enter the outer loop we print the page title and set the starting line number for the inner loop. We do the inner loop until either the line counter reaches 55 or we find the end-of-file mark. Then we exit from this loop, increment and print the page number, and eject the page. If we have not reached the end-of-file we go back to the beginning of the outer loop.

A common programming error is to leave off the .AND. .NOT. EOF from the inner loop. If we do this, what happens if we reach the end-of-file before the line counter gets to 55? We print the last record over and over until we do reach 55. If we left it off both loops, we could print the last record until we ran out of paper.

The SKIP command advances the database by one record each time the inner DO loop is executed. The line number is advanced by four each pass through the loop.

We print the ATTN line with the IF .NOT. ATTN = '   '; if it's not blank we want to print it. We need to increment the line counter by one. The print statements after this step reference the number stored in the line counter.

The last activity before each page eject is to print the page number. This example has assumed that we will have not more than 999 pages. Note that we used the STR function to print the page number. SAY should be used only with a character field or variable.

In dBASE II the RETURN command is technically optional, although using RETURN is good practice. dBASE II will recognize the EOF mark (all files have EOF marks) as a RETURN. If we do use the command RETURN, we can type as much text and comment as we like following the command without affecting the program's execution.

This is a short, simple and easy-to-read program. Its only shortcoming is that it prints the entire list each time you use it.

Menu Item 2 Print the Mailing List Alphabetically by Zip Code (MENU 3.2.CMD/.PRG)

Program 3 is very similar to the last program.

Our index file ZIP was created by using the INDEX command INDEX ON ZIP + NAME TO ZIP, then SET INDEX TO ZIP.

Again we start off by selecting the desired index

```
* Program .....:MENU3-2.CMD (or MENU3-2.PRG)
* Notes .......:This program prints the mailing list alphabetically by zip.


 SET INDEX TO Zip
GO TOP
SET FORMAT TO PRINT
SET MARGIN TO 15
STORE 0 TO page

DO WHILE .NOT. EOF
    @  6,25 SAY 'MAILING LIST FOR ZIP CODE '+ZIP+'  AS OF '+DATE()
    STORE ZIP TO mzip
   STORE 8 TO line

    DO WHILE ZIP = mzip .AND. line < 55 .AND. .NOT. EOF
      @ line,1  SAY CUSTID
      @ line,15 SAY NAME

      IF .NOT. ATTN = '        '
         STORE line+1 TO line
         @ line,15 SAY ATTN
      ENDIF
      @ line,50 SAY PHONE
      @ line+1,15 SAY ADDRESS
      @ line+2,15 SAY TRIM(CITY)+', '+STATE
      @ line+2,42 SAY ZIP
      STORE line+4 TO line
      SKIP
   ENDDO
   STORE page+1 TO page
   @ 62,40 SAY STR(page,3)
   EJECT
ENDDO

SET MARGIN TO 0
SET FORMAT TO SCREEN
 RELEASE page,line,mzip
RETURN
```

Program 3. MENU3-2.CMD/.PRG Print list alphabetically by zip code

```
FILL IN THE ITEMS YOU ARE INTERESTED IN

  NAME      :                        :
  STREET    :                     :
  CITY      :                 :
  STATE     :  :
  ZIP CODE  :     :
```

Screen 2. Screen display for printing selected records

and positioning the database to the top. We have chosen to incorporate the zip code into the page title, so we have done the title formatting inside of the DO loop.

Storing the zip code to the memory variable *mzip* allows us to insure that each new zip code will automatically begin on a fresh page. The inner loop will terminate if we find the end-of- file mark, or if the counter *line* exceeds 55, or the zip code in the field ZIP is not the same as that in the memory variable *mzip*.

Note that the test for *line* >55 occurs only at the beginning of each pass through the inner loop. It can exceed 55 during the loop. We expect that. The particular structure was selected so that a record would never be split between two pages.

The significant item discussed in this program was the use of *mzip*. We don't need to know which zip codes are in the database. We can use the data itself as a key to controlling the program.

Menu Item 4 Printing Selected Records (MENU3-4.CMD/.PRG)

In the menu examples thus far, we have printed the entire customer list each time, whether we need it or not. If our list is small, printing the whole list isn't a problem. If we have 10,000 customers, it becomes impractical.

In our next example we want to print out selected parts of the list alphabetically. We need a program that will allow us to specify exactly what we want printed. **Program 4** shows us how to set up such a system.

We display a screen that prompts us to "fill in the items we are interested in." We are provided with blanks that allow us to enter NAME, STREET, CITY, STATE, and ZIP CODE.

The idea here is that we enter something into those headings we want to select. For example, to list all of the customers in Cleveland, we enter CLEVELAND in the space provided for city and nothing in the other spaces. To list all of the customers whose names begin with CA, we enter CA in the space provided for name and nothing in the other spaces. To list all of the customers whose names begin with CA and who are in CLEVELAND: enter CA in the space provided for name, CLEVELAND in the space for city, and nothing in the other spaces.

To accomplish this, we take our basic program to print the customer list alphabetically (MENU 3-1) and add to it the dBASE II code to allow us to select the items we want for printing.

We want to select from among five different fields: name, street, city, state, and zip. The first step is to create five blank memory variables which are the same lengths as the fields they correspond to.

Next, we create a screen display that allows us to enter our selections. Note that we again use READ NOUPDATE.

Then we discard trailing blanks and convert each of our entries to upper case. It's important to note that when we TRIM a variable that is all blanks, we are left with a variable that has one blank space. We use this to test whether we entered anything at all. If we didn't we skip all the way to the bottom of the program and return to MENU3.

We are going to use the LOCATE FOR command to do our selecting. LOCATE FOR <expression> will start at the beginning of the database and search the database sequentially until a record matching the expression is found or the end-of-file mark is encountered. LOCATE NEXT n FOR <expression> will start the search from wherever you happen to be in the database. In our example we will set n = 65535, which is the maximum number of dBASE II records. We do this because if we search for the record and don't find it, we're at the end of the database and hit the end-

```
* Program .....:MENU3-4.CMD (or MENU3-4.PRG)

SET INDEX TO Customer
GO TOP
ERASE
STORE '                              ' TO mname
STORE '                         ' TO mstreet
STORE '                     ' TO mcity
STORE '  ' TO mstate
STORE '     ' TO mzip
ERASE
@ 1,10 SAY 'FILL IN THE ITEMS YOU ARE INTERESTED IN'
@ 3,10 SAY 'NAME' GET mname
@ 4,10 SAY 'STREET' GET mstreet
@ 5,10 SAY 'CITY' GET mcity
@ 6,10 SAY 'STATE' GET mstate
@ 7,10 SAY 'ZIP CODE' GET mzip
READ

STORE !(TRIM(mname)) TO mname
STORE !(TRIM(mstreet)) TO mstreet
STORE !(TRIM(mcity)) TO mcity
STORE !(TRIM(mstate)) TO mstate
STORE !(TRIM(mzip)) TO mzip

IF mname+mstreet+mcity+mstate+mzip = '      '
   RETURN
ELSE
   STORE 'LOCATE NEXT 65535 FOR ' TO command

   IF .NOT. mname=' '
      STORE command+'NAME=mname .AND.' TO command
      FIND &mname
   ENDIF

   IF .NOT. mstreet=' '
      STORE command+'mstreet$ADDRESS .AND.' TO command
   ENDIF

   IF .NOT. mcity=' '
      STORE command+'CITY=mcity .AND.' TO command
   ENDIF
```

Program 4. MENU3-4.CMD/.PRG Printing selected records *Continued on next page*

Continued from the previous page

```
      IF .NOT. mstate=' '
         STORE command+'STATE=mstate .AND.' TO command
      ENDIF

      IF .NOT. mzip=' '
         STORE command+'ZIP=mzip .AND.' TO command
      ENDIF
      STORE $(command,1,LEN(command)-5) TO command
      &command
      SET FORMAT TO PRINT
      STORE 0 TO page
      SET MARGIN TO 15
      DO WHILE .NOT. EOF
         @ 6.15 SAY DATE()+' SPECIAL CUSTOMER FILE LIST'
         STORE 10 TO LINE
         DO WHILE line<55 .AND. .NOT. EOF
            @ line.1  SAY CUSTID
            @ line,15 SAY NAME
            @ line.50 SAY PHONE

            IF .NOT. ATTN = '     '
               STORE line+1 TO line
               @ line,15 SAY ATTN
            ENDIF
            @ line+1,15 SAY ADDRESS
            @ line+2,15 SAY TRIM(CITY)+', '+STATE
            @ line+2,42 SAY ZIP
            STORE line+4 TO line
            SKIP
            &command
         ENDDO
         STORE page+1 TO page
         @ 62,40 SAY STR(page,3)
         EJECT
      ENDDO
   ENDIF
   SET FORMAT TO SCREEN
   RELEASE page,line,command,mname.mstreet,mcity,mstate,mzip
   RETURN
```

Program 4. MENU3-4.CMD/.PRG Printing selected records

of-file mark. If we do find the record, we don't want to go back to the beginning and find the record again.

Now we store the kernel of our command to the variable *command*. Then we assemble the <expression> using the series of IF/ENDIFs. Note that each additional element incorporated into the expression ends with ".AND.". Note also that if we had entered something into selection for NAME, we did a FIND on that item. This has positioned us to the first possible record that can meet our search criteria.

When we finish with the IFs we strip off the final ".AND.". dBASE II syntax will not allow a command to end with ".AND.". It will print an error message and abort the program. To get rid of the last five characters we use the LEN function inside of the substring operation:

```
STORE $(command,1,LEN(command)-5) TO
■ command
```

This reads as: store the first (n-5) characters of the variable *command* back to *command*.

Now we start our search outside of the loop by using &*command*. This is literally "execute the contents of COMMAND." We did this outside of the loop to position us to the first possible record. If there were no records, we would have hit the end-of-file flag. A caveat is that the scheme really is 100 percent reliable only if we have less than 65535 records.

The dBASE II RunTime™ package will not allow you to use a command line beginning with an "&" such as the &*command* in this example program, even though standard dBASE II will. This is one of the few differences in programming for dBASE II and RunTime. To handle a RunTime version we would pull the word LOCATE out of "command." The command line of interest would then become LOCATE &*command*.

We now enter our basic list printing routine. Note that we SKIP just prior to going back into our search routine. Why? If we are at, for example, Record 10, and we LOCATE NEXT 10 FOR <exp>, and the expression is satisfied by Record 10, we are still at Record 10. To continue our search we need to advance a record every time we do a LOCATE.

Why did we do it this way? We could have used IF with our assembled expression and put IF <expression> just after the DO WHILE of the inner do loop. The ENDIF would be just before the SKIP. This is the most common way to do the job we are trying to do. We used the LOCATE scheme because it is a lot faster.

LOCATE is essentially an assembly language search routine. To use the IF/ENDIF approach we would have a dBASE II search routine, which would require going through the loop for every record in the database. The loop takes from 30 to 50 milliseconds for each record plus the time to actually read the disk records. If we have 10,000 records this takes from 300,000 to 500,000 milliseconds. With LOCATE we reduce this to approximately the time required to read the disk, a savings of 300 to 500 seconds.

When programming in dBASE II, use the highest level command you can if you are concerned with the overall execution speed.

Menu Item 5 Printing Single-Column Labels (MENU3-5.CMD/.PRG)

Just about every organization prints labels. It's something most people loathe doing, but it's a natural for a computer.

Labels come in various sizes and in one to five columns per sheet. Sheets of labels are usually 12

```
* Program .....:MENU3-5.CMD (or MENU3-5.PRG)
* Notes .......:This program prints single column labels.

SET INDEX TO Zip
GO TOP
SET PRINT ON
SET MARGIN TO 5

DO WHILE .NOT. EOF
   ?
   ?
   ? NAME

   IF .NOT. ATTN = '     '
      ? ATTN
   ENDIF
   ? ADDRESS
   ? TRIM(CITY)+', '+STATE+'  '+ZIP

   IF ATTN = '     '
      ?
   ENDIF
   ?
   ?
   ?
   SKIP
ENDDO
SET PRINT OFF
RETURN
```

Program 5. MENU3-5.CMD/.PRG Simple label printing program

inches long instead of the standard page length of 11 inches.

We are going to use two kinds of labels in our business. The first, single column, is the easiest to deal with.

The labels we are using are 1.5 by 4 inches. Since our printer is set to print at ten characters per inch and six lines per inch, we have 40 characters available in width. The largest field we are printing has 30 characters, so we are left with a five character margin (1/2 inch) on each side of the label. Six lines per inch will allow us to print up to nine lines on each label. We are using four lines, at most.

The order in which the labels are printed is determined by the index file selected.

We select the 1/2 inch left margin with SET MARGIN TO 5.

Note that we use SET PRINT ON rather than SET FORMAT TO PRINT. The latter can be used only with @ x,y SAY command.

We have used the ? command to print the items we want. The question mark will print the items listed after it; ? issues a carriage return and a line feed. Used alone, it will advance the paper one line.

Each label uses nine lines. We need to use nine question marks. We want to print either three or four lines on a label depending on the content of the field ATTN. We print ATTN in the correct place if the field isn't blank. If the field is blank, we print an extra ? after the line containing the city, state, and zip code.

You should use single column labels only when the number of labels to be printed is reasonably small, because you put more wear and tear on the printer with single column labels. The time to print a given number of labels is also much longer than with multi-column labels because the printer uses more line feeds. Line feeds take time.

Menu Item 6 Printing Multi-Column Labels (MENU3-6.CMD/.PRG)

Labels also come in sheets with several columns of labels per sheet. We're going to use one that has 12 rows of five labels per sheet. Each label is 1 inch by 2 5/8 inches. The usable space on a label is just a little under 2.5 inches. This kind of label is best suited to printers using 12 character per inch (elite) type.

When you buy labels you should consider the length of items you need to put on them. In our example we will use a ten character per inch printer. This means that we will not be able to print all of some of the fields on a label. However, we can print the first 25 characters from each field with a 10-cpi printer. This example illustrates printing part of the contents of a field.

Program 6 illustrates why you should release memory variables as you leave each program. The five memory variables in this program require 650 bytes of memory, which represents over a third of the available dBASE II space for memory variables.

Our approach to solving this printing problem is to "typeset" an entire row of labels in memory. Once we've done the "typesetting" we'll print that row.

A row of labels corresponds to five database records. This means that we need to work our way through the database five records at a time. We will use two DO loops. The outer loop is used to set up the inner loop and to do the actual printing. The inner loop "typesets" up to five records each time. An end-of-file mark will terminate both the inner and outer loop.

Before we begin "typesetting" we store one blank space to five memory variables, *line1* through *line5*. This initializes the variables each time around.

```
* Program .....:MENU3-6.CMD (or MENU3-6.PRG)
* Notes .......:This program prints multi-column labels.

USE Customer
SET TALK OFF
SET INDEX TO Zip
GO TOP
SET PRINT ON
SET MARGIN TO 0
STORE '                                                            ' TO blanks

DO WHILE .NOT. EOF
   STORE 0 TO records
   STORE ' ' TO line1,line2,line3,line4,line5

   DO WHILE records < 5 .AND. .NOT. EOF
      STORE records +1 TO records
      STORE TRIM(CITY)+', '+STATE+blanks TO varline
      STORE line1+$(NAME,1,25)+' ' TO line1

      IF ATTN = '     '
         STORE line2+ADDRESS+' ' TO line2
         STORE line3+$(varline,1,25)+' ' TO line3
         STORE line4+ZIP+$(blanks,1,20)+' ' TO line4
         STORE line5+$(blanks,1,25)+' ' TO line5
      ELSE
         STORE line2+$(ATTN,1,25)+' ' TO line2
         STORE line3+ADDRESS+' ' TO line3
         STORE line4+$(varline,1,25)+' ' TO line4
         STORE line5+ZIP+$(blanks,1,20)+' ' TO line5
      ENDIF
      SKIP
   ENDDO
   ?
   ? line1
   ? line2
   ? line3
   ? line4
   ? line5
ENDDO
SET PRINT OFF
RELEASE line1.line2,line3.line4,line5,blanks,records
RETURN
```

Program 6. MENU3-6.CMD/.PRG Multi-column mailing labels

Our "typesetting" operation consists of building up these five lines so that each variable will print one line on each of the five labels. When we have gone through the inner loop five times, the variable *line1* will contain the first 25 characters of each of five customer names. There is also a blank space separating each of the names.

In our example, we may have records where the content of the ATTN field is blank. But we don't want to print a blank line on a label — we want to move the remaining fields up on that label. This means that as we process each record we have two possibilities to consider: we are either going to "typeset" the ATTN field or not.

line1 contains only customer names. *line2* may contain both ATTN and ADDRESS fields. Regardless of what we add to each memory variable, the addition will be 25 characters plus a space.

TRIM(CITY) is variable in length. To be sure that the line containing this item gets incremented properly, we create the variable *varline*. Then we use the first 25 characters of *varline* when we "typeset" this item.

Once we've finished our "typesetting" we print one blank line and the five memory variables. Then we go back and do it all over again.

Note that on a pass through the inner loop, we build up each of the five variables by a fixed number of characters. The items assigned to variables may be different for each record.

Note that in the setup of the program we SET MARGIN TO 0. This is just insurance — we want the printing to begin at the left edge of the page.

Chapter Seven

THE INVENTORY

The operations we want to perform with the inventory database are shown in **Screen 1**. Screen 1 is the product of **Program 1**, the menu program for our inventory system.

Of this selection of items on our menu, we are going to discuss three. These are:

- Adding items to the inventory
- Ordering books
- Updating the inventory

Programs for editing and deleting inventory records may be found in Appendix E.

Our inventory database is composed of three separate files:

The basic inventory file:	INV
The publisher file:	PUBLISH
Books on order file:	ONORDER

The database plans for each of the three files are shown in **Figure 1**. The relationship of these files is shown in **Figure 2**. In this chapter we will be working with more than two files at a time, which necessitates closing one of the open files each time we need to open a new file.

Note that INV is linked to ONORDER and to PUBLISH. The linkage between INV and ONORDER is the ISBN number; the linkage between either INV or ONORDER and PUBLISH is the publisher's identification code, which is contained within the ISBN number.

The ISBN Number

The structure of the ISBN number is complex but worth some discussion, since it illustrates how to search and verify other types of numbers. It also shows how one might construct part numbers, customer numbers, etc., that can be checked by computers.

ISBN stands for International Standard Book Numbering. The ISBN number itself is normally

```
            BOB'S BETTER BOOKS

              INVENTORY MENU

                10 OCT 83

     1 - Add Records
     2 - Edit Records
     3 - Delete Records
     4 - Order Books
     5 - Update Stock

     0 - GO BACK TO THE MAIN MENU


   : :- PICK ONE
```

Screen 1. Screen display for inventory menu

```
* Program .....:MENU4.CMD (or MENU4.PRG)
* Notes .......:This program is the Customer File Menu program.

USE Inv
GO BOTTOM
IF .NOT. #=0
  STORE ISBN+'  '+TITLE TO lastentry
ELSE
  STORE '      ' TO lastentry
ENDIF

DO WHILE T
   STORE ' ' TO choice
   ERASE
   @  2,30 SAY "BOB'S BETTER BOOKS"
   @  4,32 SAY 'INVENTORY MENU'
   @  6,34 SAY cdate
   @  8,25 SAY '1 - Add Records'
   @  9,25 SAY '2 - Edit Records'
   @ 10,25 SAY '3 - Delete Records'
   @ 11,25 SAY '4 - Order Books'
   @ 12,25 SAY '5 - Update Stock'
   @ 14,25 SAY '0 - GO BACK TO THE MAIN MENU'
   @ 17,25 SAY '  - PICK ONE'
   @ 17,24 GET choice
   READ NOUPDATE

   IF choice='0'
      RELEASE lastentry,select
      RETURN
   ENDIF

   IF choice$'12345'
      STORE 'MENU4-'+choice TO select
      DO &select
   ENDIF
ENDDO
RETURN
```

Program 1. MENU4.CMD/.PRG Inventory menu program

DATABASE FILE: INV

	FIELDNAME	TYPE	SIZE	DEC
ISBN number (part number)	ISBN	C	013	
Author's name	AUTHOR	C	030	
Title of the book	TITLE	C	040	
Subject of the book	SUBJECT	C	015	
Quantity on hand	QTYONHAND	N	003	
Minimum stock level	MINSTOCK	N	002	
Quantity sold this year so far	SOLDTHISYR	N	004	
Quantity sold last year	SOLDLASTYR	N	004	
Date of the last sale	LASTSALE	C	008	
Date last shipment received	LASTRCV	C	008	
Selling price	LISTPRICE	N	006	002
Cost to us	COST	N	006	002
Publishers (Mfgr) ID Code	PUBCODE	C	006	
Standard quantity to order	ORDERSIZE	N	003	

INDEX FILES:ISBN number	ISBN.NDX
Author	AUTHOR.NDX
Title	TITLE.NDX
Publishers Code	PUBCODE.NDX
Subject	SUBJECT.NDX

DATABASE FILE: PUBLISH

	FIELDNAME	TYPE	SIZE	DEC
Publisher's Name	NAME	C	30	
Attention (name of contact)	ATTN	C	30	
Publisher's Address	ADDRESS	C	25	
Publisher's City	CITY	C	020	
Publisher's State	STATE	C	002	
Zip Code	ZIP	C	005	
Phone number	PHONE	C	014	
Publisher's ID code	PUBID	C	007	

INDEX FILES:Publisher's ID	PUBID.NDX
Publisher's Name	PUBNAME.NDX

DATABASE FILE: ONORDER

	FIELDNAME	TYPE	SIZE	DEC
ISBN Number	ISBN	C	013	
Our Purchase Order Number	PONUMBER	N	006	
Quantity Ordered	ORDERSIZE	N	003	
Date of the Order	ORDERDATE	C	008	
Quantity Received to date	QTYRCVD	N	003	

INDEX FILES:ISBN Number	O-ISBN.NDX

Figure 1. Database plans for inventory files

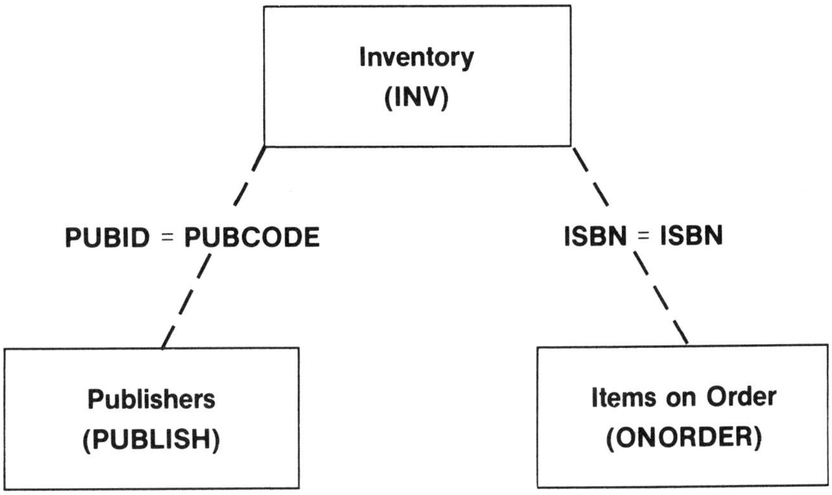

Figure 2. Relationships of files in inventory database

represented (and used) as a 13-character number. The number is comprised of four parts, normally separated by hyphens. There are actually ten digits in the four groups. Examples of ISBN numbers are:

3-88053-002-5
950-7000-10-X

The size of each of the first three groups can vary, though there are always nine digits total. The fourth group is always a single digit.

The first group is the group identifier, which is used to identify countries, geographic regions, languages, etc.

The second group identifies the publisher. The size of this group varies according to the number of titles for a publisher. Large publishers have small publisher identifiers and vice versa.

The third group is the book identification number for the publisher.

The fourth group, which is always a single digit, is the check digit.

The ISBN number can be verified by a numerical calculation involving each of its digits.

ISBN	3	8	8	0	5	3	0	0	2	5	
Digit Multiplier	10	9	8	7	6	5	4	3	2	1	
Product	30 +	72 +	64 +	0 +	30 +	15 +	0 +	0 +	4 +	5	= 220

If the product of the above operation is evenly divisible by 11 the number is a valid ISBN number. This is an example of a number that is designed for use by a computer — the number can be tested for validity.

Program 2 is used to test for the validity of an ISBN number. The first problem to solve is to get rid of the hyphens so that we can do the verification test and separate out that part of the number that identifies the publisher. This provides us the opportunity to further demonstrate the use of the @ and LEN functions.

The only digit position that we know for certain is the last — the check digit. So our first step is to separate out the check digit from the rest of the number up to the last hyphen.

Next we pull out the group identifier (the first group) by locating the first hyphen, using the @ function. The rest of the number is stored to memory variable *rem*, which contains only the publisher identifier and the book identifier (the second and third groups). Note that the memory variable *x* used in the substring operations is a number:

```
x = @('-',REM)
```

This number *x* is the position of the first hyphen in *rem*. We cannot use a substring operator where either the starting position or the size is zero. Doing so results in a syntax error. That is why we use the two IF statements that test for *x* greater than zero.

When we separated out the group identifier (the first set of numbers in the ISBN) we knew the size of *rem* was 11. We knew this because when we first broke the ISBN number into two parts, we knew that the last digit, the 13th digit, was the check digit and that the 12th digit was a hyphen. When we "pull out" the group identifier, we separate out the rest of this 11-digit character to a variable *rem*. We don't know the size of the new *rem*. However, we can get the size by using the LEN function. The number of characters in *rem* is given by LEN (*rem*). LEN(*rem*) is a number. It can be used as a number in calculations and in other dBASE II functions. We're going to use it as a number in the substring operation that extracts the book identifier digits and stores them to the memory variable *bookid*.

The DO loop performs the function of multiply-

```
* Program .....:ISBNTEST.CMD (or ISBNTEST.PRG)
* Notes .......:This program tests an ISBN number.

STORE 1 TO check
IF $(misbn,13,1)$'0123456789X'
   STORE $(misbn,13,1) TO checkdigit
   STORE $(misbn,1,11) TO rem
   STORE @('-',rem) TO X

   IF X>0
      STORE $(rem,1,X-1) TO group
      STORE $(rem,X+1,LEN(rem)-X) TO rem
      STORE @('-',rem) TO X

      IF X>0
         STORE $(rem,1,X-1) TO mpub
         STORE $(rem,X+1,LEN(rem)-X) TO bookid
         STORE group+mpub+bookid TO isbntest

         IF checkdigit='X'
            STORE 10 TO check
         ELSE
            STORE VAL(checkdigit) TO check
         ENDIF
         STORE 1 TO X

         DO WHILE X<=9
            STORE VAL($(isbntest,X,1))*(11-X)+check TO check
            STORE X+1 TO X
         ENDDO
      ENDIF FOR Test3
   ENDIF FOR Test2
ENDIF FOR Test1

IF check-INT(check/11)*11=0
   STORE T TO validtest
ELSE
   STORE F TO validtest
ENDIF
RELEASE bookid,checkdigit,rem,group,check,isbntest,X
RETURN
```

Program 2. Program to test for valid ISBN number

ing each digit by the appropriate multiplier and storing the accumulated result to the variable *check*. Note that the first line in the program stored 1 to *check*. This is a hedge against the case where there weren't any hyphens in the ISBN number. Without hyphens we could not successfully dismantle the number for the validity test. If this were the case the validity test would find *check* = 1 and the test would fail — which would be what we want to happen.

Menu Item 1 Adding Book Titles to the Inventory (MENU4-1.CMD/.PRG)

What do we want our program to do? When we add a new book to our inventory we want a lot more from the computer than a simple check as to whether the title is already in the database. We want to enter new books by their ISBN numbers. We want to insure that each ISBN number entered is a valid number. We want to verify that it isn't already in the inventory file. We want to insure that the publisher of the book is in the publisher's file, and if not, we want to add the publisher to the publisher's file.

Program 3 does all of the above. It is also our first example of using two database files at the same time. The two files we are using are the inventory file INV and the publisher's file PUBLISH.

dBASE II allows us simultaneous use of two database files. When two files are used at once, one file is identified as the primary file and one as the secondary file. We choose between them by means of the command SELECT.

How do we build the program? The file INV is already open from MENU4.CMD/.PRG when we enter the program. Since no other file is open yet, INV is the primary file. If we were to open another file at this point, INV would be closed and the second file would be the only file in use. In order to open two files at once we must SELECT SECONDARY. Any file that is now opened will be the secondary file. The primary file remains open and available for our use.

We are allowed to move about within the selected file, make changes, and add and delete records without affecting the other file. Either or both the primary and secondary files can be used with index files, as in this program. The same file may not be used as both the primary and secondary files at the same time.

When a file is opened the database is positioned to the first record. When a database is selected the database is positioned to the record that was last used. This means that we do not lose our position in the selected database, no matter what we do with the other database. In the example, INV is the primary file and PUBLISH is the secondary file.

Figure 3 shows a schematic representation of the logic used in Program 3. Diagrams like this are called flow charts. They can be used to work out the logic of a program before we try to code it. Although they are used more often in textbooks than in actual programming, they can help us understand what we want to do.

Note that most of this program consists of tests. First we test to see whether or not we have actually entered a book number. If we have, we then test the validity of the ISBN number by the command DO ISBNTEST. Remember that ISBNTEST is Program 2, and contains two memory variables, *mpub* (the publisher's identification number) and *validtest* (a logical variable that tells us whether or not the ISBN number was valid). We use these two variables in Program 3.

If we've entered a valid number we can now test to see if that number, and hence that book, is in the database. If the book is not in the database, we SELECT the publisher's file to see if there is

```
* Program .....:MENU4-1.CMD (or MENU4-1.PRG)
* Notes .......:This program adds records to the Inventory file.

SET INDEX TO Isbn,Author,Title,Pubcode,Subject
SELE SECO
USE Publish INDEX Pubid,Pubname
SELE PRIM
STORE T TO addrec
ERASE
STORE '               ' TO misbn
@ 23,1 SAY 'LAST ENTRY '+lastentry

DO WHILE addrec
   @ 21,1 SAY "ENTER THE NEW ISBN NUMBER" GET misbn PICTURE;
   "9999999999-!"
   READ NOUPDATE
   @ 20,0

   IF misbn = ' '
      STORE F TO addrec
      LOOP
   ENDIF

   DO Isbntest

   IF .NOT. validtest
      @ 20,1 SAY 'INVALID ISBN NUMBER'
      LOOP
   ENDIF
   FIND &misbn

   IF #>0
      @ 20,1 SAY 'THE BOOK '+ISBN+' NUMBER IS ALREADY IN THE INVENTORY'
      LOOP
   ENDIF
      SELECT SECO
      SET EXACT ON
      FIND &mpub
```

Program 3. MENU4-1.CMD/.PRG Add new titles to the inventory *Continued on next page*

Continued from the previous page

```
        IF #=0
           SET FORMAT TO Menu4-1A
           APPEND BLANK
           READ NOUPDATE
           REPL PUBID WITH mpub
        ENDIF

        SELE PRIM
        SET EXACT OFF
        APPEND BLANK
        SET FORMAT TO Menu4-1
        READ NOUPDATE
        REPLACE ISBN WITH misbn,PUBCODE WITH mpub
        SET FORMAT TO SCREEN
        STORE '              ' TO misbn
  ENDDO
  RELEASE addrec,misbn,oktoadd,trimisbn,mpub
  RETURN
```

Program 3. MENU4-1.CMD/.PRG Add new titles to the inventory

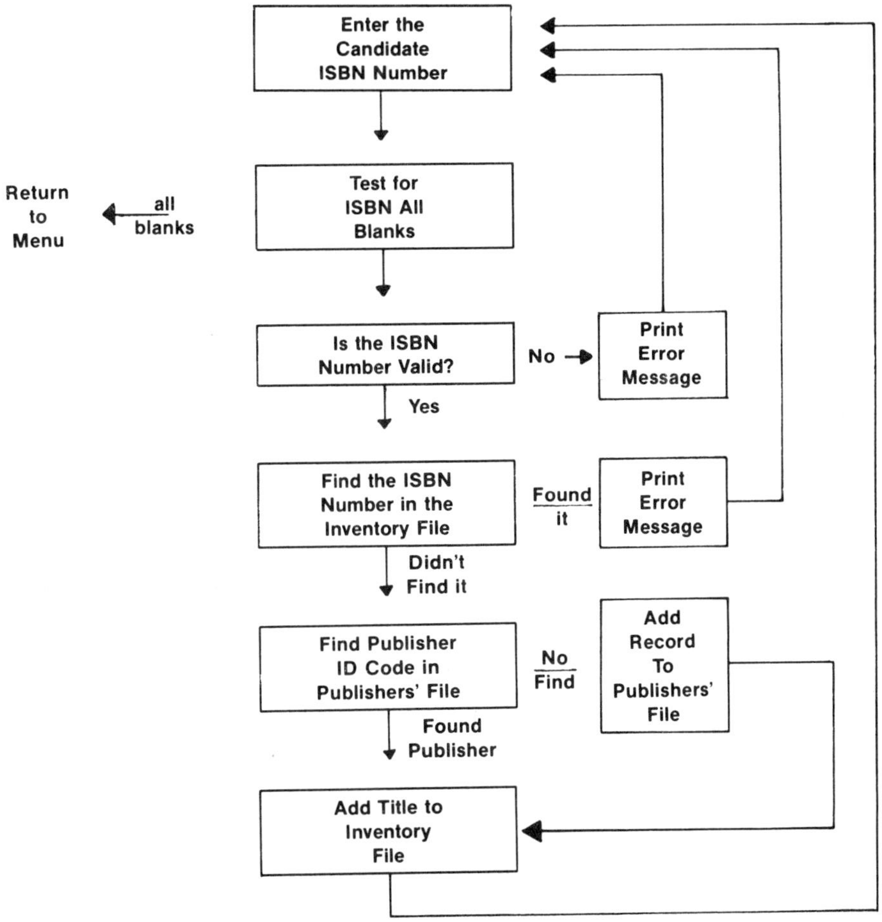

Figure 3. Logic Diagram of Program to Add Titles to the Inventory

```
* Program .....:MENU4-1A.FMT
* Notes .......:format file for adding publisher information


@  3,28 SAY "BOB'S BETTER BOOKS"
@  6,1  SAY 'PUBLISHER..... ' GET NAME PICTURE;
'!!!!!!!!!!!!!!!!!!!!!!!!!!!!!!'
@  8,1  SAY 'STREET ADDRESS ' GET ADDRESS PICTURE;
'!!!!!!!!!!!!!!!!!!!!!!!!!'
@ 10,1  SAY 'CITY.......... ' GET CITY PICTURE '!!!!!!!!!!!!!!!!!!!!'
@ 10,50 SAY 'STATE ' GET STATE PICTURE '!!'
@ 12,1  SAY 'ZIP CODE...... ' GET ZIP PICTURE '99999'
@ 14,1  SAY 'TELEPHONE..... ' GET PHONE PICTURE '(999)-999-9999'
@ 16,1  SAY 'CONTACT....... ' GET ATTN PICTURE;
'!!!!!!!!!!!!!!!!!!!!!!!!!!!!!!'
```

Screen 2. MENU4-1A.FMT Format file to add publisher information

```
* Program .....:MENU4-1.FMT
* Notes .......:format file for adding a new book title

@  3.28 SAY "BOB'S BETTER BOOKS"
@  6,1  SAY 'AUTHOR........ ';
        GET AUTHOR PICTURE '!!!!!!!!!!!!!!!!!!!!!!!!!!!!!!'
@  6,50 SAY 'ISBN NUMBER... : '+misbn
@  8,1  SAY 'TITLE......... ';
        GET TITLE PICTURE '!!!!!!!!!!!!!!!!!!!!!!!!!!!!!!'
@ 10,1  SAY 'SUBJECT....... ' GET SUBJECT PICTURE '!!!!!!!!!!!!!!!'
@ 12,1  SAY 'QUANTITY...... ' GET QTYONHAND
@ 12,25 SAY 'ORDER SIZE.... ' GET ORDERSIZE
@ 12,50 SAY 'MINIMUM STOCK. ' GET MINSTOCK
@ 14,1  SAY 'LIST PRICE.... ' GET LISTPRICE
@ 14,50 SAY 'OUR COST...... ' GET COST
@ 16,1  SAY 'PUBLISHER..... : '+NAME
```

Screen 3. MENU4-1.FMT Format file to add a new book title

already a record for that publisher. If there isn't, we add all the publisher information to the publisher file. Then we add the desired information about the book. Note that in both cases we used READ NOUPDATE for the information that was entered from the keyboard. The REPLACE command which adds the appropriate identification numbers comes after the READ.

To prevent any misidentification of publisher, we SET EXACT ON just before we try to find the publisher by means of the publisher's code *mpub* (which was not released from the ISBN test). The FIND command searches the index file for the contents of *mpub*. Normally, if *mpub* contained 19 and there was a publisher with the ID number of 19234 we would consider that a match. With SET EXACT ON we have a match only if the contents of the field PUBID contained 19 followed by blank spaces.

In this program we used two format files: MENU 4-1A.FMT for the publisher file data and MENU4-1.FMT for the book information. These files are shown as **Screens 2** and 3.

Menu Item 4 Ordering Books (MENU4-4.CMD/.PRG)

What do we want our program to do? In this example we want the computer to prepare purchase orders for books that we want to buy. The books we want to buy are those where the quantity on hand plus the quantity on order is below the minimum stock level.

A program that will do this for us is shown as **Program 4**. This program is basically composed of two parts: the first determines which books to buy; the second part actually orders the books.

How do we build the program? Determining which books to buy is a two-step process. First we assemble a list of the books we *may* want to buy. These are the books where the quantity on hand (QTYONHAND) is less than the minimum stock level (MINSTOCK). Our list of candidate books is created by the use of the COPY command. Now we have a database called TEMPFILE, where the only records are of books that we may wish to order. The records are in order of the publisher's ID code, because the database that we copied from was indexed on the publisher's code.

The next step is to eliminate all the records in this temporary file where there are enough books on order to bring the inventory up to the minimum stock level. To do this, we need to use the TEMPFILE with the ONORDER file. These two files are "linked" by the ISBN number. TEMPFILE becomes our primary file; ONORDER, our secondary.

We then step through the temporary file one record at a time, and attempt to find each book in the ONORDER file. We can do the FIND operation on the contents of the ISBN field if we first store the contents of the ISBN field to a memory variable. We also initialize a variable *qty* to the current value of QTYONHAND.

To do the FIND operation we must select the secondary file, ONORDER. You can only move about within a file while it is selected. There may be more than one record in the ONORDER file for the book of interest. The inner DO loop will update the variable *qty* by the number of books on order. Note that if the book was not on order, the inner DO loop would be ignored.

Now we go back to the primary file. It's important to note that we automatically returned to the record we were using before we went off to look at the secondary file. If the variable *qty* is now larger than MINSTOCK we delete the record. Then we advance a record and do it all over again. The SKIP command is a "relative" addressing technique. The syntax is SKIP n. If n is one, it is

```
        * Menu4-4.CMD   Order Books

ERASE
SET INDEX TO Pubcode
COPY TO Tempfile FOR QTYONHAND<MINSTOCK
  USE Tempfile
IF #>0
  SELE SECO
  USE Onorder INDEX O-isbn
  SELE PRIM

  DO WHILE .NOT. EOF
   STORE F TO delerec
   STORE QTYONHAND TO qty
   STORE ISBN TO misbn
   SELE SECONDARY
   FIND &misbn

   DO WHILE misbn=S.ISBN .AND..NOT.EOF
     STORE S.ORDERSIZE+qty TO qty
     SKIP
   ENDDO

   SELECT PRIMARY
   IF qty>MINSTOCK
    DELETE
   ENDIF
   SKIP
  ENDDO

  SET DELETE ON
  GO TOP
  RESTORE FROM Ponumber ADDITIVE
  ERASE
  @ 5,1 SAY 'TURN THE PRINTER ON!'
  SET MARGIN TO 15
  SET FORMAT TO PRINT
  DO WHILE .NOT. EOF
    STORE m.ponumber+1 TO m.ponumber
    STORE PUBCODE TO mpubid
    STORE 0 TO subtotal
    DO WHILE PUBCODE=mpubid .AND..NOT.EOF
    SELECT SECONDARY
    USE Publish INDEX Pubid
    FIND &mpubid
```

Program 4. MENU4-4.CMD/.PRG Program to order books *Continued on next page*

Continued from the previous page

```
  SELECT PRIMARY
    @  6.1   SAY 'PURCHASE ORDER'+STR(M.PONUMBER,5)
    @  6.62 SAY cdate
    @  7,30 SAY "BOB'S BETTER BOOKS"
    @  8,29 SAY '10150 JEFFERSON BLVD'
    @  9,32 SAY 'CULVER CITY, CA'
    @ 11,1   SAY NAME
    @ 12,1   SAY ADDRESS
    @ 13.1   SAY TRIM(CITY)+', '+STATE+'  '+ZIP
    @ 15,1   SAY 'ISBN NUMBER'
    @ 15,15 SAY 'BOOK TITLE/AUTHOR'
    @ 15,55 SAY 'QTY'
    @ 15,64 SAY 'COST'
    @ 15,75 SAY 'TOTAL'
    STORE 17 TO line
    SELE SECO
    USE Onorder INDEX O-isbn
    SELE PRIM
    DO WHILE PUBCODE=mpubid .AND. LINE<55 .AND..NOT.EOF
      @ line.1 SAY ISBN
      @ line,15 SAY TITLE
      @ line,55 SAY STR(ORDERSIZE,3)
      @ line,60 SAY STR(COST,8,2)
      @ line,70 SAY STR(COST*ORDERSIZE,10,2)
      @ line+1,15 SAY AUTHOR
      STORE line+3 TO line
      STORE COST*ORDERSIZE+subtotal TO subtotal
      SELE SECO
      APPEND BLANK
      REPLACE S.ISBN WITH P.ISBN, S.ORDERSIZE WITH P.ORDERSIZE,;
    PONUMBER WITH m.ponumber, ORDERDATE WITH DATE()
      SELE PRIM
      SKIP
    ENDDO
     IF PUBCODE#mpubid .OR. EOF
      @ line+1,60 SAY 'TOTAL'
      @ line+1.70 SAY STR(SUBTOTAL,10,2)
     ENDIF
    EJECT
 ENDDO
 ENDDO
   SET FORMAT TO SCREEN
   SELECT SECONDARY
   USE
   SELECT PRIMARY
   SAVE ALL LIKE ponumber TO Ponumber
```

Program 4. MENU4-4.CMD/.PRG Program to order books

Continued on next page

Continued from the previous page

```
ENDIF
     USE Inv
     SET MARGIN TO 0
     DELETE FILE Tempfile.dbf
     SET DELETE OFF
     RETURN
```

Program 4. MENU4-4.CMD/.PRG Program to order books

understood. (We can skip backwards as well as forwards.)

This part of our example program is representative of the use of two database files. These two files were "cross-referenced" by means of the ISBN number in much the same way you would do it without a computer.

Now we have our list of books to order. Those we will not be ordering have been "crossed out" (deleted). We have a choice of ways to "get rid" of our deleted records. We can use PACK and physically remove them. Or we can SET DELETE ON and logically remove them. When we use SET DELETE ON, dBASE II will pretend that they aren't there. So, in effect they're not.

In the second part of our program we want to actually order the books by preparing a purchase order for each publisher we are buying from (see **Figure 4**). (Throughout this book we will "create" our own forms. Quite often, it is not convenient to use printed forms unless a computer and its printer are dedicated to one particular task. If they are not, each time you want to do something new, you have to stop and change forms. A reasonably high-quality printer is usually adequate for producing "self-generated" forms.)

We also want to prepare a record of the purchase of each book. This part of the program will use three database files for each purchase order prepared: TEMPFILE, PUBLISH, and ONORDER. TEMPFILE is our source of books to be ordered. PUBLISH provides the name and address of each publisher we are ordering from. ONORDER is our record of the order for each book.

In this program, TEMPFILE will be the primary file at all times. The other two files, PUBLISH and ONORDER, will alternate as the secondary file. We can change the file designated as the secondary each time we use a new file.

To prepare for the second part of our program, we need to re-position the database to the beginning. This is called rewinding, and the command is GO TOP. This takes us to the first logical record in the database. If there are no indexes in use we go to the first physical record. The next step is a simple reminder from dBASE II to the user to turn the printer on.

Each order needs a purchase order number. For our example we retrieve the last purchase order used from a .MEM file. We keep the purchase order number stored in memory (*ponumber*) during this program, incrementing it for each purchase order issued. When we finish we save the last number used back to the disk file from whence it came.

To do the ordering we have used three embedded DO loops. The outer loop is to continue the process until all of the books in TEMPFILE have been ordered. The second loop is to handle all of the books for a specific publisher. The final loop is to take care of the case where we are ordering more books than will fit on a single page.

On each pass through the outer loop we prepare a purchase order. We need to increment the purchase order number, store the publisher's code to memory to act as a control for the two inner loops, and initialize a variable to store the subtotals for the purchase order. Note the "m." in front of the variable *m.ponumber*. We have a field named PONUMBER in the ONORDER file. Since field operations take precedence over memory variables, when we have a field and a memory variable with the same name, the result of an operation on the variable is not always what we wanted.

We do not use the *m.* in the target name when using the STORE command. *m.var* is a legitimate variable name.

STORE PONUMBER TO *ponumber* will store the contents of the field PONUMBER to the memory variable *ponumber*.

```
PURCHASE ORDER 1006                                  23 JULY 1983

                         BOB'S BETTER BOOKS
                        10150 JEFFERSON BLVD
                          CULVER CITY, CA

ODYSSEY BOOKS
4545 SW AVE. 43
PORTLAND, OR  97742
ATTN:  STEVE

ISBN NUMBER       BOOK TITLE/AUTHOR            QTY   COST    TOTAL

0-912677-99-7     EVERYMAN'S DATABASE PRIMER    10   19.95   199.50
                  BYERS, ROBERT

0-912677-01-5     REFERENCE ENCYCLOPEDIA FOR    10   69.95   699.50
                  THE IBM PERSONAL COMPUTER
                  PHILLIPS, GARY/KAREN

0-931988-84-5     MERCANTILE INTERESTS           3   19.95    59.85
                  SMITH, SHARON

0-89588-042-3     THE ORDER OF THE DAY           1    1.95     1.95
                  RAND, ANN

                                                   TOTAL    960.80
```

Figure 4. Purchase order

STORE PONUMBER TO *m.ponumber* will store the contents of the field PONUMBER to the memory variable *m.ponumber*.

STORE *m.ponumber* TO *newnumber* will store the contents of the memory variable *ponumber* to the variable *newnumber*.

With TEMPFILE as our primary file, our first step in the second loop is to use the publisher's file, PUBLISH, so that we can print the purchase order heading. Note that the heading makes use of *cdate*, the "English" date from the main menu program. Then, while still in SECONDARY, we use the ONORDER file. Now we select the primary before entering the third loop.

The purpose of the third loop is to process the individual books that are being ordered from a publisher. The line counter monitors the space available on the page.

In this loop we print detailed information for each book we are ordering. We also keep a running subtotal of the dollar amount for each purchase order. Quantity of books ordered comes from the field ORDERSIZE in the primary file. For each book ordered we add a record to the ONORDER file containing the ISBN number, the number of books ordered, the purchase order number and the system date.

In this example, ORDERSIZE is common to both the primary (TEMPFILE) and secondary (ONORDER) files. We distinguish which is which by preceding the FIELDNAME with a "P." or "S." — an important step in this application. Without the file specification we would store ORDERSIZE back to itself, netting us nothing. The same is true for PONUMBER; we want to replace the content of the field PONUMBER with the content of the memvar *ponumber*.

When we exit from the third loop, we test to see if we are really through with the publisher. If so we print the content of the subtotal variable, eject the page, and go on to the outer loop.

Next, a little cleanup is in order: out goes the secondary file. It doesn't really hurt to have one, but *not* having one avoids confusion and insures that we haven't selected the same file as both primary and secondary. To avoid this, employ the USE command without an accompanying filename while SECONDARY is selected. This closes the database file in use without opening another.

Before returning to the menu, we go back to the primary file and use the database file INV. Each of the programs that is called from MENU4 assumes that INV is in use and that it is the primary file.

Menu Item 5 Updating the Inventory (MENU4-5.CMD/.PRG)

What do we want our program to do? When a shipment of books is received, we want to do the following: update the quantity on hand in the inventory file, close out (delete) the records in the ONORDER file, and do a printout of the items updated. **Program 5** accomplishes these tasks.

The next job is to enter the books received into a temporary file. The COPY command can be used to create the file structure that we want to use for our temporary file. We really want only part of the structure copied, and no records. By specifying the fields to be copied, the structure we want to use in our temporary file can be defined. The FOR clause uses an impossible condition — quantity received greater than 10000 — which guarantees that our new database file will have no records. The command NEXT 1 speeds up the process by keeping dBASE II from reading the entire ONORDER file.

How do we build the program? We want to start our data entry process with INV as the primary file and our new file UPDATE as the secondary file. As items are entered into UPDATE, we want as many as possible to remain on the screen. A typical entry

```
* Program .....:MENU4-5.CMD (or MENU4-5.PRG)
* Notes .......:This program updates the Inventory.

ERASE
USE Onorder
COPY NEXT 1 FIELDS ISBN,QTYRCVD TO Update FOR QTYRCVD>10000
USE Inv INDEX Isbn
SELE SECO
USE Update
STORE T TO mupdate
STORE '             ' TO misbn
@ 1,1 SAY 'ISBN NUMBER   QTY    TITLE'
STORE 2 TO line
SET COLON OFF

DO WHILE mupdate
   @ LINE.1  GET misbn PICTURE "9999999999-!"
   READ NOUPDATE

   IF .NOT. misbn = ' '
      SELE PRIM
      FIND &misbn

      IF #=0
         @ line,20 SAY misbn+' IS NOT IN THE DATABASE'
         LOOP
      ENDIF
      @ line,20 SAY TITLE
      SELE SECO
      APPEND BLANK
      @ line,15  GET QTYRCVD
      READ NOUPDATE
      CLEAR GETS
      REPLACE ISBN WITH misbn
      SELE PRIM
      REPLACE QTYONHAND WITH QTYONHAND+QTYRCVD, LASTRCV WITH
                                                DATE() NOUPDATE
```

Program 5. MENU4-5.CMD/.PRG Update inventory

Continued on next page

Continued from the previous page

```
    IF line<23
      STORE line+1 TO line
    ELSE
      ?
    ENDIF
    STORE '                  ' TO misbn
  ELSE
    STORE F TO mupdate
  ENDIF
ENDDO

SET COLON ON
SELE SECO
USE
SELE PRIM
USE Onorder INDEX O-isbn
UPDATE FROM Update ON ISBN RANDOM ADD QTYRCVD
GO TOP
STORE 0 TO excess
STORE '     ' TO misbn
DO WHILE .NOT. EOF
  IF ORDERSIZE>QTYRCVD .AND. ISBN=misbn .AND. excess>0
    REPL QTYRCVD WITH QTYRCVD+excess
  ENDIF

  IF QTYRCVD>ORDERSIZE
    STORE QTYRCVD-ORDERSIZE TO excess
    STORE ISBN TO misbn
  ENDIF

  IF ORDERSIZE<=QTYRCVD
    DELETE
  ENDIF
  SKIP
ENDDO
```

Program 5. MENU4-5.CMD/.PRG Update inventory

Continued on next page

Continued from the previous page

```
SELE PRIM
USE Inv INDEX Isbn
SELE SECO
USE Update
ERASE
? 'MAKE SURE THE PRINTER IS TURNED ON'
SET FORMAT TO PRINT

DO WHILE .NOT. EOF
   STORE 9 TO line
   @ 5,30 SAY 'INVENTORY UPDATE FOR '+cdate
   @ 7,15 SAY 'ISBN NUMBER'
   @ 7,35 SAY 'QTY'
   @ 7,45 SAY 'TITLE'

   DO WHILE .NOT.EOF .AND. line<55
      @ line,15 SAY ISBN
      @ line,35 SAY QTYRCVD
      STORE ISBN TO misbn
      SELE PRIM
      FIND &misbn
      @ line.45 SAY TITLE
      STORE line+1 TO line
      SELE SECO
      SKIP
   ENDDO
   EJECT
ENDDO
SET FORMAT TO SCREEN
USE
SELE PRIM
RELEASE mupdate,misbn,line,excess
RETURN
```

Program 5. MENU4-5.CMD/.PRG Update inventory

screen might look like Screen 3. Normally, when data are entered using the GET command, colons define the beginning and end of the data entry area. In this example we don't want these colons to appear, so SET COLON OFF is used.

Only the ISBN number and the quantity of books received will be entered, in two columns. As each item is entered, the book title will be retrieved from the inventory database and displayed in the third column. If the book isn't found in the inventory, we display the message "item is not in the database" in the third column. Before the DO LOOP is entered, we display the column headings. These remain on the screen until we've entered 22 items. At that point the screen display scrolls up one line for each entry — and each new entry is entered on Line 23.

The ISBN number is entered into a memory variable *misbn* with the help of PICTURE. We attempt to FIND the contents of *misbn* in our inventory file. If it's not found, we go back and try again. If it is, we display the title and select the secondary file, add a blank record, enter the quantity received into the field QTYRCVD, and move the contents of the memory variable *misbn* into the field ISBN. We now have a complete record of the item being updated.

Now we go back to our INV database. It was positioned to the correct record with the previous FIND. We update the fields for quantity on hand and last received date. Notice that the content of a field is used in the secondary file to help with the updating. Remember, the NOUPDATE command inhibits updating of index files. No indexed item was changed.

CLEAR GETS prevents our moving the cursor back to "correct" an earlier entry. Because of the way this program was structured, we cannot go back to make corrections. In addition, we can have only 64 "gets" between either an ERASE or CLEAR GETS.

When we've finished entering the books into the temporary file, our inventory file has also been updated. Our next step is to delete the appropriate records from the ONORDER file.

The UPDATE command is used to update one file with the data stored in another. The file being updated is ONORDER; the file we are updating from is the temporary file UPDATE. These two files are linked by the ISBN number. In this case the ISBN numbers in UPDATE may not be in order. To use UPDATE here, the file being updated must be indexed on the linkage (as it is), and the word RANDOM must be used in the command statement. ADD QTYRCVD adds the value in the file UPDATE to the value in the same field in the file ONORDER.

Part of programming is anticipating what can happen. There might be more than one record in the ONORDER file for a record in the UPDATE file. This last operation would have updated only the first of the records in the ONORDER file. It is also possible that the quantity updated is larger than that ordered by the record.

Now we want to step through the ONORDER file one record at a time. For each record there are three possibilities. The quantity received can be greater than, less than, or equal to the order size. If the quantity is less than the order size we ignore the record. If the quantity is equal to the order size we delete the record. If the quantity is greater than the order size we store the excess to a memory variable and delete the record. Then we check the next record. If the ISBN number is the same and the quantity is less than the order size and the amount stored in EXCESS is greater than zero, we replace the quantity with excess and test the quantity with the order size.

Now we print out the contents of our temporary file. To do this we use the inventory file together with the temporary file so that we can print the book title.

ASHTON·TATE

Chapter Eight

SALES ORDER ENTRY

Sales order entry is the process of entering new orders for goods into the computer, so that these orders can be filled. Once filled, they become invoices and are used by Accounts Receivable to prepare billings.

Developing an order entry system can be challenging. Frequently a sales order translates into more than one database record, and the standard dBASE II data entry facility provides for *single* record entry. The challenge is to make the entry process natural for the user.

In our business example, the information to be entered in each record consists of an order identification number, and:

who has ordered the books
what titles and quantities of books
when the order was entered.

We want to maintain order records "on-line" for a period of a year. We have chosen to use three database files for our order entry system. These three files are represented pictorially by **Figure 1**.

The three database files SALES, SALESDET, and OPENORD are linked by the sales order number SONUMBER (see **Figure 2**). The SALES file is a master listing of all orders that have been entered into the system, whether they have been filled or not. The SALESDET file contains sales details on each order. The file OPENORD is a listing of orders that have not yet been filled.

In order to save disk space, we have chosen to use two files, SALES and SALESDET, rather than a single file. If our business processes 20 orders each day and the average order is for ten different titles, and there are 200 business days in a year. SALES will have 4000 records and SALESDET will have 40,000.

Combined into a single file, each of the 40,000 records would take 51 bytes of disk space (50 bytes of data plus one byte of overhead). This works out to over 2,000,000 bytes of disk storage. Our two-file approach takes less than 1,300,000 bytes — saving about 700,000 bytes.

Sales orders are entered as they are received and sales order numbers are assigned sequentially. In

SALES DATABASE

Sales Order Number	Customer I.D. Code	Date	Customers P.O. Number
100211	016215	09/21/83	A6125A3
100212	321311	09/21/83	B-2314
100213	116161	09/22/83	D-6524
100214	553131	09/22/83	X-63-83
100215			
100216			
100217			
100218			

SALES DETAIL DATABASE

Sales Order Number	ISBN Number	QTY	Price
100211	X — — — — —	23	8.75
100211	— — — — — —	14	21.63
100211	— — — — — —	39	— — — — — —
100212	— — — — — —	64	— — — — — —
100212	— — — — — —	101	— — — — — —
100213	— — — — — —	98	— — — — — —

OPEN ORD

Sales Order No.
100214
100215

Figure 1. Pictorial representation of the sales order database

Database file: SALES

	FILENAME	TYPE	SIZE	DEC
Sales order number	SONUMBER	C	6	
Customer ID code	CUSTID	C	6	
Customer purchase order number	PONUMBER	C	8	
Date order was entered	DATE	C	8	

Database file: SALESDET

Sales order number	SONUMBER	C	6	
Book ISBN number	ISBN	C	13	
Quantity ordered	QTY	N	3	
Price to customer	PRICE	N	6	2

Database file: OPENORD

Sales order number	SONUMBER	C	6	

Figure 2. Schema for sales order entry

```
* Program .....:MENU5.CMD (or MENU5.PRG)
* Notes .......:This program is the Sales Order Menu.

DO WHILE T
   STORE ' ' TO choice
   ERASE
   @  2,30 SAY "BOB'S BETTER BOOKS"
   @  4,31 SAY 'SALES ORDER MENU'
   @  6,34 SAY cdate
   @  8,25 SAY '1 - Enter a Sales Order'
   @  9,25 SAY '2 - Edit a Sales Order'
   @ 10,25 SAY '3 - Void a Sales Order'
   @ 11,25 SAY '4 - Print Sales Orders'
   @ 12,25 SAY '5 - Prepare Sales Report'
   @ 13,25 SAY '6 - Outstanding Orders'
   @ 14,25 SAY '7 - Delete Orders More than 1 Year Old'
   @ 15,25 SAY '0 - GO BACK TO THE MAIN MENU'
   @ 18,25 SAY '  - PICK ONE'
   @ 18,24 GET choice
   READ NOUPDATE

   IF choice = '0'
      RELEASE lastentry,select
      RETURN
   ENDIF

   IF choice $'1234567'
      STORE 'MENU5-'+choice TO select
      DO &select
   ENDIF
ENDDO
```

Program 1. MENU5.CMD/.PRG Menu program for sales order entry

our example, we will take advantage of this and develop our order entry system without using *any* index files. We will also take advantage of the fact that the most recently entered data is the data of greatest interest, which is true for many business and personal files.

In the remainder of this chapter we are going to discuss five programs from **Program 1** (MENU 5):

MENU5-1 — Entering a sales order
MENU5-4 — Printing a sales order
MENU5-5 — Preparing a sales report
MENU5-6 — Displaying outstanding orders
MENU5-7 — Clearing out old orders

MENUS 5-2 and 5-3 may be found in Appendix E.

Menu Item 1 Entering a Sales Order (MENU5-1.CMD/.PRG)

Program 2, which allows entry of sales orders, is diagrammed in **Figure 3**. The program prompts the user to enter the customer's identification code, checks to see if that code matches the last entry, locates the customer's record, and displays information about the customer. The user can now enter the ISBN number and quantity of each book ordered. When all the ordered books have been entered, the sales order number is added to the open orders file.

Our program is entirely contained within the loop *salesorder*. When we enter the loop we select the primary file. This is done because a little later in the program, when the secondary file is selected, we could encounter a situation which would take us back to the beginning of the loop.

It is good to be alert to the consequences of commands while programming. dBASE II does not allow you to choose the same file as both primary and secondary. Opening the program with USE SALES would produce a dBASE II error message.

This program displays a placeholder each time the user is prompted to enter a customer identification code. The placeholder displays the customer's name for the last order entered. Providing a placeholder is often overlooked by programmers. Without a placeholder, a data entry worker who gets distracted between orders has no clue as to which order was last entered.

Our first step in the program is to use the sales file to obtain the variables *nextentry* and *mcustid*. (We will use *nextentry* later in the program when the sales record is added to the databases SALES, SALESDET, and OPENORD.) We will perform the test for a sales order record every time a sales order is entered. MCUSTID is used to locate the customer record — for the last sales order.

This program requires that the user enter the customer's identification code to initiate a sales order. We could have used the customer name or, as in an earlier example, either the name or the ID code, but in that case additional programming would be needed that did not contribute to the item of interest, order entry.

Our next step is to test the variable *mcustid*. If a <RETURN> is entered rather than a customer code, it's back to the menu. The next test covers the case where the customer code entered is the same as that for the last sales order. Here an option is provided: starting over or entering a new order. Next, we attempt to find the customer code in the customer file. If the try is unsuccessful an error message is displayed and we start over.

If we flag an error and need to start over, the error messages will remain on the screen for as long as it takes to open the files and locate the last entry record. This is not long but is adequate to inform the user, and eliminates the need to keep track of error messages and clear parts of the screen as we move through the program.

We elected to use the INPUT command to provide the special queries to the user. This minimizes

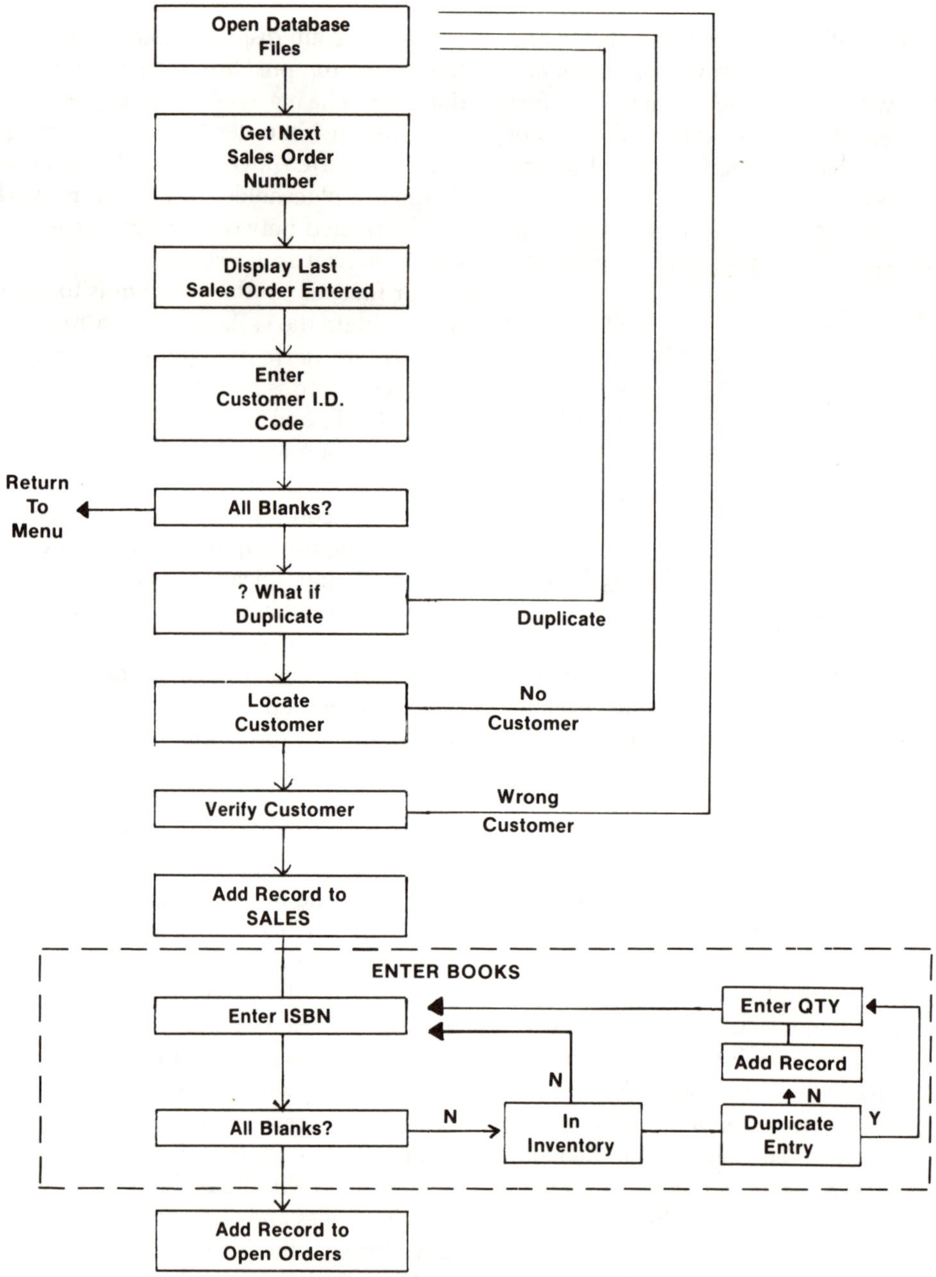

Figure 3. Diagram of Program 2

```
* Program ......:MENU5-1.CMD (or MENU5-1.PRG)
* Notes ........:This program is for Sales Order Entry.

STORE T TO salesorder
DO WHILE salesorder
   SELE PRIM
   USE Sales
   GO BOTTOM

   IF #>0
      STORE VAL(SONUMBER)+1 TO nextentry
   ELSE
      STORE 100000 TO nextentry
   ENDIF

   STORE CUSTID TO mcustid
   SELE SECO
   USE Customer INDEX Custid
   FIND &mcustid

   IF nextentry = 100000
     STORE '                ' TO lastentry
   ELSE
     STORE 'LAST ENTRY: '+SONUMBER+'   '+NAME+'    '+P.DATE TO lastentry
   ENDIF

   ERASE
   @  1,20 SAY 'SALES ORDER ENTRY SYSTEM'
   @ 23,1  SAY lastentry
   STORE '      ' TO mcustid
   @  3,0  SAY 'ENTER CUSTOMER IDENTIFICATION NUMBER ';
           GET mcustid PICTURE '999999'
   READ NOUPDATE

   IF mcustid = '    '
      STORE F TO salesorder
      LOOP
   ENDIF

   IF P.CUSTID = mcustid
      INPUT 'CUSTOMER ID MATCHES LAST ENTRY - ENTER ANYWAY (Y/N)? ' ;
TO query

      IF .NOT. query
```

Program 2. MENU5-1.CMD/.PRG Sales order entry program *Continued on next page*

Continued from the previous page

```
        LOOP
    ENDIF

ENDIF

FIND &mcustid

IF #=0
   @  4,1  SAY 'INVALID CUSTOMER ID NUMBER - TRY AGAIN'
   LOOP
ENDIF

ERASE
@  $,1  SAY NAME

IF .NOT. ATTN = '  '
   @ $+1,1 SAY ATTN
ENDIF

@ $+1,1 SAY ADDRESS
@ $+1.1 SAY TRIM(CITY)+', '+STATE+'  '+ZIP
?
INPUT 'IS THIS THE CORRECT CUSTOMER (Y/N)? ' TO query

IF .NOT. query
   LOOP
ENDIF

@  5,0
@  6,0
SELE PRIM
APPEND BLANK
REPL SONUMBER WITH STR(nextentry,6),DATE WITH DATE(),CUSTID WITH mcustid
STORE SONUMBER TO mso
@  6,1  SAY "CUSTOMER'S P.O. NUMBER " GET PONUMBER
READ
@  6,1  SAY 'ISBN NUMBER          QTY       TITLE
USE Salesdet
SELE SECO
USE Inv INDEX Isbn
SELE PRIM
STORE T TO detail
STORE 22 TO line
```

Program 2. MENU5-1.CMD/.PRG Sales order entry program *Continued on next page*

Continued from the previous page

```
DO WHILE detail
   STORE '             ' TO misbn
   @ line,1  GET misbn
   READ
   CLEAR GETS

   IF misbn = '  '
      STORE F TO detail
      LOOP
   ENDIF

   SELE SECO
   FIND &misbn

   IF #=0
      DO Isbntest

      IF .NOT. validtest
         @ line,30 SAY misbn+' IS NOT VALID    '
      ELSE
         @ line,30 SAY misbn+' NOT IN INVENTORY'
         STORE line+1 TO line
      ENDIF

      LOOP
   ENDIF

   @ line,30 SAY TITLE
   @ line,65 SAY LISTPRICE
   SELE PRIM
   GO BOTTOM

   DO WHILE SONUMBER = mso .AND. .NOT. ISBN = misbn .AND. .NOT. #=0
      SKIP -1
   ENDDO

   IF .NOT. (SONUMBER = mso .AND. misbn = ISBN)
      APPEND BLANK
      REPLACE SONUMBER WITH mso,ISBN WITH misbn,PRICE WITH listprice
   ELSE
      @ line,0
      @ line,1 SAY misbn
      @ line,30 SAY '----DUPLICATE ENTRY----'
   ENDIF
```

Program 2. MENU5-1.CMD/.PRG Sales order entry program *Continued on next page*

Continued from the previous page

```
         @ line,20 GET QTY
         READ
         CLEAR GETS

         IF line >= 23
            ?
         ELSE
            STORE line+1 TO line
         ENDIF

      ENDDO
      SELE PRIM
      USE Openord
      APPEND BLANK
      REPLACE SONUMBER WITH mso
   ENDDO
   RELEASE salesorder,nextentry,mcustid,query,mso,detail,line,misbn,mpub,;
   validtest
   SELE SECO
   USE
   SELE PRIM
   RETURN
```

Program 2. MENU5-1.CMD/.PRG Sales order entry program

the chance that the user will "type through" the query. INPUT requires a <RETURN> before the entry is accepted.

After locating the customer record, we check the accuracy of the customer code by displaying the code and providing a chance to escape. Note how the customer data is displayed. The $ uses the current screen line (Line 1 immediately after the ERASE), a terrific way to handle cases where we may want an item included in the display. The disadvantage of the $ as a position command is that we don't know where we are on the screen. In order to be sure we have erased the INPUT query, we erase both Lines 5 and 6.

Once we have the desired customer, we APPEND a blank record to the SALES file and enter the sales order number (this comes from the variable *nextentry* created at the beginning of the program), the system date and the customer code. We could have chosen to make the customer name a part of the file, which would give us a marginal speed advantage but double the size of the file.

Now we allow the user to enter the customer's purchase order number (PONUMBER). At this point we have created the master sales record. The next step is to enter the books ordered into the SALESDET file.

When we enter the books being ordered into the file, we use the ISBN number. Our program looks up the title in the inventory file and displays the title and the price to be charged the customer. Then we enter the quantity of that item being ordered. A representative display of this order entry screen is shown as **Screen 1**.

Again, we need to make a number of tests: to determine whether to terminate the data entry process, to see if the ISBN number is already in the inventory, and to test the validity of the ISBN number.

If a <RETURN> is entered rather than an ISBN number, the process is terminated. If a number had been entered, we try to find that number in the inventory database. If we don't find the number, one of two things has happened: either we do not stock the book, or the number was entered incorrectly. In the space where the title is normally printed, we print an error message which includes the number entered and go to the beginning of this part of the program. We printed the number as part of the error message because all blanks are stored back to the entry variable *misbn* on each pass through the program. This message allows the user to determine what was wrong.

If a number was found, we display the title and the price. Before any further activity takes place, we verify that we have not already entered the title for this sales order.

If a duplicate entry exists, it is somewhere near the end of our non-indexed database. To look for it, we search backwards from the end of the database.

SKIP n is a relative addressing command. It moves you by the amount n (either positive or negative) from the current record. With SKIP, you don't need to know where you are. It cannot take you past the end (or the beginning) of the database. Direct addressing GOTO 20000 produces a dBASE II error message if there were fewer than 20,000 records in the database. SKIP 20000 takes you to the end of the file and no further, without producing an error message.

Our loop will move us backwards as long as the content of SONUMBER matches the content of *mso* and we do not encounter the ISBN number. Note the term .AND..NOT.#=0. This is the equivalent of the EOF (end of file) function for the beginning of the file. We need it here — even though we will be using it only in the first sales order entered.

If we do not locate a duplicate, we add a blank record to the database and replace the sales order field with the contents of *nextentry*, the ISBN field

```
TEDIOUS TECHNICAL TOMES
GEOFFREY D. MARTINDALE III
2123 MONTMORENCY PLACE
CITY OF INDUSTRY, CA 91232

 ISBN NUMBER          QTY      TITLE                           PRICE

0-13-196519-0          5   MICROPROCESSORS                      7.14
0-8306-0082-5          2   FOREE'S FAMOUS FORTH FIGURES         9.11
```

Screen 1. CRT display for sales order entry

with the variable *misbn*, and the PRICE field with the contents of the LISTPRICE field in the database INV. Although it is already in the database INV, we add the price here because we want to insure that the customer is charged the appropriate amount if we change the price (in INV) before the next billing.

If a duplicate entry is found, we erase the entry line on the screen, write the ISBN number using a SAY command, and print the message DUPLICATE ENTRY where the title was.

In both cases we are now prompted to enter the quantity. If the record is being edited the value previously entered is visible. This allows the operator to edit a previous record by deliberately entering a duplicate number. We will void a record by entering a 0 for the quantity.

Each time the READ command was used for data entry we followed with the CLEAR GETS command. There are two reasons for this: we did not want the user to be able to back up (on screen) and think he had changed the entry; also, we are limited to 64 uses of the GET command before we *must* issue either a CLEAR GETS or an ERASE.

Now we increment the line counter and enter the next book. The approach being used allows us to have up to 24 titles on the screen at a time. As we may need to enter more than 24 titles for a single order, we stop incrementing the line counter when Line 23 is reached. At that point a single ? is used each time we pass through the loop. The ? on Line 23 will cause the screen contents to scroll up one line. From this point on, each new entry will be on Line 23, since dBASE II counts Lines 0 to 23.

After entering the order, we choose our control file OPENORD (the list of sales orders that have not been filled) as the primary file.

When all orders are entered, we clean up by closing out the secondary file and releasing all unneeded memory variables.

Menu Item 4 Printing Out Sales Orders(MENU5-4.CMD/.PRG)

Chances are that we'll want to print out a sales order; we want our printed sales order to look like the entry "form" of **Screen 1**. Our printing program is shown as **Program 3**.

The first step is to find the sales order in our database system. Remember, we did not index these files. Normally, we would use LOCATE, but LOCATE searches sequentially from the beginning of the file, and the records that we want to print are usually near the end of the file. Since the sales orders are entered sequentially, the sales order numbers can be used to find the record we are interested in.

The first thing to do is store the starting and ending sales order numbers to memory variables. We will use these two numbers to validate the sales order number entered as the sales order to print. It's important to avoid entering a number that is either larger or smaller than any number in the database. Note that even though the sales order numbers are stored as characters, we are able to compare them as if they were numeric fields.

Once we've entered a number that falls within the valid range we estimate the record number for the record.

STORE VAL(mso)-VAL(start) + 1 TO *place*

We've used the VAL function to allow us to use these character string variables in arithmetic. It was necessary to add one to the difference, since our desired sales order *mso* could be the first record in the database (*start*).

If our database is perfect and there are no missing records, GO PLACE will position us directly at the desired record. We have the choice of either GO or GOTO *place*. When direct addressing is used, we must be going to a valid record number.

```
* Program .....:MENU5-4.CMD (or MENU5-4.PRG)
* Notes .......:This program prints a Sales Order.

USE Sales
STORE SONUMBER TO start
GO BOTTOM
STORE SONUMBER TO end
ERASE
@  1,1  SAY 'PRINT OUT SALES ORDER'
STORE T TO printout

DO WHILE printout
   STORE '      ' TO mso
   @  3,1  SAY 'ENTER SALES ORDER NUMBER TO BE PRINTED ';
           GET mso PICTURE '999999'
   READ

   IF mso = '      '
      STORE F TO printout
      LOOP
   ENDIF

   IF mso > end
      @  5,1  SAY 'NUMBER TOO LARGE'
      LOOP
   ENDIF

   IF mso < start
      @  5,1  SAY 'NUMBER TOO SMALL'
      LOOP
   ENDIF
   STORE VAL(mso)-VAL(start)+1 TO place
   GO PLACE

   DO WHILE mso>SONUMBER .AND. .NOT. EOF
      SKIP
   ENDDO

   DO WHILE mso<SONUMBER .AND. #>0
      SKIP -1
   ENDDO

   IF SONUMBER = mso
      SET FORMAT TO PRINT
      SET PRINT ON
      SET MARGIN TO 15
```

Program 3. MENU5-4.CMD/.PRG Printout of sales order *Continued on next page*

Continued from the previous page

```
    @  6.1  SAY 'SALES ORDER '+SONUMBER+'   DATED: '+DATE
    STORE CUSTID TO mcustid
    STORE PONUMBER TO mpo
    SELE SECO
    USE Customer INDEX Custid
    FIND &mcustid
    @  9,1  SAY NAME
    @  9,45 SAY 'CUSTOMER P.O. '+mpo

    IF .NOT. ATTN = '  '
       @ 10,1  SAY ATTN
       @ 11,1  SAY ADDRESS
       @ 12,1  SAY TRIM(CITY)+', '+STATE+'  '+ZIP
    ELSE
       @ 10,1  SAY ADDRESS
       @ 11,1  SAY TRIM(CITY)+', '+STATE+'  '+ZIP
    ENDIF
    USE Salesdet
    SELE PRIM
    USE Inv INDEX Isbn
    SELE SECO
    DO Search

    DO WHILE SONUMBER = mso .AND. .NOT. EOF
       @ 14,1  SAY 'ISBN NUMBER        QTY        PRICE    TITLE'
       STORE 16 TO line

       DO WHILE SONUMBER = mso .AND. .NOT. EOF .AND. line<55
          @ line.1  SAY ISBN
          STORE ISBN TO misbn
          @ line.20 SAY QTY
          SELE PRIM
          FIND &misbn
          @ line,30 SAY PRICE
          @ line,40 SAY TITLE
          SELE SECO
          SKIP
          STORE line+1 TO line
       ENDDO
       EJECT
    ENDDO
    STORE F TO printout
  ENDIF
ENDDO
```

Program 3. MENU5-4.CMD/.PRG Printout of sales order *Continued on next page*

Continued from the previous page

```
RELEASE line,printout.selection.start,end,mso,mpo,place,jumpsize,;
findstart,misbn
SET MARGIN TO 0
SET FORMAT TO SCREEN
SET PRINT OFF
SELE SECO
USE
SELE PRIM
RETURN
```

Program 3. MENU5-4.CMD/.PRG Printout of sales order

If, for whatever reason, our database is not perfect, we can home in on the record we want by skipping either forward or backward using the two DO loops following the positioning command. If our candidate number is larger than the content of SONUMBER for the record we positioned to, we haven't gone far enough. If it's smaller, we've gone too far. Only the applicable loop will apply. If we tried to go to a number in the valid range that is not in the database, we will eventually end up at either the beginning or the end of the file with no harm done.

If the record is found, we enter a relatively standard display routine — even if it does use several files. The item of interest in this display loop is the command DO SEARCH.

In our main sales order file SALES we have one record for each sales order, so that there is a correlation between sales order number and record number. In our sales detail file SALESDET we can have several records for each sales order, so we cannot predict exactly where the data of interest begins. However, the sales orders are still sequential within the file. There are a number of approaches that can be used to locate the records we want.

The approach we have chosen is of general applicability to any file where the records are in sequential order. Any sorted file where we would be searching on the sort key could use this approach *if* the records are in sequential order. A program to implement our search is shown as **Program 4**.

The general scheme is to first check the beginning and the end of the database to insure that neither of these records is the desired one and that the desired record is in a valid range. Next we go to the middle. If the record content is too large we go halfway to the beginning; if it's too small we jump halfway to the end. We keep jumping in this seesaw manner until we get within a certain range of the record we want. Each time we jump, the jump is only half as far as the last. When we are within range, and in front of the record, we can use:

```
LOCATE NEXT N FOR ......
IF ......
```

The whole idea here is to get close enough so that LOCATE doesn't take excessive time. This technique is a variation of a "Binary Search."

Another technique that we could use is to skip backwards in steps of 100 until we reach a sales order that is smaller than the one we want and then employ the LOCATE command. If we know that the record we want is at or near the end of the database, this is a much more efficient approach. The more specialized your need, the more optimum use you can make of your searching algorithm.

A third possible technique is to add a field to the SALES database. This field contains the record number of the first detail record in the database SALESDET for the sales order. The field becomes a "pointer" and our system becomes quasi-hierarchical. This is a particularly workable scheme if we never do random deletions in either database. When deleting, we delete only a block of records at the beginning of the database SALES. After the database is packed, select the SALESDET as the secondary file, then:

DELETE WHILE S.SONUMBER<P.SONUMBER
PACK
SELECT PRIMARY
GO TOP
STORE *pointer* -1 TO *adjust*
REPLACE ALL *pointer* WITH *pointer-adjust*

Though this would have been a particularly powerful technique to use in this set of examples and would speed up parts of the process considerably, it is not without pitfalls. One potential

```
*search command

GO BOTTOM
IF .NOT. mso=SONUMBER
 STORE # TO end
 STORE INT(#/2) TO jumpsize

 SKIP -jumpsize
ENDIF


IF .NOT. mso=SONUMBER
DO WHILE .NOT.mso=SONUMBER .AND. jumpsize > 3
STORE INT(jumpsize/2) TO jumpsize
IF mso>SONUMBER
  SKIP -jumpsize
ENDIF
IF MSO<SONUMBER
  SKIP -JUMPSIZE
ENDIF
ENDDO
ENDIF

DO WHILE mso>SONUMBER .AND..NOT.EOF
  SKIP
ENDDO
DO WHILE mso<SONUMBER .AND. #>0
 SKIP -1
ENDDO

STORE T TO findstart
DO WHILE findstart .AND. #>0
 SKIP -1
 IF MSO#SONUMBER
   SKIP
   STORE F TO findstart
   LOOP
 ENDIF
ENDDO
```

Program 4. Search command

problem area is if the "pointers" get out of kilter; if you are writing the program for someone else, don't even try it. Generally speaking, fine tuning performance usually comes with risk.

Menu Item 5 The Daily Sales Report (MENU5-5.CMD/.PRG)

Program 5 prepares a daily sales report or summary of the day's activities, which would look like **Screen 2**.

Our first step is to determine the number of sales orders entered during the day. We do this by selecting SALES as our primary file and storing the last record number to a memory variable *bottom* with STORE # TO *bottom*.

Next we skip backwards through the database one record at a time until we encounter either the beginning of the database (# = 0) or the date differs from the desired date. The number of orders is simply the difference between the stored record number *bottom* and the current record number. Note that the current record number is for the record just before the first record of the date of interest. We are going to store this result as a character string to the variable *sales*:

STORE STR(*bottom* -#,5) TO *sales*

Now if we skip one record we will be positioned at the first sales order of the day. We need to store the sales order number to a variable *mso*, the variable used by our search routine in the last section. SALESDET is selected as our secondary file. Then use the program SEARCH to position at the first sales order record of the day in the secondary file SALESDET.

The next step is to obtain the total quantity of books sold during the day, the value of those books, and the number of titles (records in the secondary file) entered during the day. All of this is done with:

SUM NEXT 6500 QTY,QTY*PRICE,1 TO
■ *sold,worth,entries*

Why the *next* 65000? We want to sum the expressions listed from the point we were at in the database to the end of the database. The SUM command terminates automatically at the end of the database. NEXT causes the SUM command to begin at the positioned record. We chose 65000 just to be sure that we used a number that was larger than the number of records between where we were and the end of the database.

The final step is to print out the report. We have collected all the needed information. The number of books sold during the day is in the variable *sold*. The number of books per sales order is just the total number of books sold divided by the number of sales orders. Note that we had to multiply the expression *sold/sales* by 1.0.

The number of decimal places displayed as a result of a dBASE II arithmetic operation depends upon the number of decimal places used directly in the expression. This is technically correct, although it is somewhat of a nuisance. For example, if we divide four by five, dBASE II will tell us 4/5 = 0 even though it has actually carried out the arithmetic operation properly. It has displayed the result in accordance with the rules for arithmetic operations.

To get dBASE II to display the result we want, we need either to include the desired number of decimal points in the expression as in *sold/sales* *1.0, or we can display the result as a part of a string operation as in STR(*entries/sales*,10,1). With the string operation, we display the quotient of *entries/sales* as a character string with a length of 10, including one decimal place.

```
Sales Report for 08/01/83

SALES ORDERS PROCESSED              18

NUMBER OF BOOKS SOLD                260

AVG BOOKS PER SALES ORDER           14.4

AVG VALUE PER SALES ORDER           170.94

NUMBER OF TITLES PER S/O            1.1

TOTAL VALUE OF SALES ORDERS         3077.00
```

Screen 2. Daily sales report

```
* Program .....:MENU5-5.CMD (or MENU5-5.PRG)
* Notes .......:This program produces the Daily Sales Report.

ERASE
SELE PRIM
USE Sales
GO BOTTOM
STORE # TO bottom
STORE DATE TO salesday

DO WHILE DATE = salesday .AND. #>0
   SKIP -1
ENDDO
STORE bottom-# TO sales
SKIP
STORE SONUMBER TO mso
SELE SECO
USE Salesdet
DO Search
SUM NEXT 65000 QTY,QTY*PRICE,1 TO sold,worth,entries

SET FORMAT TO PRINT
SET MARGIN TO 15
@  6,1  SAY 'Sales Report for '+DATE
@  9,1  SAY 'SALES ORDERS PROCESSED'
@  9,30 SAY sales
@ 11,1  SAY 'NUMBER OF BOOKS SOLD '
@ 11,30 SAY sold
@ 13,1  SAY 'AVG BOOKS PER SALES ORDER '
@ 13,30 SAY sold/sales*1.0
@ 15,1  SAY 'AVG VALUE PER SALES ORDER '
@ 15,30 SAY worth/sales
@ 17,1  SAY 'NUMBER OF TITLES PER S/O '
@ 17,30 SAY STR(entries/sales,10,1)
@ 19,1  SAY 'TOTAL VALUE OF SALES ORDERS '
@ 19,30 SAY worth
RELEASE bottom,salesend,detailend,sales,salesday,mso,findstart,jumpsize,end
EJECT
SET FORMAT TO SCREEN
SELE SECO
USE
SELE PRIM
USE
RETURN
```

Program 5. MENU5-5.CMD/.PRG Daily sales report

Menu Item 6 Display of Outstanding Sales Orders (MENU5-6.CMD/.PRG)

The file OPENORD, the list of sales orders that have not yet been filled, is the controlling file for processes that use the sales order system. Since sales orders are removed from this file after they are filled, this file will not be very large.

From time to time we want to know the status of this file, which orders have not been filled, and who they belong to. **Program 6** is intended to provide a video display of this status with an option for a printed copy.

Three files are to be used in preparing this report: OPENORD, SALES, and CUSTOMER. An example of the product of this program is shown as **Screen 3**.

The items displayed are the sales order number, the date the order was entered, the customer purchase order number (if any), the customer's identification code, and the customer's name.

In the process of preparing this report we skip through the file OPENORD one record (sales order) at a time. For each record in this file we first select SALES as our secondary file, go to the bottom of the file SALES, and skip backwards until we find the record where the sales order number matches the sales order number in our primary file. Then we display the sales order number, the date, the purchase order number, and the customer code, using the ? command (optionally we could have used DISPLAY OFF).

We have not displayed the name even though we want the name displayed on the same line as the other items. To get the name, we store the sales order number to the memory variable *mcustid*. Now select the file CUSTOMER indexed on CUSTOMERID. Alternating between secondary files is slow. Speed in this case is of little importance, however, since the number of records to be processed is small, averaging 20 per day.

Next we find the desired record in the customer file and display the customer's name using the ?? command. ?? is the same as the single question mark except that it does *not* issue a carriage return or a line feed. It displays items beginning with the last position of the cursor or the printhead.

If we have chosen not to print the display, the ACCEPT command is used (with a <RETURN>) to cause the screen display to pause. This prevents the program from terminating and returning to the menu before we finish reading the information displayed on the screen.

Menu Item 7 Deleting Old Sales Order Records (MENU5-7.CMD/.PRG)

In order to get rid of the records that are more than a year old, use **Program 7** to purge the two database files SALES and SALESDET. Since neither file is indexed, this program is reasonably simple and markedly faster than it would be if such large files were indexed.

The records that we want to delete from the two files occur in blocks at the beginning of each. First we delete records from the file SALES. Here a simple date criterion can be used. We are literally going to delete everything that is more than one year old by reducing the year in the current system date by one.

The current date previously stored at the introduction to the menu system is the variable *mdate*. *mdate* is in the form MM/DD/YY. To use the date as a part of a comparison operation, we need to turn it around so that the variable is in the form YY/MM/DD. This can be done physically by creating variables in this form, or logically by naming the pieces within the command string.

```
S. O. #   DATED   P. O. #    ID #    NAME
100010 08/01/83            100001    TEDIOUS TECHNICAL TOMES
100011 08/01/83 45         100002    BAKER'S BILIOUS BOOKS
100013 08/01/83 89         100002    BAKER'S BILIOUS BOOKS
100014 08/01/83 99         100003    ODYSSEY BOOKS
100015 08/01/83 45678/78 100001    TEDIOUS TECHNICAL TOMES
Press <RETURN> to return to the menu.
```

Screen 3. Screen display of open orders

```
* Program .....:MENU5-6.CMD (or MENU5-6.PRG)
* Notes .......:This program gives the Open Sales Orders report.

ERASE
@  1,30 SAY 'OPEN SALES ORDERS AS OF '+DATE()
STORE ' ' TO query
@  3,1  SAY 'DO YOU WANT A PRINTED COPY (Y/N)? ' GET query PICTURE '!'
READ
@ 3,0

IF query = 'Y'
   SET PRINT ON
   SET FORMAT TO PRINT
   SET MARGIN TO 15
   @  6,1  SAY 'OPEN SALES ORDERS AS OF '+DATE()
   ?
ENDIF
? 'S. O. #   DATED   P. O. #   ID #   NAME'
SELE PRIM
USE Openord

DO WHILE .NOT. EOF
   SELE SECO
   USE Sales
   GO BOTTOM

   DO WHILE .NOT. SONUMBER = P.SONUMBER .AND. #>0
      SKIP -1
   ENDDO

   ? SONUMBER, DATE, PONUMBER, CUSTID
   STORE CUSTID TO mcustid
   USE Customer INDEX Custid
   FIND &mcustid
   ?? '  ',NAME
   SELE PRIM
   SKIP
ENDDO

IF .NOT. query = 'Y'
   ACCEPT 'PRESS THE RETURN KEY TO RETURN TO THE MENU ' TO query
ENDIF
RELEASE mso,query,selection,mcustid
EJECT
```

Program 6. MENU5-6.CMD/.PRG Open sales orders report

Continued on next page

Continued from the previous page

```
SET MARGIN TO 0
SET PRINT OFF
SET FORMAT TO SCREEN
SELE SECO
USE
SELE PRIM
RETURN
```

Program 6. MENU5-6.CMD/.PRG Open sales orders report

```
* Program .....:MENU5-7.CMD (or MENU5-7.PRG)
* Notes .......:This program deletes Sales records over one year old.

ERASE
@  5,1  SAY 'CLEARING OUT OLD RECORDS TAKES TIME - RELAX '
USE Sales
STORE STR(VAL($(mdate,7,2))-1,2)+$(mdate,1,6) TO repldate
DELETE WHILE $(DATE,7,2)+$(DATE,1,6) < repldate
SET TALK ON
PACK
GO TOP
STORE SONUMBER TO mso
USE Salesdet
DELETE WHILE SONUMBER < mso
PACK
SET TALK OFF
RELEASE mso,repldate
RETURN
```

Program 7. MENU5-7.CMD/.PRG Delete records over one year old

In this example both have been done. First we create the variable *repldate*. *repldate* is actually of the form YYMM/DD/. That the slashes are in the wrong place doesn't matter as long as what we compare it to has the slashes in the same place as *repldate*. *repldate* begins with the year, which is one less than the current year.

Records are deleted where the "reorganized" date matches *repldate*. We use DELETE WHILE as opposed to DELETE FOR to avoid reading the entire database, which substantially speeds up the operation.

Once we have packed the database SALES, it is necessary to go back to the beginning and store the first sales order number to the variable *mso*. GO TOP is the dBASE II command to position you to the beginning of the database. If the database is not indexed, then GO TOP will take you to Record One, the first record in the database. If the database is indexed, GO TOP takes you to the first logical record in the database.

Next we select the file SALESDET. Once again we want to delete a block of records at the beginning of the database file. USE positions us to Record One in the file SALESDET. We want to get rid of all of the records up to, but not including, the record where the sales order number is stored in *mso*. Again, we use the DELETE WHILE command to do this.

Deleting and packing records in large databases is a slow operation. Packing involves physically rearranging the database file. If we delete 100 records from the beginning of the file, the first remaining record would be Record 101. When we PACK the file, Record 101 is physically moved to the disk position formerly occupied by Record One. Record 102 is moved to the position formerly occupied by Record Two, and so forth. Disk operations of this type are slow. On many computer systems, particularly systems with Winchester drives, there isn't much of an indication that the computer is really doing anything.

In our example program we first display the message that the process may take a long time. Then we SET TALK ON so that dBASE II's normal activity display will be routed to the screen enabling the user to have some feel for what the computer is doing. We need to remember to SET TALK back OFF before we exit this program.

ASHTON·TATE

Chapter Nine

ORDER FULFILLMENT AND INVOICING

Once a sales order has been entered into the computer, the next step is to fill the order and prepare an invoice. The invoice is printed for the customer and stored to the invoices file for use by Accounts Receivable in the monthly billing.

Another task of order fulfillment is to set up a system for back ordering books. If a customer order exceeds books in stock, we need to create a record of owing the customer so many copies of a particular book at the original order price. When the books come in, we ship them to the customer and prepare a billing invoice.

The order fulfillment system consists of the sales order files, inventory file, customer file, invoice files, and a back orders file (see **Figure 1**).

In this chapter, we are going to discuss programs to convert sales order records to invoice and back order records, and a program to print the customer's invoice. In **Program 1**, the menu program for the order fulfillment system, these tasks are shown as Item 1, Filling a Sales Order, and Item 3, Reprinting an Invoice. The programs developed on these items illustrate one of the major concepts of structured programming: calling other programs.

The menu program itself was pirated from previous menus and modified to be the Order Fulfillment Menu. Of particular interest on this menu is the second IF group. In this group there are program selections that do not exist because we copied this menu from the Main Menu in Chapter Four. To protect against a syntax error we use the dBASE II file function:

```
IF FILE('filename')
```

This function is used to test for the existence of a file on a disk. The filename must include the file identifier, and be enclosed by both delimiters and parentheses.

In our example, we have stored a part of the filename to the variable *select*. We could have concatenated .CMD to *select* so that *select* would con-

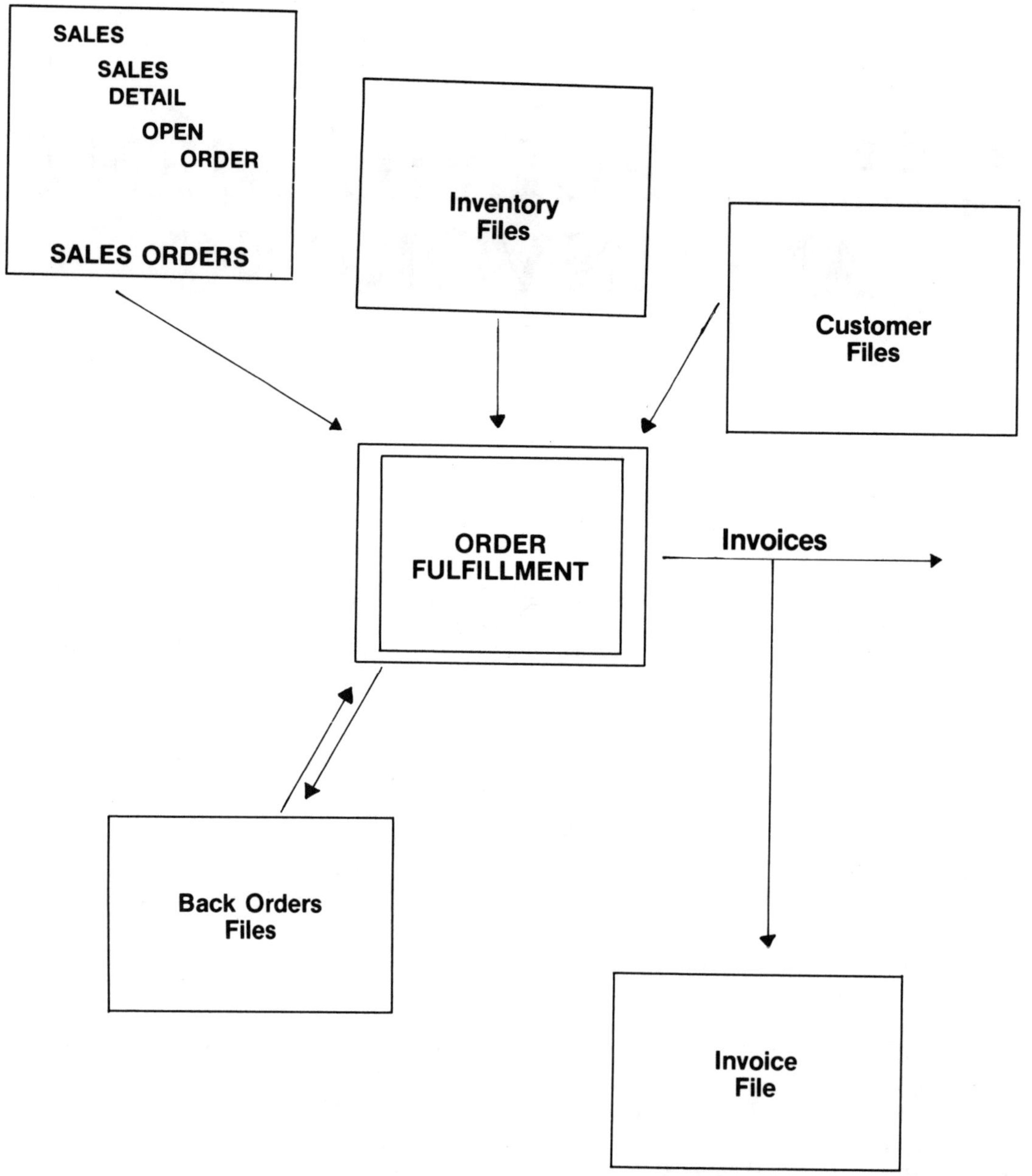

Figure 1. Diagram of order fulfillment system

```
* Program .....:MENU6.CMD (or MENU6.PRG)
* Notes .......:This program is for filling Invoices.

DO WHILE T
   STORE ' ' TO choice
   ERASE
   @  2,30 SAY "BOB'S BETTER BOOKS"
   @  4,31 SAY 'ORDER FULFILLMENT MENU'
   @  6.34 SAY cdate
   @  8,25 SAY '1 - Fill a Sales Order'
   @  9,25 SAY '2 - Display Backorders'
   @ 10,25 SAY '3 - Reprint an Invoice'
   @ 15,25 SAY '0 - GO BACK TO THE MAIN MENU'
   @ 18,25 SAY '  - PICK ONE'
   @ 18,24 GET choice
   READ NOUPDATE

   IF choice = '0'
      RELEASE lastentry,select
      RETURN
   ENDIF

   IF choice $'1234567'
      STORE 'MENU6-'+choice TO select

      IF FILE ('&select..CMD')
         DO &select
      ENDIF
   ENDIF
ENDDO
```

Program 1. MENU6.CMD/.PRG Menu program for order fulfillment system tain the entire filename. Then we would have IF FILE('&*select*') instead of IF FILE ('&*select*' ..CMD'). If we had selected Menu Item 1, for example, this would then read IF FILE('MENU 6-1.CMD').

Instead, we have chosen to concatenate the .CMD to *select* within the expression. This is done by the period (.) between .CMD and &*select*. That period "tells" dBASE II where the end of the macro title is. When used in this way the variable *select* is referred to as a "macro." The way it is used is called macro substitution.

Sales Order Fulfillment

In our dynamic book distributor's operation, a copy of the sales order is printed for the warehouse to use in filling the order. After the order is filled, the copy of the sales order is returned to the computer clerk. If the warehouse was unable to ship the requested number of books for a given title, the actual number shipped is written on the sales order form.

We could have adjusted the inventory value for quantity on hand for each title when the sales order was issued, before the order was sent to the warehouse. We have chosen not to do so for the following reason: computers process orders first in, first out (FIFO), whereas warehouse workers tend to process orders last in, first out (LIFO). Most orders go into an in basket with the last order on top. A warehouse worker who picks up one of the top orders in the basket might not realize that available stock has been assigned to a previous order. S/he will see that the book has been back ordered and think that the computer has made a mistake.

Later in the day, the worker gets down to the earlier sales order that the computer had assigned the stock to, and now there is not enough stock. The worker thinks that the computer has been wrong twice in one day. All records on these orders then have to be corrected back at the office to adjust the computer to the reality of the warehouse. It is a lot simpler to let the warehouse control the inventory in the first place — especially since it is likely to do so anyway. Adjusting stock quantities after the order is filled gives us a better match with the realities of our inventory. It also involves simpler software.

Of the seven programs in this chapter, order fulfillment is handled with Programs 2, 3, 4 and 6. The main program in this group is **Program 2. Program 3** is auxiliary to Program 2, and incorporates the search program used in the last chapter. A diagram of the overall program is shown as **Figure 2.**

If you look over Program 2, you will notice that the program is mostly composed of various tests of one type or another. The rest of the program consists of procedures for moving and manipulating records. Program 2 uses nine separate database files, of which only three, CUSTOMER, INVOICES and INV (inventory), are indexed.

The sequence of activities in this program is:

- Identify the sales order to the computer, enter the sales order number.
- Verify that the correct sales order was entered, display the customer's name and address.
- Check for any back-ordered items, do special back order processing.
- Assign an invoice number to the transaction (there may be more than one invoice per sales order).
- Create invoice records similar to sales order records.
- Print out the invoice.

Program 2 begins by selecting OPENORD as the primary file and CUSTOMER, indexed on the customer identification code, as the secondary file. OPENORD contains only the sales order numbers

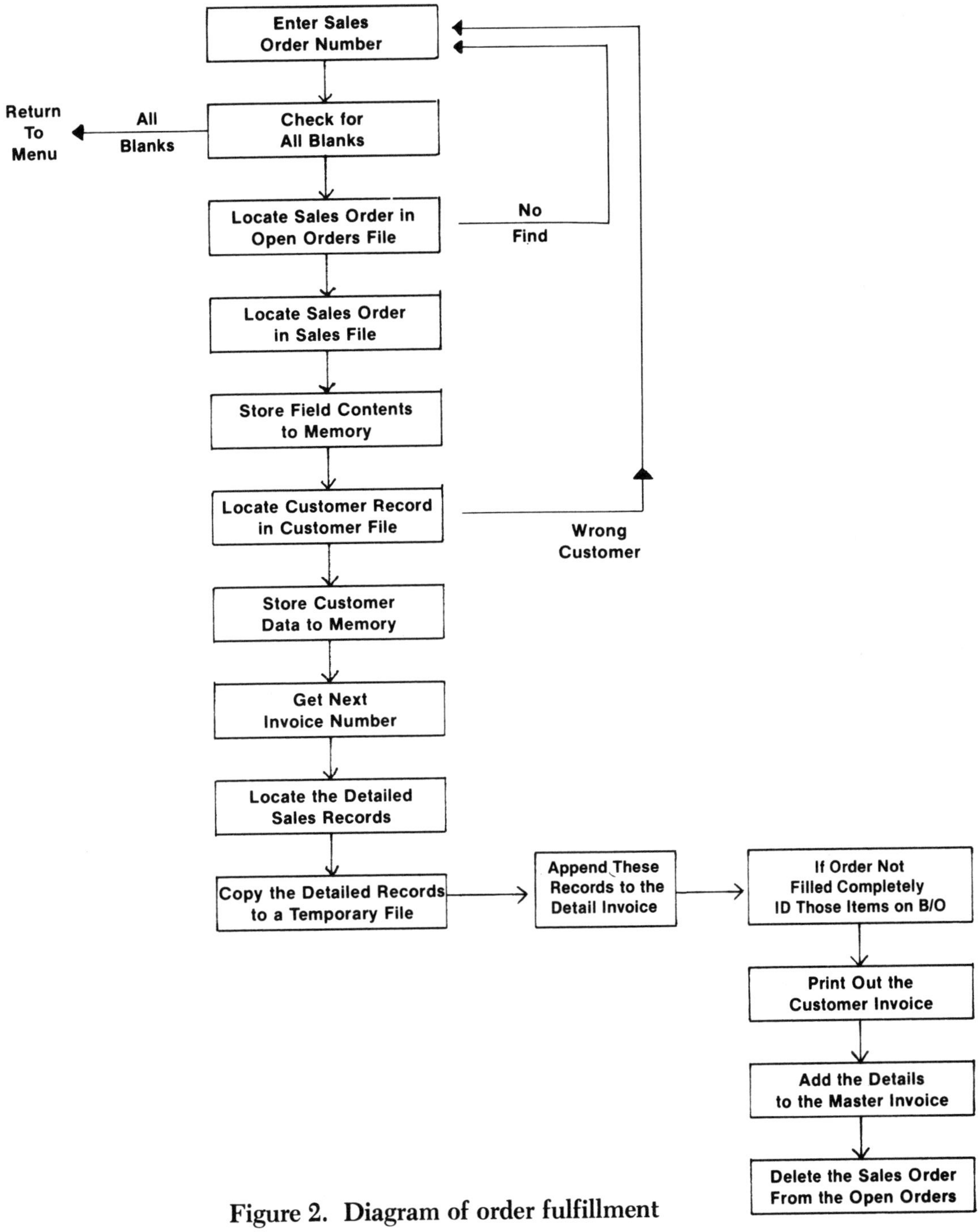

Figure 2. Diagram of order fulfillment

```
* Program --------:Menu6-1.CMD/.PRG
* Notes ----------:program to close out sales orders and prep
* ----------------:invoices

ERASE
STORE T TO program

USE Openord
SELECT SECONDARY
USE Customer INDEX Custid
SELE PRIM

DO WHILE program

@ 1,20 SAY 'ORDER FULFILLMENT AND INVOICES SYSTEM'

STORE '      ' TO mso
@ 3,1 SAY 'ENTER SALES ORDER NUMBER' GET mso PICTURE '999999'
READ

IF mso='      '
   STORE F TO program
   LOOP
ENDIF

LOCATE FOR SONUMBER=mso

IF EOF
   @ 5,1 SAY 'SALES ORDER '+mso+' IS NOT OPEN'
   LOOP
ENDIF

@ 5,0
USE Sales
GO BOTTOM
DO WHILE .NOT. mso=SONUMBER
  SKIP -1
ENDDO

STORE CUSTID TO mcustid
SELECT SECONDARY
FIND &mcustid
SELECT PRIMARY

STORE NAME TO name
STORE ADDRESS TO address
```

Program 2. MENU6-1.CMD/.PRG Program to prepare invoices for filled orders *(Continued)*

Continued from the previous page

```
STORE TRIM(CITY)+', '+STATE+'  '+ZIP TO city
STORE ATTN TO attn

@ $,1 SAY m.name
@ $+1,1 SAY m.address
@ $+1,1 SAY m.city

@ $+2,0
STORE ' ' TO query
DO WHILE .NOT. query $ 'YNyn'
@ $,1 SAY 'IS THIS THE CORRECT CUSTOMER (Y/N)? ' GET query
READ
ENDDO  ----------- for answer checking loop

IF .NOT. query $ 'Yy'
   USE Openord
   ERASE
   LOOP
ENDIF

CLEAR GETS

STORE ' ' TO query
DO WHILE .NOT. query $ 'YNyn'
@ $,1 SAY 'IS THIS ORDER COMPLETELY FILLED (Y/N)? ' GET query
READ
ENDDO  ----------- for answer checking loop

DO Menu6-1a
STORE mso TO savemso
STORE m.invoice TO mso
STORE DATE() TO date

IF  query$'Nn'
DO Menu6-1b
ENDIF
DO Menu6-3p

USE Invoices
INDEX I-custid
APPEND BLANK
REPLACE INVOICE WITH m.invoice, DATE WITH DATE(), CUSTID WITH mcustid,;
   PONUMBER WITH m.ponumber, AMOUNT WITH m.amount
```

Program 2. MENU6-1.CMD/.PRG Program to prepare invoices for filled orders *(Continued)*

Continued from the previous page

```
  USE Openord
  LOCATE FOR savemso=SONUMBER
  DELETE
  PACK

  ERASE
  SELECT SECONDARY
  USE Customer INDEX Custid
  SELECT PRIMARY

  ENDDO --------------- for main program loop

  RELEASE program,mso,mcustid,name,city,address,attn,query,invoice,;
 ponumber,end,jumpsize,findstart,savemso,date,amount,page,line,misbn
  SELE SECO
  USE
  SELE PRIM
  RETURN
```

Program 2. MENU6-1.CMD/.PRG Program to prepare invoices for filled orders

of orders that have not been filled. When an order is filled (by this program), the order number will be deleted from OPENORD. We expect that this database is not going to be very large — especially at seven bytes per sales order (an average of 140 bytes per day if our burgeoning business has 20 orders a day).

As usual, the bulk of the program is contained within a DO loop. DO loops simplify the code through the various error tests that are made. Whenever an error is detected an error message is printed, and we LOOP back to the beginning of the program. It's often worthwhile putting the program in a DO loop even if commands inside the loop are executed only one time.

The first step is to set up the screen and the key memory variable, *mso*. Remember, the PICTURE clause prohibits our entering any characters except numbers into the variable, which simplifies error checking to a small degree. The first thing to do is check to see if we want to stop, which we do by entering a <RETURN>.Next we check to see if the sales order number is in the file.

If it is, we get the computer to help us verify whether the right number has been entered by finding the customer record and displaying the customer's name and address. At the same time we store the customer information to memory variables, so that if we have the correct customer, we can print the information. Though there is a lot more work to do before we are ready to print the invoice, storing the data to memory allows us to avoid looking up the customer again when it is time to print. Information we need to print accumulates as we go along; memory variables allow the program to be simpler (and faster) by eliminating frequent opening and closing of files.

Following the display of customer data, we query the user as to whether the computer has found the correct record. We have confidence that the computer has found the record the user asked for; the query checks whether or not the user entered the number actually desired.

A word on queries: Many programs overdo asking the user if data is correct. If asked at every step, the user automatically begins to answer "yes" and the purpose is defeated. Rather than simply asking if the user has done the correct thing, it is better to display data reinforcing the record in question.

Another important check in the program deals with back orders. Since our book distributor runs a reasonably tight ship, the program asks a single question regarding back orders. The answer then leads irretrievably down one of two paths. Such brevity (with no checks) is not really a good practice. A better choice would be always to enter the equivalent of **Program 4**, the program to process incomplete orders. This way, the user has to take a more positive action to make a choice. Program 2 illustrates calling a program (in this case, Program 4) as a result of an action by the user.

At this point we want to bring the next invoice number into the program. The two principal ways to save the invoice number are to a disk memory (.MEM) file or in a database. We have chosen to use a database with one record and one field, INVOICE. Our database name is CONTROL.

The idea of using a database for storing various control parameters used in the program system is one that should be examined for each software system. The task is to open the file, extract the parameter, increment it and close the file. Though it's tempting (and easy) to open the system once and operate entirely from memory variables, if something goes wrong — you trip over the computer's power cord, for instance — recovery may be more difficult than if there were only a single parameter increment to recover to.

Note that the invoice number is stored as a character string.

The next step is to use the file SALESDET, which contains the detailed sales records for the

```
* Program -------- :MENU6-1A.CMD/.PRG
* Notes  --------- :called from  Menu6-1,  processes  completely
* -----------------:filled orders.  Starting databases are  sales
* -----------------:prim and customer second

SELECT SECONDARY
USE controls
IF # = 0
  APPEND BLANK
  REPLACE INVOICE WITH 200000
ENDIF
REPLACE INVOICE WITH INVOICE+1
STORE STR(invoice,6) TO invoice
STORE PONUMBER TO ponumber

SELECT PRIMARY
USE Salesdet
DO Search

* ----------:At this point the sales order gets split into two
* ----------:parts -- the invoiced items and back orders.
* --- Don't forget to add the qty ordered somewhere.
* --- The  file Invoiced contains the entire order with the  added
* --- field Qtyship.

COPY TO Tfile WHILE SONUMBER=mso
USE Tfile
REPLACE ALL SONUMBER WITH m.invoice,QTYDEL WITH QTY
USE Invoiced
APPEND FROM Tfile
DELETE FILE Tfile
RETURN
```

Program 3. MENU6-1A.CMD/.PRG Program to process complete orders. Auxillary program to MENU6-1.

sales order being filled. Using SALESDET automatically saves the previous file CONTROL and writes it back to the disk. To find the desired record in SALESDET, we "call" the pseudo-binary search program SEARCH (Program 4 in Chapter Eight). This positions us to the first record with the sales order number we have asked for.

The object here is to move sales records either to the back order file or to the invoice file INVOICED, which is the invoice system counterpart to the file SALESDET. The structure of INVOICED is the same as that of SALESDET except for the addition of a field QTYDEL, the quantity actually shipped. Most of the time, quantity shipped (QTYDEL) will be the same as quantity ordered (QTY). The database plans for the two invoice files are shown in **Figure 3**.

We first move all the records in the relevant sales order to a temporary file. Then we "tack on" the records in this temporary file to the end of the file INVOICED. This is shown pictorially in **Figure 4**.

The process for moving the records may appear somewhat roundabout, but it is ultimately faster than the alternative approach, which would be to USE INVOICED and APPEND FROM SALESDET FOR SONUMBER= *mso*. Though this alternative approach is simpler, it causes dBASE II to read SALESDET in its entirety. Since SALESDET is a large file (over a megabyte), this "simpler" approach would actually take much longer. The copying process we will use reads only the records of interest.

In our plan for the file INVOICED we have used the fieldname SONUMBER for the field containing the index numbers. This allows us to use the APPEND FROM operation to add the records from the temporary file TFILE to INVOICED. Here we want the entire file anyway, so APPEND FROM is the "fastest" option.

Note that we replace the sales order number in the index file with the invoice number before moving these records to the invoice file. This is done to preclude the possibility that the sales order number is the same as the last invoice number used. When the records have been moved to the invoice file, the QTYDEL will be zero because there is no QTYDEL field in the sales file. Initially, the quantity delivered is set to the quantity ordered. This allows us to change the quantity delivered by exception since most items are completely filled. We take advantage of this situation when we enter the back order data, if there is any.

We "call" the program to enter back order information, **Program 4**, only if we had entered a "no" to the query, "Is this order completely filled?" Program 4 allows us to identify records where there is a back order through a relatively simple technique. We ask the user to enter each ISBN number that is to be back ordered. We locate the record by searching the database backwards, since we know that we are dealing with the last few records in the database INVOICED. Then we allow the user to change the quantity shipped (QTYDEL).

This process continues until the user enters a <RETURN> instead of an ISBN number. At this point, the program developer needs to make a "human factors" decision. The user is much more likely to enter inadvertently a <RETURN> than to enter a more deliberate response such as STOP or END. We can just as easily detect a STOP or END in the memory variable as we can detect all blanks. In either case, the capability for editing these files to correct an error must be provided. It is not always provided within a program for users who are facile in dBASE II, but for those who are not, it is a must.

Once we have "edited" the records, we need to move copies of them to the back orders file, BACKORD. We retain these records in INVOICED so that we can reprint the invoice at any time. Moving copies of these records to the back orders file is done by using a temporary file as the

DATABASE FILE: INVOICES

	FIELDNAME	TYPE	SIZE	DEC
Invoice number	INVOICE	C	6	
Customer ID code	CUSTID	C	6	
Cust.purc.order number	PONUMBER	C	8	
Date of invoice	DATE	C	8	
Amount of invoice	AMOUNT	N	8	2

DATABASE FILE: INVOICED

Invoice number	SONUMBER	C	6	
ISBN number	ISBN	C	13	
Quantity ordered	QTY	N	3	
Quantity shipped	QTYDEL	N	3	
Unit price	PRICE	N	6	2

Figure 3. Database plans for invoice files

SALES

SO #	CUST ID	DATE	PO #
221212	123456	09/21/83	A282
221213	837211	09/21/83	129-83
221214	161171	09/21/83	1876-11

SALESDET

SO #	ISBN	QTY	PRICE
221212	848374	7	643
221213	123456	10	895
221213	678435	5	714
221213	897343	30	934
221214			

OPENORD

SO #
221213

INVOICES

INVOICE #	CUST ID	DATE PO #	AMOUNT
121613	123456	09/21/81	24.95
121616	837211	09/22/83	86.21

INVOICED

SO #	ISBN	QTY	PRICE	QTY DEL
121615	845763	11	9.45	6
121616	123456	10	8.95	5
121616	674939	5	7.14	5
121616	894737	30	6.00	30

BACKORD

SO #	ISBN	QTY	PRICE	QTY DEL
221213	123456	10	8.95	5

Figure 4. Pictorial representation of moving sales order records to the invoice and back orders files

```
* Program ------------ Menu6-1B.CMD/.PRG
* Notes------------ Program to enter back orders.  File in use is
* ----------------------Invoiced.

STORE 'x' TO misbn
ERASE
DO WHILE .NOT. misbn= '    '
STORE '              ' TO misbn
?
@ 23.1 SAY 'ISBN NUMBER' GET misbn
READ
IF .NOT. misbn='   '
GO BOTTOM
DO WHILE mso=SONUMBER .AND. .NOT. ISBN=misbn .AND..NOT. #=0
  SKIP -1
ENDDO

IF .NOT. misbn=ISBN
   @ 23.30 SAY 'DID NOT LOCATE ISBN '+misbn
   LOOP
ENDIF

@ 23.30 SAY 'ENTER QUANTITY SHIPPED' GET QTYDEL
READ

IF QTYDEL>QTY
@ 23.30 SAY 'PROBABLE ERROR ON ENTRY'
ENDIF
ENDIF  -- for case where no number entered

ENDDO

GO BOTTOM
DO WHILE mso=SONUMBER .AND. .NOT. ISBN=misbn .AND..NOT. #=0
  SKIP -1
ENDDO
SKIP

COPY NEXT 65000 TO Tfile FOR QTYDEL<QTY

USE Backord
```

Program 4. **MENU6-1B.CMD/.PRG Program to process incomplete orders. Auxillary program to MENU6-1.**

Continued on next page

Continued from the previous page

```
APPEND FROM Tfile
REPLACE SONUMBER WITH savemso FOR SONUMBER=m.invoice
USE Invoiced

DELETE FILE Tfile

RETURN
```

Program 4. MENU6-1B.CMD/.PRG Program to process incomplete orders. Auxillary program to MENU6-1.

--- INVOICE ---

BOB'S BETTER BOOKS
10150 JEFFERSON BLVD
CULVER CITY, CA 90230

01 AUG 1983
Invoice Number 200048
dated: 08/01/83

ODYSSEY BOOKS
4545 SW AVE. 43
PORTLAND, OR 97742
ATTN: STEVE

CUSTOMER NUMBER 1000003
REF: PURCHASE ORDER 12345678

TITLE ORDERED/ISBN	QTY	PRICE	TOTAL
BARDOLATRY 0-201-14471-9	21	10.50	220.50
THE PRINCESS AND THE PEA 0-911979-00-X	22	11.00	242.00
THE IDOL OF THE IDLE 0-8359-9517-8	23	11.50	264.50
POESIE 0-89588-047-4	24	12.00	288.00
PRIMITIVE RIGHTS 0-13-110163-3	25	12.50	312.50
RENE' AND THE MILKMAID 0-87835-025-X	26	13.00	338.00
A WALKING TOUR OF AVON 0-89588-048-2	27	13.50	364.50
GOOD QUEEN BESS 0-931988-84-5	28	14.00	392.00
THE COMPLEAT IDIOT'S GUIDE TO COMPUTERS 0-89588-042-3	29	14.50	420.50
THE SINK OR SWIM SCHOOL OF PROGRAMMING 0-89588-066-0	30	15.00	450.00
	Total Due		3292.50

Figure 5. Example of invoice

transfer medium. This allows us an easy way of replacing the invoice number with the sales order number, which then links back order records to the original sales order. This allows us to respond to a customer's query about an order.

Once we get back to the main program, we store the sales order variable *mso* to *savemso*, store the variable *invoice* to *mso*, and store the system date to *date*. These operations are done so that we can use the same program, **Program 6**, to print the invoices here and in menu selection 3, Reprint an Invoice. We will discuss the printing program in the section on Reprinting an Invoice. The invoice printed by the program is shown as **Figure 5**.

After we've printed the invoice we add a record to the main invoice file INVOICES. The replacement operation uses a variable *amount*. This variable was created by the printing program.

Now we go back to the starting database file, OPENORD (the list of open sales orders), and "close out" the order by deleting the record corresponding to the sales order number we have just filled. Now we can either fill the next order or return to the Fulfillment Menu.

Reprinting Invoices

There are any number of reasons why we might want to reprint an invoice, not the least of which is that the printer ran amok and crunched the paper during the original printing. We should be able to reprint most of the paper products of our business system.

In our example we can reprint the invoice for some period of time. In **Program 5**, the program to reprint invoices, we test the invoice number that was entered to see if it is in the database by simply looking at the first record and the last. A diagram of Program 5 is shown as **Figure 6**.

In our business system we discard the invoices that have been billed at the end of each month. This allows us to use the LOCATE command to find the invoice record. LOCATE will always "find" the record by searching the entire database. In an interactive system with a large database, this can take more time than the user would like.

If the database were really small, it might be faster to just use the LOCATE command as the existence test. In our example we have assumed that the range test takes much less time than the LOCATE command. If that were not the case, we would have been better off using LOCATE.

Even if the invoice number is within the valid range for invoice numbers, it might *not* be in the database file. If it is not, we must do the test for actually finding the invoice.

In order to print the invoice once it has been found, we store all of the parameters describing the invoice to memory variables. We will need these parameters at various points within the printing program, and it's more convenient to take them from memory than to stop and reopen the invoices file.

Next we locate the customer record and store all of the customer's parameters to memory variables. Again we use memory for our later convenience.

Part of the rationale for these procedures is to have this printing operation and the original invoice printing operation, Menu Item 1, use the same printing program.

In order to print the desired invoice we will need the stored memory variables and the database files INVOICED and INV (inventory). These two files contain the details of the transactions.

On the first page of the invoice (Figure 5) we print a page heading. This heading is printed by calling **Program 7**. On subsequent pages, if any, we print the invoice page number and the invoice number. You should note that the date printed is the original invoice date and not the current date.

```
* Program-----------Menu6-3.CMD/.PRG
* Notes ------------Program to reprint invoices

ERASE
STORE T TO program

USE Invoices
SELECT SECONDARY
USE Customer INDEX Custid
SELE PRIM

DO WHILE program

@ 1,30 SAY 'REPRINT AN INVOICE'

STORE '      ' TO mso
@ 3,1 SAY 'ENTER INVOICE NUMBER' GET mso PICTURE '999999'
READ

IF mso='      '
   STORE F TO program
   LOOP
ENDIF

GO TOP
STORE INVOICE TO start
GO BOTTOM
STORE INVOICE TO end
IF INVOICE>=start .AND. INVOICE<=end
LOCATE FOR INVOICE=mso
ENDIF

IF EOF .OR. INVOICE>end .OR. INVOICE<start
   @ 5,1 SAY 'INVOICE '+mso+' IS NOT AVAILABLE FOR PRINTING'
   LOOP
ENDIF

@ 5,0

STORE CUSTID TO mcustid
STORE PONUMBER TO ponumber
STORE DATE TO date
STORE INVOICE TO invoice
SELECT SECONDARY
FIND &mcustid
SELECT PRIMARY
```

Program 5. MENU6-3.CMD/.PRG Main section of program to print invoices *(Continued)*

Continued from the previous page

```
STORE NAME TO name
STORE ADDRESS TO address
STORE TRIM(CITY)+', '+STATE+'  '+ZIP TO city
STORE ATTN TO attn

DO Menu6-3p

ERASE
SELECT SECONDARY
USE Customer INDEX Custid
SELECT PRIMARY
USE Invoices
ENDDO --------------- for main program loop

RELEASE program,mso,start,end,mcustid,ponumber,date,invoice,name,;
address,city,attn.amount.page.findstart,line,misbn
SELE SECO
USE
SELE PRIMARY
RETURN
```

Program 5. MENU6-3.CMD/.PRG Main section of program to print invoices

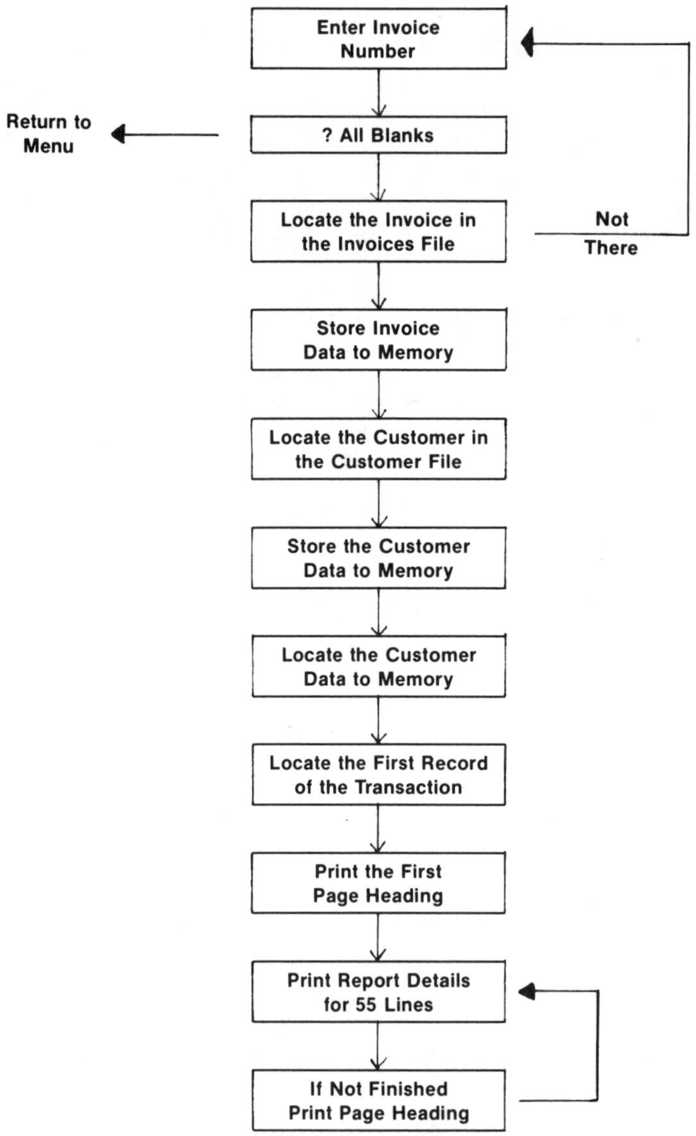

Figure 6. Diagram of program to reprint invoices

```
* Program ------------MENU6-3P.CMD/.PRG
* Notes --------------program to print invoices

SET FORMAT TO PRINT
SET MARGIN TO 15
ERASE
STORE 0 TO amount,page
SELECT SECONDARY
USE Inv INDEX Isbn
SELECT PRIMARY
USE Invoiced
DO SEARCH
DO WHILE SONUMBER=MSO .AND..NOT.EOF
  STORE page+1 TO page
  IF page=1
      DO Pagehead
      @  18,1 SAY 'TITLE ORDERED/ISBN                    QTY      PRICE;

    TOTAL'
     STORE 20 TO line
  ELSE
      @  6,1 SAY 'PAGE '+STR(page,2)
      @  7,1 SAY 'INVOICE # '+INVOICE
      @  18,1 SAY 'TITLE ORDERED/ISBN                    QTY      PRICE;

    TOTAL'
     STORE 20 TO line
  ENDIF


 DO WHILE line< 55 .AND. SONUMBER=mso .AND. .NOT. EOF

 STORE P.ISBN TO misbn
 SELECT SECONDARY
 FIND &misbn
 @ line,1  SAY TITLE+' '+STR(QTYDEL,3)+' '+STR(PRICE,10,2)+STR;
(PRICE*QTYDEL,10,2)
 @ line+1,5 SAY misbn
 IF QTYDEL<QTY
  @ LINE +1,42 SAY 'B/O'
 ENDIF
 STORE line+3 TO line
 STORE PRICE*QTY+AMOUNT TO AMOUNT
 IF SELECT='MENU6-1'
 REPLACE QTYONHAND WITH QTYONHAND-QTYDEL, SOLDTHISYR WITH
   SOLDTHISYR+QTYDEL,; LASTSALE WITH DATE()  NOUPDATE
 ENDIF
```

Program 6. MENU6-3P.CMD/.PRG Print routine for MENU6-1 and MENU6-3 *(Continued)*

Continued from the previous page

```
SELECT PRIMARY
SKIP

   ENDDO ------- inner loop

  IF SONUMBER#mso .OR. EOF
      @ line+1,47  SAY 'Total Due'
      @ line+1,56  SAY STR(m.amount,10,2)
  ENDIF
EJECT

ENDDO -------- OUTER LOOP
SET FORMAT TO SCREEN
SET MARGIN TO 0
RETURN
```

Program 6. MENU6-3P.CMD/.PRG Print routine for MENU6-1 and MENU6-3

```
* pagehead ------prints heading for MENU6-3P

@ 5,25 SAY '--- INVOICE ---'
@ 6,1  SAY "BOB'S BETTER BOOKS"
@ 6.55 SAY cdate
@ 7,1  SAY '10150 JEFFERSON BLVD'
@ 7,45 SAY 'Invoice Number '+INVOICE
@ 8,1  SAY 'CULVER CITY, CA   90230'
@ 8,45 SAY 'dated: '+m.date
@ 13.1  SAY m.name
@ 13,44 SAY 'CUSTOMER NUMBER '+mcustid
@ 14,1  SAY m.address
IF .NOT. ponumber='    '
@ 14,38 SAY 'REF: PURCHASE ORDER '+ponumber
ENDIF
@ 15,1  SAY m.city
IF .NOT.attn='  '
@ 16.1  SAY 'ATTN: '+attn
ENDIF
```

Program 7. Program to print invoice page headings

The bulk of the invoice is printed by the inner loop, which also tracks how many lines have been printed. On each pass through the loop we process one record from the file INVOICED.

The detailed information printed consists of data from two databases. The title comes from the inventory database; the quantity, quantity shipped, price, and ISBN number come from the invoice database. Note that in this case we have printed the data on two lines. There is not enough line space in 10 character per inch pica type to print each record on a single line and still maintain a margin.

We alert the customer to back orders by printing B/O under the quantity shipped. Note that we have not printed the quantity ordered.

If we are printing the invoice from Menu Selection 1, we also want to update the inventory fields QTYONHAND, SOLDTHISYR, and LASTSALE at this time. REPLACE NOUPDATE prevents the index file ISBN from being tested and saves a little time.

When we exit the inner loop, we test to see if we are done before ejecting the page. After printing invoice records, the total value of the invoice is printed.

Chapter Ten

ACCOUNTS RECEIVABLE - BILLING

Though our business sends out an invoice with each shipment, the actual billing is done once a month. In this chapter, five programs involved in monthly billing will be discussed: an accounts summary program for the month, two programs to produce monthly statements, a program to post the monthly activity to an ageing file, and a program to produce an ageing report. As usual, each of these programs is "called" from a menu program, **Program 1. Screen 1** is the menu selection produced by the menu program.

This system of programs will make use of three separate database files: the CUSTOMER file, the INVOICES file, and a PAYMENTS file. Records in the PAYMENTS and INVOICES files are produced by other programs within the overall system. The programs in this menu system use those files to produce the desired result. For convenience, we have combined the CUSTOMER file with an ageing file, which adds several new fields to the CUSTOMER file and allows us to simplify the overall process (see **Figure 1**).

The original CUSTOMER file ended after the customer ID number field. If we wanted, we could put the remaining 15 fields into a separate ageing file. There is one ageing record for each record in the CUSTOMER file. If we did have two separate files, we would need a CUSTID field in the ageing file to link the two together, and we would need to index the file on CUSTID. However, since we have enough fields available in our CUSTOMER file, it makes sense to combine these files, as we have done. Though the current index file CUSTID would work for a separate ageing file, we cannot use the same index file for both primary and secondary files.

The ageing fields M1CHG through M6CHG contain the subtotals of invoices for five months back. M1PAY through M6PAY are for the payment subtotals. HISTORY combines payments and invoices for all previous months. Each month we shift everything one month (M1CHG will become M2CHG, etc.). DATEOFBILL is the billing date. BALANCE is the amount due as of the billing date.

The database plans for the PAYMENTS file and

```
            BOB'S BETTER BOOKS

          CUSTOMER BILLING MENU

                10 JUL 83

     1 - Monthly Activity Summary
     2 - Prepare Customer Statements
     3 - Prepare Single Customer Statement
     4 - Post Data to History Files
     5 - Prepare Ageing Report
     0 - FINISHED


    : :  ENTER YOUR SELECTION
```

Screen 1. Customer billing menu display

```
* Program .....:MENU7.CMD (or MENU7.PRG)
* Notes .......:This program is the Billing Menu.

USE Customer INDEX Customer
STORE ' ' TO selection

DO WHILE .NOT. selection = '0'
   ERASE
   STORE ' ' TO selection
   @ 3,25 say "BOB'S BETTER BOOKS"
   @ 5,23 SAY 'CUSTOMER BILLING MENU'
   @ 7,30 SAY cdate
   @ 10,20 SAY '1 - Monthly Activity Summary'
   @ 11,20 SAY '2 - Prepare Customer Statements'
   @ 12,20 SAY '3 - Prepare Single Customer Statement'
   @ 13,20 SAY '4 - Post Data To History Files'
   @ 14,20 SAY '5 - Prepare Ageing Report'
   @ 15,20 SAY '0 - FINISHED '
   @ 20,24 SAY 'ENTER YOUR SELECTION'
   @ 20,19 GET selection
   READ

   DO CASE
      CASE selection = '1'
         DO Menu7-1
      CASE selection = '2'
         DO Menu7-2
      CASE selection = '3'
         DO Menu7-3
      CASE selection = '4'
         DO Menu7-4
      CASE selection = '5'
         DO Menu7-5
   ENDCASE
ENDDO
RETURN
```

Program 1. MENU7.CMD/.PRG Billing menu program

DESCRIPTION	NAME	TYPE	WIDTH	DEC
CUSTOMER NAME	NAME	C	030	
ATTENTION	ATTN	C	030	
STREET ADDRESS	ADDRESS	C	025	
CITY	CITY	C	020	
STATE	STATE	C	002	
ZIP CODE	ZIP	C	005	
PHONE NUMBER (999)-999-9999	PHONE	C	014	
DATE BECAME CUSTOMER	DATE	C	008	
CUSTOMER ID NUMBER	CUSTID	C	006	
CURRENT BALANCE	BALANCE	N	008	002
DATE OF LAST BILLING	DATEOFBILL	C	008	
INVOICES FOR LAST BILLING	M1CHG	N	008	002
INVOICES FOR PRIOR MONTH	M2CHG	N	008	002
INVOICES TWO MONTHS BACK	M3CHG	N	008	002
INVOICES THREE MONTHS BACK	M4CHG	N	008	002
INVOICES FOUR MONTHS BACK	M5CHG	N	008	002
INVOICES FIVE MONTHS BACK	M6CHG	N	008	002
PAYMENTS AS OF LAST BILLING	M1PAY	N	008	002
PAYMENTS PRIOR MONTH	M2PAY	N	008	002
PAYMENTS TWO MONTHS BACK	M3PAY	N	008	002
PAYMENTS THREE MONTHS BACK	M4PAY	N	008	002
PAYMENTS FOUR MONTHS PACK	M5PAY	N	008	002
PAYMENTS FIVE MONTHS BACK	M6PAY	N	008	002
PREVIOUS ACCOUNT SUMMARY	HISTORY	N	008	002
	RECORD SIZE		261 BYTES	

```
INDEXES             NAME ........... CUSTOMER.NDX
                    CUSTID ......... CUSTID.NDX
                    ZIP+NAME ....... ZIP.NDX
```

Figure 1. Database plan for CUSTOMER.DBF (combined customer and ageing file)

DESCRIPTION	NAME	TYPE	WIDTH	DEC
CUSTOMER ID NUMBER	CUSTID	C	006	
DATE OF PAYMENT	DATF	C	008	
AMOUNT OF PAYMENT	AMOUNT	N	008	002
	RECORD SIZE		23 BYTES	
INDEXES	CUSTID ...... P-CUSTID.NDX			

Figure 2A. Database plan for PAYMENTS database file

DESCRIPTION	NAME	TYPE	WIDTH	DEC
CUSTOMER ID NUMBER	CUSTID	C	006	
INVOICE NUMBER	INVOICE	C	006	
DATE OF PAYMENT	DATE	C	008	
AMOUNT OF PAYMENT	AMOUNT	N	008	002
	RECORD SIZE		29 BYTES	
INDEXES	CUSTID ...... I-CUSTID.NDX			

Figure 2B. Database plan for INVOICES database file

Figure 2. Database plans for PAYMENTS and INVOICES database files the INVOICES file are shown in **Figure 2**. A good argument could be made for combining the two files, since the time involved with running the programs would be significantly reduced. (On PC-type computers using DOS 2.0, opening and closing files is particularly time consuming.) Though it would be less time consuming, we have not combined files because we are trying to demonstrate the use of multiple files.

Menu Item 1 Monthly Activity Summary (MENU7-1.CMD/.PRG)

At billing time, we need a report summarizing financial activity for each customer. This report, produced by **Program 2**, is shown as **Figure 3**. A logic diagram of Program 2 is shown as **Figure 4**. This particular program demonstrates the use of the SUM command as well as the use of multiple files to print one line of text.

To produce this report we use all three files for each line of the report. The primary file CUSTOMER supplies the customer name and the current balance. The secondary file PAYMENTS provides the payments received during the month; the secondary file INVOICES provides customer charges for the month.

The program uses two loops: the outer loop takes us through the entire customer database a record at a time; the inner loop handles the fact that there are more customers than will fit on a single page. On each page, we need to increment the page number and print the page heading. When we've finished with the page, we need to advance the printer to the next page.

Upon entering the inner loop, the primary file CUSTOMER is selected. The first step is to select the secondary file. Next, we store the customer ID number from the primary file to the memory variable *mcustid*. Notice that we were able to do this even though we had already selected the secondary file. This is because we prefaced CUSTID with P. (for primary). The secondary file also has a field CUSTID. Had we not prefaced CUSTID with P. we would have been in trouble, since we would have stored the customer ID number from the secondary file to the variable. (If we had done the store before we entered the secondary file we could have omitted the P. from the command.) It is a good practice always to use the file designator P. or S. when a field is common to both the primary and secondary files.

To obtain the value of each customer's payments and the amount of each customer's invoices, the SUM command is used. Any command that can be used with the FOR clause can be used with the WHILE clause.

```
SUM AMOUNT TO custpay WHILE
■ S.CUSTID=mcustid
```

is equivalent to

```
STORE 0 TO custpay
DO WHILE S.CUSTID=mcustid
■.AND..NOT. EOF
STORE custpay + AMOUNT to custpay
SKIP
ENDDO
```

The preferable choice depends upon the computer you are using, the number of records for each customer, and whether or not you would be doing more than adding up quantities for each record. In general, if there are very few records the second approach will be a little faster. This is because the SUM command is in the dBASE II overlay file. If we need to reposition the disk head to read the command into memory we pay a little time overhead. However, if there are many records for each customer, SUM will be faster.

```
Page 1                                                  01 AUG 1983

                       BOB'S BETTER BOOKS

                     MONTHLY ACTIVITY SUMMARY
```

CUSTOMER NAME	STARTING BALANCE	PAYMENTS RECEIVED	CURRENT BILLING	NEW BALANCE
BAKER'S BILIOUS BOOKS	125.00	275.00	619.34	469.34
ODYSSEY BOOKS	100.00	100.00	234.56	234.56
TEDIOUS TECHNICAL TOMES	0.00			0.00
TOTALS	225.00	375.00	853.90	703.90

Figure 3. Monthly activity report

```
* Program .....:MENU7-1.CMD (or MENU7-1.PRG)
* Notes .......:This program prepares the Monthly Activity Summary.

STORE 0 TO totalbal,totalpay,totalchg,page
SET FORMAT TO PRINT

DO WHILE .NOT.EOF
   STORE page+1 TO page
   @ 6,15 SAY 'Page '+STR(page,1)
   @ 6,75 SAY cdate
   @ 8,41 SAY "BOB'S BETTER BOOKS"
   @ 10,41 SAY 'MONTHLY ACTIVITY SUMMARY'
   @ 12,15 SAY  '                        STARTING    PAYMENTS    CURRENT;
    NEW'
   @ 13,15 SAY 'CUSTOMER   NAME          BALANCE     RECEIVED    BILLING;
    BALANCE'
   @ 14,15 SAY '---------------------------------------------------------;
-----------------'
   STORE 15 TO line

   DO WHILE line<56 .AND. .NOT. EOF
      SELE SECO
      STORE P.CUSTID TO mcustid
      USE Payments INDEX P-custid
      FIND &mcustid
      SUM AMOUNT TO custpay WHILE S.CUSTID = mcustid
      USE Invoices INDEX I-custid
      FIND &mcustid
      SUM AMOUNT TO custchgs WHILE S.CUSTID = mcustid
      @ line,15 SAY NAME
      @ line,45 SAY STR(BALANCE,8,2)

      IF .NOT. custpay = 0
         @ line,57 SAY STR(custpay,8,2)
      ENDIF

      IF .NOT. custchgs = 0
         @ line,68 SAY STR(custchgs,8,2)
      ENDIF
```

Program 2. MENU7-1.CMD/.PRG Monthly activity summary program *(Continued)*

Continued from the previous page

```
         @ line.78 SAY STR(BALANCE-custpay+custchgs,8,2)
         STORE line+1 TO line
         STORE totalbal+BALANCE TO totalbal
         STORE totalpay+custpay TO totalpay
         STORE totalchg+custchgs TO totalchg
         SELE PRIM
         SKIP
      ENDDO

      IF EOF
         STORE line+2 TO line
         @ line,15 SAY 'TOTALS'
         @ line.44 SAY STR(totalbal,9,2)
         @ line,56 SAY STR(totalpay.9,2)
         @ line.67 SAY STR(totalchg,9,2)
         @ line,77 SAY STR(totalbal-totalpay+totalchg.9,2)
      ENDIF
      EJECT
   ENDDO
   RELE totalbal.totalpay,totalchg,custpay.custchgs,page
   SET FORMAT TO SCREEN
   SELE SECO
   USE
   SELE PRIM
   RETURN
```

Program 2. MENU7-1.CMD/.PRG Monthly activity summary program

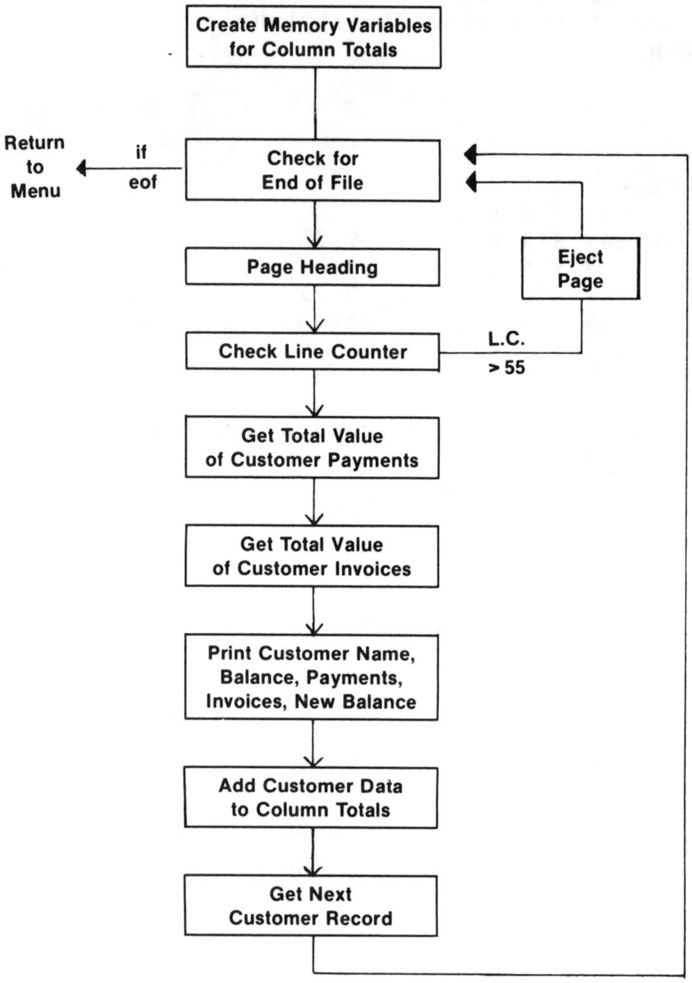

Figure 4. Diagram of Activity Summary Program

Note that in neither case do we need to be concerned with finding the customer ID number in the secondary file. If we didn't find the ID number, the secondary database was positioned to Record 0. The contents of the field CUSTID cannot match *mcustid*. Also, when using SUM WHILE we do not need to worry about the end of file.

Once we've accumulated the payments and invoices subtotals, we print the line. In this example we have elected not to print the customer payments or customer invoices if their value is zero. Not printing zero balances makes them stand out and be more easily noticeable than printing 0.00. Note that when we print the new balance we use a field and two memory variables within that print statement.

```
@ line,78 say str (BALANCE-custpay +
■ custchgs,8,2)
```

Next we add each of these items to the appropriate column totals. There are four columns. The fourth column total can be printed simply by knowing the other three totals.

Now we go back to the primary file and advance a single record.

This program does not disturb the contents of any of the databases nor does it affect the indexes. It can be run as often as desired during the month.

Menu Item 2 Customer Monthly Statement (MENU7-2.CMD/.PRG)

For the monthly customer billing we want to produce a two-page statement. The first page is a simple summary of the customer's monthly activities. The second page contains a listing of each of the invoices for the month. These invoices are printed "three up" — each row on the statement contains three invoices. A sample statement produced by the program for monthly billing is shown as **Figure 5** and **Figure 6**.

Program 3 is essentially the same as the monthly activity summary except that we are doing a lot more print formatting. Other than that, the logic is pretty much the same. Again, we will print customer statements in alphabetical order. This makes it a little easier to match statements with labels printed by a label printing program. If we fold the statements properly we can use window envelopes instead of labels. Even though these envelopes cost a little more than regular envelopes, they are more professional in appearance, and can save us some time in preparing the monthly billing.

Much of Program 3 deals with printing page headings. If we had used a standard page heading in the other programs, such as the one for book ordering, we could save about 20 lines of programming in this program alone. This is part of the rationale for structured programming. With a small program for printing headings, we would replace the page heading code with DO HEADING. Having fewer lines of code per program increases clarity and understanding.

When we "call" another program such as a heading program, opening the command file takes a fraction of a second. In this particular example, the limited time taken to open a file would be lost in the printing and paper handling time anyway. When a large number of command file calls is used, however, the opening times could significantly affect the overall execution speed. All that this means is that we should temper our zeal to make a program smaller with a little common sense.

The positioning of the printing of each invoice on Page 2 of the customer monthly statement is handled by DO CASE. On each pass through the loop we evaluate the last column value and adjust

```
* Program .....:MENU7-2.CMD (or MENU7-2.PRG)
* Notes .......:This program does Monthly Statements.

SET FORMAT TO PRINT
  GO TOP
DO WHILE .NOT. EOF
   STORE CUSTID TO mcustid
   @ 6,15 SAY "BOB'S BETTER BOOKS"
   @ 6,70 SAY cdate
   @ 7,15 SAY '10150 JEFFERSON BLVD'
   @ 8,15 SAY 'CULVER CITY, CA   90230'
   @ 13,15 SAY NAME
   @ 13.50 SAY 'CUSTOMER NUMBER '+CUSTID
   @ 14,15 SAY ADDRESS
   @ 15,15 SAY TRIM(CITY)+', '+STATE+'   '+ZIP

   IF .NOT.ATTN='  '
      @ 16,15 SAY 'ATTN: '+ATTN
   ENDIF
   @ 18,45 SAY 'STATEMENT'
   @ 19,15 SAY '---------------------------------------;
-----------------------------'
   @ 21,15 SAY 'BALANCE DUE AS OF: '+DATEOFBILL
   @ 21,50 SAY STR(BALANCE,8,2)
   STORE CUSTID TO mcustid
   SELE SECO
   USE Invoices INDEX I-custid
   FIND &mcustid
   SUM AMOUNT TO custchg WHILE CUSTID=mcustid
   @ 22,15 SAY 'CHARGES FROM '+DATEOFBILL+' TO '+DATE()
   @ 22,50 SAY STR(custchg,8,2)
   USE Payments INDEX P-custid
   @ 23.15 SAY 'PAYMENTS RECEIVED'
   FIND &mcustid
   STORE 23 TO line
   STORE 0 TO custpay

   DO WHILE CUSTID=mcustid .AND. .NOT. EOF
      @ LINE,50 SAY STR(AMOUNT,8,2)+' '+DATE
      STORE AMOUNT+custpay TO custpay
      SKIP
      STORE line+1 TO line
   ENDDO
```

Program 3. MENU7-2.CMD./PRG Program to produce monthly statements *(Continued)*

Continued from the previous page

```
@ line+2,15 SAY 'AMOUNT NOW DUE: '
@ line+2,50 SAY STR(BALANCE-custpay+custchg,8,2)+'  TERMS ARE NET
                                                    10 DAYS'

SELE PRIM
EJECT
@ 6,15 SAY "BOB'S BETTER BOOKS"
@ 6,70 SAY cdate
@ 7,15 SAY '10150 JEFFERSON BLVD.'
@ 8,15 SAY 'CULVER CITY, CA   90230'
@ 13,15 SAY NAME
@ 13,50 SAY 'CUSTOMER NUMBER '+CUSTID
@ 14,15 SAY ADDRESS
@ 15,15 SAY TRIM(CITY)+', '+STATE+'   '+ZIP

IF .NOT.ATTN='   '
   @ 16,15 SAY 'ATTN: '+ATTN
ENDIF
@ 18,45 SAY 'STATEMENT DETAIL'
@ 19,15 SAY '-----------------------------------------------------;
--------------------------'
@ 20,15 SAY 'INVOICE                       INVOICE               ;
INVOICE'
@ 21,15 SAY 'NO.     DATE     CHARGE      NO.      DATE       CHARGE;
 NO.      DATE       CHARGE'
@ 22,15 SAY '-----------------------------------------------------;
--------------------------'
SELE SECO
USE Invoices INDEX I-custid
FIND &mcustid
STORE 24 TO line
STORE 15 TO col

DO WHILE CUSTID=mcustid .AND. .NOT. EOF
   @ line,col SAY INVOICE NO
   @ line,col+7 SAY DATE
   @ line,col+16 SAY STR(AMOUNT,7,2)

   DO CASE
      CASE col=15
         STORE 42 TO col
```

Program 3. MENU7-2.CMD./PRG Program to produce monthly statements *(Continued)*

Continued from the previous page

```
            CASE col=42
               STORE 69 TO col
            CASE col=69
               STORE 15 TO col
               STORE line+1 TO line
         ENDCASE
         SKIP
      ENDDO
      EJECT
      SELE PRIM
      SKIP
   ENDDO
   SET FORMAT TO SCREEN
   SELE SECO
   USE
   SELE PRIM
   RELEASE mcustid,line.col.custchg,custpay
   RETURN
```

Program 3. MENU7-2.CMD./PRG Program to produce monthly statements

```
BOB'S BETTER BOOKS                                              01 AUG 1983
10150 JEFFERSON BLVD
CULVER CITY, CA  90230


BAKER'S BILIOUS BOOKS                          CUSTOMER NUMBER 100002
2731 W. 24TH STREET
NEW YORK, NY  21223
ATTN:  BARTHOLOMEW BAKER
                           STATEMENT
--------------------------------------------------------------------

BALANCE DUE AS OF:  06/30/83                   125.00
CHARGES FROM 06/30/83 TO 08/01/83              619.34
PAYMENTS RECEIVED                              125.00 07/05/83
                                               150.00 07/15/83


AMOUNT NOW DUE:                                469.34  TERMS ARE NET 10 DAYS
```

Figure 5. Monthly customer statement, page 1

BOB'S BETTER BOOKS
10150 JEFFERSON BLVD
CULVER CITY, CA 90230

01 AUG 1983

BAKER'S BILIOUS BOOKS
2731 W. 24TH STREET
NEW YORK, NY 21223
ATTN: BARTHOLOMEW BAKER

CUSTOMER NUMBER 100002

STATEMENT DETAIL

INVOICE NO.	DATE	CHARGE	INVOICE NO.	DATE	CHARGE	INVOICE NO.	DATE	CHARGE
892345	07/15/83	153 45	456283	07/31/83	465.89			

Figure 6. Monthly customer statement, page 2

```
* Program .....:MENU7-3.CMD (or MENU7-3.PRG)
* Notes .......:This program prints out a single Customer Statement.

STORE T TO printout
ERASE

DO WHILE printout
   STORE '                              ' TO customer
   @ 5,10 SAY 'PRINT OUT INDIVIDUAL CUSTOMER STATEMENTS'
   @ 7,10 SAY 'CUSTOMER NAME' GET customer
   READ NOUPDATE
   FIND &customer

   IF customer = '  '
      STORE F TO printout
      LOOP
   ENDIF

   IF #=0
      @ 9,1 SAY 'NOT ABLE TO FIND CUSTOMER AS ENTERED'
      LOOP
   ENDIF
   @ 9,0

   COPY NEXT 1 TO Tempfile
   USE Tempfile
   DO Menu7-2
   USE Customer INDEX Customer
   CLEAR GETS
ENDDO
DELETE FILE Tempfile
RELEASE customer,printout
RETURN
```

Program 4. MENU7-3.CMD/.PRG Program for selected customer statements

the contents of the variables *line* and *col* accordingly.

This program does not affect the content of any database and can be run as often as desired. In general, it is not advisable to have a printing program affect database content, because if something happens to the printer during the program run, we can't just fix the printer and do it over again. Wherever possible, one should try to separate printing from database change.

Menu Item 3 Print Selected Customer Monthly Statements (MENU7-3.CMD/.PRG)

Program 3 is a production program: you turn it on and do something else while it prints out the monthly billing. What do you do, though, if something *does* happen to one of the statements during printing? You don't want to have to print out hundreds of statements in order to reproduce a single damaged statement.

In this case, we use **Program 4**, a program for printing selected customer monthly statements.

In this example, selectivity is provided by the copy command. Since each of the programs in this menu system assumes that the CUSTOMER file (indexed on customer name) is in use when the program is called, we can cheat a little.

We go to the desired record within the file CUSTOMER and copy that one record to the file TEMPFILE. Then we call Program 3, MENU7-2. Though MENU7-2 is used to print statements for all of the records in the file CUSTOMER, it doesn't know that it's not using CUSTOMER. So it prints statements for all of the records in the file TEMPFILE (one record).

Menu Item 4 Post Monthly Activity to Ageing — Customer File (MENU7-4.CMD/.PRG)

This is the most interesting program in this particular menu system. **Program 5** stores the summaries of payments and invoices to the CUSTOMER file. The PAYMENTS and INVOICES files are then cleared out to begin the next month's activities.

Once this program has run to completion, the monthly billing process is all over. We cannot do the billing if we accidentally run this program first. At the same time, we do not want to post automatically when we do the billing. For successful operation we need to depend on a combination of reasonable good sense on the part of the operator and a little help from a program. When the billing is completed, the operator should run this program before any new items are entered into either the PAYMENTS or INVOICES files. We can provide reasonable protection against overlapping billing by checking the date of last billing in the customer file and using code in the programs to add payment and invoice records. To prevent premature posting we have the operator enter a code to enable program execution.

Upon entering the program, the user is informed that this program is in use. S/he must take deliberate action to run the program. (This prevents the program from running if a single wrong key is pressed in the menu.) We have chosen to have the sequence ABCDEF entered in order for the program to run. ABCDEF is simple enough not to be disagreeable and long enough to prevent a spontaneous, erroneous action.

The first thing that we want to do is shift the data in each monthly field one month downstream. The oldest debit is added and the oldest credit subtracted from the history field. Strictly speaking, we don't really need the balance and date of bill fields. The former can be computed from the data in the monthly and history fields. The latter can be handled as a permanently saved variable in the file DATE.MEM. But since we have only a couple of hundred customers in our file, the penalty associated with carrying these items isn't significant. If we were dealing with thousands of customers, we would want to carefully evaluate how to store this information.

We use REPLACE ALL <exp> to do our field shifting. The order in which we do this — from the oldest to the newest data — is important. Note that we turned the *index* off before we do the replacements, which means that we are working with the physical ordering of the records. With the index on, the replacements would take place in the logical order controlled by the index file. Except in a pathological case, working with the logical ordering would require a lot more disk head movement. Even with a couple of hundred records the time involved could be significant. Several minutes is a long time compared to turning an index on and off.

Here, REPLACE ALL <exp> is a particularly long command: four lines separated by semicolons. (As you may remember, we can have up to 254 characters in a command, and, at the end of a line, we mark the continuation of a command with semicolons.)

Note that the fields for the current month are set to zero. This takes care of cases where a customer had no activity for the current month.

The next step is to use the TOTAL command to create a temporary file containing the subtotals for each customer number. Since the secondary file INVOICES is indexed on the customer number, the temporary file TOTINV has one record for each customer number in the INVOICES file. The structure of TOTINV is the same as that of INVOICES. The contents of the AMOUNT field contain the subtotal of AMOUNT for each customer number. Once again, if the file is large this process can be slow.

A word of caution: when TOTAL is used in this manner, the fields that are totalled must be large enough to contain the sum. dBASE II does not change the field size if there is an overflow. Unfortunately, as of this writing, there isn't even an indication of error.

We cannot use UPDATE directly. UPDATE allows us to add to the contents of a field only when the fieldnames are identical.

Once we have the subtotals file TOTINV we want to clear out the current contents of the invoices file. The straightforward way to this is:

```
DELETE ALL
PACK
```

Here again, using an index file works against us. A 1000-record file (on a floppy disk) can take about a half hour to delete and pack. Turning off the index can cut this time to about three minutes. The technique that we are using cuts the time to a few seconds.

We want to get rid of everything but the structure, so we copy the structure to a temporary file. Then we delete the invoices file. Note that the command USE is used all by itself. We cannot delete the file we are using and we cannot rename it. So we step back to a point where we are not using either file, delete INVOICES, and rename NEWINV to INVOICES. Note that we did not need to add the file identifier .DBF. Next we need to straighten out the index file I-CUSTID, which still thinks there are 1000 records. The solution here is to INDEX. Indexing a file without records is pretty fast.

Now we go back to our primary file and select the index for customer number CUSTID. This allows us to use the UPDATE command to update

```
* Program .....:MENU7-4.CMD (or MENU7-4.PRG)
* Notes .......:This program posts monthly account records back to the
* ............:customer file as a summary.

ERASE

TEXT

    ***** WARNING *******  WARNING ******  WARNING ***** WARNING *****

       YOU HAVE ENTERED THE PROGRAM TO POST PAYMENTS AND INVOICES

      PAYMENTS AND INVOICES JOURNALS WILL BE CLEARED AT COMPLETION

ENDTEXT

? "      TODAY'S DATE IS "+DATE()+"      LAST BILLING WAS "+DATEOFBILL
STORE '      ' TO enable
@ 11,10 SAY 'ENTER  ABCDEF  to POST, anything else to ABORT' GET enable
READ NOUPDATE

IF enable='ABCDEF'
   SET INDEX TO
   REPL ALL HISTORY WITH HISTORY+M6CHG-M6PAY,M6PAY WITH M5PAY,;
        M5PAY WITH M4PAY,M4PAY WITH M3PAY,M3PAY WITH M2PAY,M2PAY WITH M1PAY
   REPL ALL M6CHG WITH M5CHG,M5CHG WITH M4CHG,M4CHG WITH M3CHG,;
        M3CHG WITH M2CHG,M2CHG WITH M1CHG,M1CHG WITH 0,M1PAY WITH 0
   SELE SECO
   USE Invoices INDEX I-custid
   TOTAL ON CUSTID TO TOTINV
   COPY STRU TO Newinv
   USE
   DELETE FILE Invoices
   RENAME Newinv TO Invoices
   USE Invoices
   INDEX ON CUSTID TO I-custid
```

Program 5. MENU7-4.CMD/.PRG Program to post payments and invoices to the customer ageing file *Continued on next page*

Continued from the previous page

```
    SELE PRIM
    SET INDEX TO Custid
    UPDATE FROM TOTINV ON CUSTID RANDOM REPLACE M1CHG WITH AMOUNT
    SELE SECO
    USE Payments INDEX P-custid
    TOTAL ON CUSTID TO Totinv
    COPY STRU TO Newpay
    USE
    DELETE FILE Payments
    RENAME Newpay TO Payments
    USE Payments
    INDEX ON CUSTID TO P-custid
    SELE PRIM
    UPDATE FROM Totinv ON CUSTID RANDOM REPLACE M1PAY WITH AMOUNT
    SET INDEX TO
    REPLACE ALL BALANCE WITH BALANCE-M1PAY+M1CHG,DATEOFBILL WITH DATE()
    SET INDEX TO Customer
    DELE FILE Totinv
ENDIF
RETURN
```

Program 5. MENU7-4.CMD/.PRG Program to post payments and invoices to the customer ageing file

the customer file with the data stored in TOTINV.

We repeat the process for the PAYMENTS file, turn the index off, and do our final replacement.

UPDATE and TOTAL are relational operations. Each of these is much faster than trying to write code to accomplish the same result. They cannot be used in all cases, but they are truly effective when they fit.

Menu Item 5 The Ageing Report (MENU7-5.CMD/.PRG)

The ageing report shows the invoices and payments subtotals over time, so that we can determine who doesn't pay up. In our business, as long as the customer pays within the month, all is well.

The program to produce the report (**Program 6**) is very simple. Each customer record contains two lines: invoices are on the top line and payments on the bottom line. The report prepared by this command is shown as **Figure 7**.

```
* Program .....:MENU7-5.CMD (or MENU7-5.PRG)
* Notes .......:This program prints the Ageing Report.

GO TOP
SET INDEX TO c
SET MARGIN TO 15
SET FORMAT TO PRINT
DO WHILE .NOT. EOF
   @ 6,32 SAY 'AGEING REPORT FOR '+cdate
   @ 8,1 SAY 'CUSTOMER NAME                        BALANCE  LAST MO     30-60;
     60-90       90-120'
   STORE 10 TO line

   DO WHILE line<55 .AND. .NOT. EOF
      @ line,1 SAY NAME
      @ line,31 SAY BALANCE
      @ line,40 SAY M1CHG
      @ line,50 SAY M2CHG
      @ line,60 SAY M3CHG
      @ line,70 SAY M4CHG
      @ line+1,31 SAY DATEOFBILL
      @ line+1,40 SAY M1PAY
      @ line+1,50 SAY M2PAY
      @ line+1,60 SAY M3PAY
      @ line+1,70 SAY M4PAY
      STORE line+3 TO line
      SKIP
   ENDDO
   EJECT
ENDDO
SET FORMAT TO SCREEN
SET MARGIN TO 0
RETURN
```

Program 6. MENU 7-5.CMD/.PRG Print ageing report

CUSTOMER NAME	BALANCE	LAST MO.	30-60	60-90	90-120
BAKER'S BILIOUS BOOKS	125.00	0.00	275.00	200.00	210.00
	08/01/83	275.00	200.00	210.00	220.00
ODYSSEY BOOKS	100.00	100.00	100.00	0.00	0.00
	08/01/83	100.00	0.00	0.00	0.00
TEDIOUS TECHNICAL TOMES	0.00	100.00	110.00	120.00	130.00
	08/01/83	110.00	120.00	130.00	140.00

Figure 7. Ageing report

Section Three

Special Topics

ASHTON·TATE

ASHTON·TATE

Chapter Eleven

THINGS YOU CAN DO WITH REPORT

The REPORT command deserves this chapter of its own. The inability of many of us to make full use of it is probably the reason we learn to program with dBASE II in the first place. The REPORT command is extremely powerful, much more so than it seems initially.

Modifying Reports

When a report is created, dBASE II prompts us to answer a series of simple questions. Our answers to these questions are stored as a report form file (.FRM) on the disk, so that on subsequent requests for the report, we do not have to go through the prompt questions. This stored report form can be modified by use of MODIFY COMMAND, or by most word processors, providing that the proper word processing mode is used — for example, Option N in WordStar.

In Chapter One, Screen 13, we demonstrated the process of creating a report form. That form has been reproduced here for your convenience as **Screen 1**.

This particular use of REPORT produced the result shown in **Figure 1**. The report isn't bad, but we would like to improve it cosmetically by moving MIN over one space, moving the column entries for MIN STOCK under the "O" in STOCK, and putting the column headings UNIT PRICE and STOCKVALUE on two lines.

To do this we simply invoke:

```
.MODIFY COMMAND SAMPLE.FRM
```

This will produce the screen display shown as the left column in **Screen 2**. Note that this display contains only the answers to the questions shown in Screen 1. We can make the changes we want by moving the cursor to the desired position on the screen and typing in the changes. The revised report is shown as the right column, with the changes underlined.

The changes to the minimum stock heading

```
 . REPORT
ENTER REPORT FORM NAME:  B:SAMPLE
ENTER OPTIONS, M=LEFT MARGIN, L=LINES/PAGE. W=PAGE WIDTH
PAGE HEADING? (Y/N)  Y
ENTER PAGE HEADING:  SAMPLE DATABASE REPORT
DOUBLE SPACE REPORT? (Y/N)  N
ARE TOTALS REQUIRED? (Y/N)  Y
SUBTOTALS IN REPORT? (Y/N)  N
SUMMARY REPORT ONLY? (Y/N)  N
COL      WIDTH,CONTENTS
001       20,PARTNAME
ENTER HEADING:  PART NAME
002       3 QTY
ENTER HEADING:  QTY
ARE TOTALS REQUIRED? (Y/N)  Y
003       5,MINSTOCK
ENTER HEADING:  MIN  STOCK
ARE TOTALS REQUIRED? (Y/N)  N
004       10.UNITPRICE
ENTER HEADING:  UNIT PRICE
ARE TOTALS REQUIRED? (Y/N)  N
005       10.QTY*UNITPRICE
ENTER HEADING:  STOCKVALUE
ARE TOTALS REQUIRED? (Y/N)  Y
006
```

Screen 1. Example of report form preparation

```
PAGE NO. 00001
10/15/82

                SAMPLE DATABASE REPORT

       PART NAME        QTY MIN    UNIT PRICE STOCKVALUE
                            STOCK

HAMMER, 10 OZ BALL        5     3        8.15       40.75
HAMMER, 16 OZ CLAW        6     6       10.88       65.28
PLIERS, 8 IN GAS         11     5        3.89       42.79
WRENCH, 3/4 BOX           8     5        6.19       49.52
WRENCH, 5/8 BOX           4     6        4.29       17.16
** TOTAL **
                         34                        215.50
```

Figure 1. Sample database report

```
Y
SAMPLE DATABASE REPORT
N
Y
N
N
20,PARTNAME
PART NAME
3.QTY
QTY
Y
5,MINSTOCK
MIN  STOCK
N
10.UNITPRICE
UNIT PRICE
N
10,QTY*UNITPRICE
STOCKVALUE
Y
```

```
Y
SAMPLE DATABASE REPORT
N
Y
N
N
20,PARTNAME
PART NAME
3.QTY
QTY
Y
5.STR(MINSTOCK,3)
MIN STOCK
10.UNITPRICE
>UNIT ;PRICE
N
10.QTY*UNITPRICE
>STOCK;VALUE
Y
```

Screen 2. Before and after report form SAMPLE.FRM

were accomplished by simply placing a space before MIN and removing one space from after MIN. The numbers were centered under the “o” by the use of STR(MINSTOCK,3). STR(FIELDNAME,NUMBER) causes dBASE II to treat a numeric field as though it were a character field. The value of the NUMBER can be greater than or equal to the size of the field. We are able to do this because we are not going to total the column. Note that we needed to delete the next line which contained an “N” in response to a request for totals. Merely blanking out the “N” would have terminated the report at that column.

The headings UNIT PRICE and STOCKVALUE were each put onto two lines by inserting a semicolon at the place where we wanted the line to break. The titles were “right justified,” or placed at the right hand side of the 10-space column, by the use of the “ > ”. The “ < ” would have caused the title to appear at the left hand edge of the column. (Of course, we could have saved ourselves some trouble by setting up the headings as five spaces in the first place.) Note that we did not need a semicolon for the MIN STOCK title. This is because the title width was greater than the column width. However, we did leave a space before and after MIN to fill the initial 5-space allotment.

The modified report is shown as **Figure 2**.

Printing Items Vertically

Quite often people want to print reports that have the fields arranged vertically. For example:

```
Aardvark, Anthony A.     Home 213-555-3700
2543 W. 45th St.         Work 213-567-1212
New York, NY
  13090

Allen, Steve W.          Home 454-123-4567
 etc.                         etc.
```

Let’s suppose that the database has the following fields:

NAME	C	30
ADDRESS	C	25
CITY	C	20
STATE	C	2
ZIP	C	5
HOMEPHONE	C	12
WORKPHONE	C	12

In setting up our report format, we can arrange these fields vertically in three columns. When asked to enter the width and contents, the first column is defined as:

```
30,NAME + ADDRESS + ';'
■ + TRIM(CITY) + ', '+ STATE + '; ' + ZIP
```

The “30” applies to all lines in the first column. If the size of the content of the column is greater than the specified column width, as in this case, the item will be printed on multiple lines within the column. All of these items are character fields. This means that we can concatenate them (join them together) by using the plus sign (+). The column width was chosen as the size of the largest of the fields (NAME). Since NAME filled the first line of the column completely, ADDRESS began at the beginning of the second line. ADDRESS, however, has only 25 characters. The semicolon was inserted at this point to make CITY begin on the third line. TRIM(CITY) was used to eliminate the trailing blanks in the CITY field, allowing the insertion of a comma and STATE in their normal positions. The semicolon after STATE forces another line break. The two blank spaces provide the offset, forcing ZIP to be printed two spaces to the right of the column edge.

The column containing the horizontal titles “Home” and “Work” is created simply by:

```
4,'HomeWork'
```

```
PAGE NO   00001
10/15/82
                              SAMPLE DATABASE REPORT


       PART NAME          QTY   MIN          UNIT          STOCK
                               STOCK         PRICE         VALUE

HAMMER, 10 OZ BALL          5     3           8.15         40.75
HAMMER, 16 OZ CLAW          6     6          10.88         65.28
PLIERS, 8 IN GAS           11     5           3 89         42.79
WRENCH, 3/4 BOX             8     5           6-19         49.52
WRENCH, 5/8 BOX             4     6           4.29         17-16
** TOTAL **
                           34                             215.50
```

Figure 2. Sample database report, revised

No semicolon was required because the column size of 4 forces the line to be broken between "Home" and "Work." The text was enclosed by delimiters because there is no field entry for this item.

Finally, the column containing the phone numbers is created simply by:

12,HOMEPHONE + WORKPHONE

Again we need no semicolon linebreak here, although if we had wanted the two phone numbers separated by a blank line we could insert a semicolon (in quotes) between the two field titles.

Note that the display shows a blank line separating the data from the two records. This is accomplished by double spacing the report. Double space inserts a blank line between the printed database records; blank lines within a record area are controlled by the use of semicolons.

Grouping Data

Now, suppose that we want to print out class rosters for a school. A class consists of the students in a grade and room (each room can have students from different grades). The rosters are to contain only the names of students. We can use REPORT to prepare the rosters. Assume that the database we are using is indexed on GRADE + ROOM + NAME.

To get REPORT to prepare the rosters we must lie a little. When asked ARE TOTALS REQUIRED?, answer yes — even though we have no intention of actually using any numeric fields. Similarly, when asked SUBTOTALS IN REPORT?, answer yes. You will then be asked to:

ENTER SUBTOTALS FIELD:

The "subtotals" field can be an expression. This allows us to enter:

ENTER SUBTOTALS FIELD: 'GRADE:
■ ' + GRADE + '   ROOM: ' + ROOM

This takes care of the first step, combining grade and room. Two REPORT questions further on you will be asked:

EJECT PAGE AFTER SUBTOTALS? (Y/N):

Answering yes (Y) causes each class roster to begin on a separate sheet of paper. The column will begin with:

* GRADE: 6   ROOM 11

followed by the list of names. The next question asks for a subtotals heading. This is intended as text to be inserted between the asterisk and any text created by the subtotals expression. Generally, you won't need to enter anything in response to this question.

Normally you can use the semicolon to control line spacing, but it doesn't work here. The only way that you can get a blank line between the subtotals printing and the first name in a new class is to add a long set of blanks at the end of the subtotals expression.

The above approach also works when you really do want to subtotal.

Substituting Text for Field Contents

There are times when you may want to substitute text for the contents of a field. For example, suppose you have a field named DATE which contains dates entered as MM/DD/YY. A typical entry might be 10/15/82 which you want printed as Oct 15, 1982. This can be accomplished under certain conditions.

First we must create two memory variables:

```
STORE 'JanFebMarAprMayJun
■JulAugSepOctNovDec' TO month
STORE '01 02 03 04 05 06 07 08 09 10 11 12'
■TO code
```

We have constructed two memory variables where the beginning of the numeric code for *month* lines up with the English abbreviation. This allows us to make use of "@", the substring operator, which yields an integer value indicating where one string appears in the other. For example:

```
@('05',code)
```

is equivalent to the number of the starting position of the sequence 05, in the character string *code*; in this case 13.

We then make use of the substring operator "$" to extract the specified portion of the string from the given starting position,

```
$(month,13,3)
```

which is, of course, May. Now we can put these two together as:

```
$(month,@('05',code),3)
```

To relate this to the content of the field DATE, remember that the month is the first and second characters of the field. This brings us to the next substitution:

```
$(month,@($(DATE,1,2),code),3)
```

which, if entered as the expression for field content, would cause REPORT to print the corresponding English month instead of the actual field content. To get the entire desired result we would enter the column width and content as:

```
12,$(month,@($(DATE,1,2),code),3) + ' '
■ + $(DATE,4,2) + ', 19' + $(DATE,7,2)
```

This expression transforms the entry 10/15/82 to the printed result: Oct 15, 1982.

You can use this scheme for any number of substitutions, but you can also get into some trouble with it. If there is an entry for which you have no code, you will get a SYNTAX ERROR and the whole thing will grind to a halt. Nevertheless, with reasonable care you can make profitable use of this trick.

One other obvious use for this trick is with true/false entries. If you use a character field with T and F you can get a printout with more than just columns of.T. and.F. With our school example, if we wanted a printout to contain FAIL if a student failed and nothing if s/he had passed, we would:

```
STORE 'FAIL      ' TO text
STORE 'F      T  ' TO code
```

The entry in REPORT would be:

```
4,$(text,@(FAILED,code),4)
```

Margin Control

The first request you encounter when you enter REPORT is:

```
ENTER OPTIONS, M=LEFT MARGIN,
■L=LINES/PAGE, W=PAGE WIDTH
```

The default setting for the left margin is eight character spaces. This is 8/10 of an inch using a 10 character per inch printer. This size of margin is barely adequate if you want to put the reports into a three-ring binder, and is completely inadequate if you are using a 12 or 16 cpi printer. To change the left margin to some larger number, 15 for instance, type M = 15 in response to the question. This will begin the report 15 spaces from the left edge of the paper.

You can also change the left margin from the keyboard without fussing with the REPORT margin setting. SET MARGIN TO 10, for example, will cause everything to be offset by ten spaces. This means that the report would have an 18 character left margin (ten spaces from SET MARGIN TO and eight from the standard default). SET MARGIN TO affects only the printer, not the screen. It also produces a margin for other print commands such as LIST.

Similarly, the page width is the number of character spaces from the left edge before the report begins to wrap around. The default is 80. (This protects the platen on the printer). If you are using a 12 or 16 cpi printer or 15-inch paper you will probably want to increase the width to a number appropriate to your print size and paper size. **Figure 3** gives you some comparisons of numer of characters per line for different page widths and type sizes.

Page length is the number of lines on the page. The default is 57. This gives satisfactory results with 11-inch paper and no double spacing. If you wish a larger bottom margin try changing the number of lines to something less than 57.

Page Headings

REPORT allows you to define headings other than the standard title. The additional heading is printed on the line containing the page number. This allows you to include specific text pertinent to the day that you run the report and insert it at the top of the page without having to modify the report. For example:

```
SET HEADING TO SPECIAL REPORT AS
■OF THE DAY BEFORE INVENTORY
```

You can make particular use of this feature from within programs. For example, you might have the same report structure for several clients. The program could:

```
STORE 'INVENTORY FOR ABERCROMBIE
■AND CZYNCOWICZ' TO title

SET HEADING TO &title

REPORT FOR INVENTRY='A & C'
```

You would have to enter the STORE command for each client and then let the program do the actual inventory listings for each.

Reports Using Two Databases

You can use two databases to produce a single report under certain conditions. The second database must be an extension of the first. That is, the records must match on the basis of record numbers. When this is the case, the report setup is:

```
.SELECT SECONDARY
.USE FILE2
.SELECT PRIMARY
.USE FILE1
.SET LINKAGE ON
.REPORT
```

REPORT can select fields from either database. If two fields have the same fieldname you must discriminate by using "S." and "P." immediately preceding the fieldname (i.e. S.ADDRESS). Should

Width	10 cpi	12 cpi	16 cpi
8 1/2	85	102	136
15	150	180	240

Figure 3. Number of characters on line

you elect to prepare a report using two files, remember to always have both files selected and each file positioned to Record 1.

Selective Reporting

REPORT can be used to select only specific items for a report. There are two mechanisms for selecting records — FOR and WHILE.

If the desired records are scattered throughout the database, the FOR condition is the best technique. For example, suppose we have a student database which has been indexed by student name, but we want REPORT to prepare a class roster for only one room and grade.

```
.REPORT FOR ROOM='11' .AND. GRADE='6'
```

Here is a perfect example for the use of the HEADING. Prior to using the last command, enter:

```
.SET HEADING TO ROOM 11 GRADE 6
```

This will annotate the report with ROOM 11 GRADE 6 printed on the top line.

If your database is indexed on both GRADE and ROOM you could also prepare the identical report using WHILE. First you must position the database to the desired record.

```
.FIND 611
```

will position the database to the first record for grade 6 and room 11. The report can be prepared by:

```
.SET HEADING TO ROOM 11 GRADE 6
.REPORT WHILE ROOM='11' .AND.
■ GRADE='6'
```

REPORT is an extremely powerful command. The best way to try it out is using the screen with a short database file. Since REPORT is a read only command, there is no way that you can do damage to the contents of a database. The very worst thing that can happen when you do something wrong is to get a SYNTAX ERROR; then you know you need to try another tack.

ASHTON·TATE

Chapter Twelve

THE DATE

The "date" deserves special attention. It is an item we use frequently in a variety of different applications.

The System Date

The system date is stored in memory at a location named DATE( ). If you have a PC type computer (16-bit), the system clock is read when dBASE II is loaded and the date is set automatically. With an 8-bit computer, you are asked to enter the date when dBASE II is loaded.

The system date is written to the database header whenever a change is made to the database. Reports prepared with REPORT use the system date, and it may also be used by a variety of applications programs.

For a number of reasons, the system date might not be set properly. Many people are prone to hit the <RETURN> key when asked for the date by the operating system or by dBASE II. On non-PC machines the date-setting operation is completely bypassed when a program is loaded at the same time that dBASE II is loaded. (You can load dBASE II and a program with a single command — type DBASE followed by the program name.)

Testing and Setting the System Date

We can easily check the system date to verify whether or not it has been set. On computers where the system clock is automatically read, the date will be set to some arbitrary base date (such as 01/01/80) if we bypassed setting the clock when we brought up the computer. On 8-bit computers where the date is *not* read, the date is set to 00/00/00. We can test for the date by looking at DATE( ).

The date can be set directly using SET DATE TO. A simple program to test and set the date is shown as **Program 1**.

```
SET TALK OFF
IF $(DATE(),7,2)+$(DATE(),1,5)<'8301/01'
     STORE DATE() TO mdate
     ERASE
     @ 1,1 SAY 'ENTER THE DATE AS MM/DD/YY' GET mdate PICTURE '99/99/99'
     READ
     SET DATE TO &mdate
ENDIF
RETURN
```

Program 1. Test and set the system date

Note the syntax of the command SET DATE TO &*mdate*. Without the ampersand (&), which permits the use of the stored value of a memory variable in a command line, 00/00/00 would be installed as the system date.

Validating the Date

Program 1 does not validate the date — we could enter, and the system would accept, 15/32/83 as a valid date. There are a couple of ways to test for illegal data, although it's terribly difficult to test for erroneous "legitimate" dates.

The first method sets up a small database with only one field, DAYS, a numeric field with a field length of two for the number of days in the month. The record number corresponds to the month. (Record 1 has the entry 31, etc.) We call this database DATES. The program to verify the date (month and day only) is shown as **Program 2**.

Program 2 illustrates the use of a DO loop in error testing, the use of the VAL function, and the use of DO CASE.

In Program 2, we first set a system flag, *baddate* to True, and create a memory variable *mdate*. Then we set up a DO loop that will keep running as long as our flag *baddate* is True. Why use a DO loop? Without it, we must assume that the user will enter the correct date on the first try. But if this is the case, we don't need to test the data in the first place. On each pass through the loop we have the user enter a date. PICTURE provides a first level filter for bad data; only blank spaces or numeric data can be entered into the variable.

Our next step is to test for valid month and day. We create two numeric variables, *month* and *day*, from the appropriate parts of the character string *mdate*. This is done with the VAL function. Once we have these variables we can perform our test, which we do in two steps. First, we check for a valid month. If the month isn't valid we inform the user by printing INVALID MONTH on the screen. If the month tests okay, we then check for the day of the month. GO *month* positions the database to the record corresponding to the month. We have chosen to use DO CASE for our test.

This is a particularly good illustration of the use of DO CASE. The CASES are tested in order until one (or none) is satisfied. The ordering of the cases is significant. The first test insures that the operator actually entered a positive date (the PICTURE command doesn't protect against minus signs). Had we placed the third case first, a -6, for example, would have been honored as valid. The second case is a test for leap years. If either the second or third case is satisfied, the loop flag is set to False to terminate the loop.

Note that there are separate error messages for each of the possible errors. On each pass through the loop we erased screen Line 3 with @ 3,0. This prevents any ambiguity in the error message that would result if the user made the two possible errors on successive tries.

Program 3 is an alternative implementation of a date validation program. It illustrates the use of the @ function to select a desired item from a second character string. It also illustrates using substring comparisons of character representations of "numeric" data (the dates).

This is a much "slicker" implementation than Program 2, although it isn't as easy to follow. On many systems it will "come up" much quicker than Program 2 because we are not "opening" a database file.

The variables *monthmask* and *daymask* are to be used to determine the number of days in a particular month. Note that the number of days (*daymask*) line up exactly with the month in *monthmask*. You should also note that months less than "10" are represented with a leading "0." The tech-

```
SET TALK OFF
IF $(DATE(),7,2)+$(DATE(),1,5)<'8301/01'
     USE Dates
     STORE T TO baddate
     STORE DATE() TO mdate
     ERASE
     DO WHILE baddate
     @ 1,1 SAY 'ENTER THE DATE AS MM/DD/YY' GET mdate PICTURE '99/99/99'
     READ
     @ 3,0
     STORE VAL($(MDATE,1,2)) TO month
     STORE VAL($(MDATE,4,2)) TO day
     IF month>=1 .AND. month<=12
        GO Month
        DO CASE
           CASE day<=0
             @ 3,20 SAY 'INVALID DAY'
           CASE month=2 .AND. $(mdate,7,2)$'84,88' .AND. day<=DAYS+1
             STORE F TO baddate
           CASE day<=DAYS
             STORE F TO baddate
           OTHERWISE
             @ 3,20 SAY 'INVALID DAY'
        ENDCASE
     ELSE
       @ 3,1 SAY 'INVALID MONTH'
     ENDIF
     ENDDO
     SET DATE TO &mdate
     RELEASE mdate, month, day, baddate
ENDIF
RETURN
```

Program 2. Test, validate and set the system date

```
SET TALK OFF
IF $(DATE(),7,2)+$(DATE(),1,5)<'8301/01'
    STORE DATE() TO mdate
    STORE '01 02 03 04 05 06 07 08 09 10 11 12' TO monthmask
    STORE '31 28 31 30 31 30 31 31 30 31 30 31' TO daymask
    STORE T TO baddate
    ERASE
    DO WHILE baddate
    @ 1,1 SAY 'ENTER THE DATE AS MM/DD/YY' GET mdate PICTURE '99/99/99'
    READ
    @ 3,0
    SET DATE TO &mdate
    STORE DATE() TO mdate
    IF $(mdate,1,2)$monthmask
       STORE  $(daymask,@($(mdate,1,2),monthmask),2) TO days
       IF $(mdate,1,2)='02' .AND. $(mdate,7,2)$'84,88'
          STORE '29' TO days
       ENDIF
       IF $(mdate,4,2)>='01'.AND. $(mdate,4,2)<=days
          STORE F TO baddate
       ELSE
          @ 3,20 SAY 'INVALID DAY'
       ENDIF
    ELSE
      @ 3,1 SAY 'INVALID MONTH'
    ENDIF
    ENDDO
    SET DATE TO &mdate
    RELEASE mdate, days, baddate,monthmask, daymask
ENDIF
RETURN
```

nique we are going to use is very fast but, if you aren't careful, potentially disastrous.

After *mdate* has been "read" we store it into DATE( ) using SET DATE TO &*mdate* and then take it out again. This allows us to take advantage of the fact that DATE always stores a numeric digit, 0 thru 9, in each of the positions for data. Character positions 3 and 6 are always a "/". We need this characteristic to avoid problems in the next line.

The first IF checks to see if the first two characters of *mdate* are to be found in the *monthmask*. If not, we get the error message INVALID MONTH. Had we allowed the possibility of a blank space in the first character of *mdate*, we could locate a January date as beginning one character space before the "10" in *monthmask*. That would line us up incorrectly with the number of days check.

The next line, where we create the variable *days*, is particularly instructive. It uses the first two characters of *mdate* to store the maximum number of days in a month directly to *days*. Note that *days* is a character string. Now let's explain what is happening on this line.

Suppose that the first two characters of *mdate* are 09. The function @($(*mdate*,1,2), *monthmask*) returns a number that is the starting position of 09 in the string *monthmask*. The substring function always takes the form:

$(<variable name>, starting location, length)

All we are doing is using @, the substring search function, to place us at the starting location. This ends up by storing the two characters directly below the 09 to *days*, a character string.

Next we test for leap year. If it's February, and if it's a leap year, we store the characters "29" to days.

Now we compare the fourth and fifth characters to our limits. Note here that we can compare character strings exactly as if they were numbers. This is because, in actuality, we are comparing ASCII values. Furthermore, we have insured that each of the character positions must be a numeric character. If we pass the test, we set our flag *baddate* to False and escape; otherwise we display the error message INVALID MONTH and do it all over again.

The Date as a Menu Item

In all systems, you can enter a program directly from the operating system by typing DBASE followed by the name of the program. In a CP/M system, this bypasses the process wherein dBASE II asks you to enter the system date.

Bypassing the date at the operating system or upon entering dBASE II prohibits the use of the system date as a source for data entry. One way around this is to have the menu program display the date, and to have one of the menu selections provide an option to change the date.

A way to provide a source for the date is to keep the latest date stored on the disk in a memory file (.MEM). Then, when the program is loaded, one of the program commands will read the disk file and use that file for the system date.

Program 4 demonstrates restoring (reading) memory variables from a disk file, and incorporating a date and a date change program into the menu. The former is accomplished with the command RESTORE FROM DATE ADDITIVE. The word ADDITIVE is optional. However, without it any memory variables in use when the RESTORE command is used are erased.

Not explicitly shown is the fact that we have restored two memory variables: *mdate* and *cdate*. *mdate* has the date in the conventional format of

```
SET TALK OFF
RESTORE FROM Date ADDITIVE
SET DATE TO &mdate
DO WHILE T
ERASE
STORE ' ' TO choice
@ 5,30 SAY 'BOB'S BETTER BOOKS'
@ 7,35 SAY cdate
@ 9,30 SAY '1 - CHANGE THE DATE'
@ 10,30 SAY '2 - CUSTOMER MENU'
@ 11,30 SAY '3 - INVENTORY MENU'
@ 12,30 SAY '4 - SALES ORDER ENTRY'
@ 13,30 SAY '5 - MAILING LISTS MENU'
@ 14,30 SAY '6 - INVOICE MENU'
@ 15,30 SAY '0 - QUIT'
@ 18,32 SAY '- PICK ONE'
@ 18,29 GET CHOICE
READ
DO CASE
  CASE choice='1'
     DO Date
  CASE choice='2'

      ETC


ENDCASE
ENDDO
```

Program 4. Menu program using displayed date

MM/DD/YY. *cdate* is the "longhand" version of the same date. If *mdate* contains 10/11/82, *cdate* contains 11 Oct 1982. We use *cdate* as the date display because all of us, at one time or another, transpose the day and month when they are presented as numbers. Program 4 provides the user with a positive visual validation of the date.

Program 5, the program called to change the date, begins with the command CLEAR GETS. We did not erase the screen when we entered this program; the menu is still displayed. CLEAR GETS is used to prevent the cursor from moving to the screen area for CHOICE.

Then we create three memory variables to verify the date and convert it to "longhand." These are kept outside of the DO loop as there is no need to re-create these variables on each pass through the loop. (Keep as much as you can out of the loop).

The balance of this program is basically the same as that shown in Program 2, except that we have changed the position on the screen we are using. Note that we erased Line 7 before we entered the DO loop. Line 7 is where the date had been displayed. If our new Line 7 does not completely overlap the previous text, part of both will be displayed, causing confusion. It's better to be sure and erase the line first.

Once we leave the loop, having entered a valid date, we convert the date to "longhand" using the two command lines involving *cdate*. Although these two lines could be incorporated into a single command, we used two steps due to the size of the command on the page.

To store our dates safely back to the disk we use the command SAVE ALL LIKE ?*date* TO DATE. This command allows us to write only those variables that have five-character names and that end in DATE to the disk file. The ? is a wild card — meaning any character or a space. ?DATE is the "skeleton" of the variable name.

The Date as a Field

Dates are popular fields: birthdates, enrollment dates, transaction dates, promotion dates, etc. Yet the date poses a particular problem for the dBASE II programmer. In America we like to write dates as MM/DD/YY. Europeans prefer DD/MM/YY, while the Japanese use YY/MM/DD. Only the Japanese use dates in a form that is natural for the computer.

If we want to test whether a date falls between two other dates (earliest date < testdate < latest date), the dates must be in the arrangement YY/MM/DD. This is because the standard comparison begins with the most significant character (or digit) and that is the character on the left. Let's take three dates: A, B, and C.

A. 02/01/82
B. 11/11/83
C. 01/01/84

You want to arrange these dates in the order A, B, C — from earliest to latest. Without other manipulation the computer would order them as C, A, B.

Dates are most frequently entered as character fields, usually with a width of eight. This can further compound the problem. Here we see dates entered in a variety of ways:

```
D.  01/01/82
E.   2/ 1/82
F.  1 /1 /82
```

To the computer, date E is less than date D. The comparison is made from left to right according to the ASCII value of each character. The ASCII values for characters are shown in Appendix D.

```
* Program .....:MENU1.CMD (or MENU1.PRG)
* Notes .......:This program stores the date to a memory file.

CLEAR GETS
STORE '01 02 03 04 05 06 07 08 09 10 11 12' TO monthmask
STORE '31 28 31 30 31 30 31 31 30 31 30 31' TO daymask
STORE 'JANFEBMARAPRMAYJUNJULAUGSEPOCTNOVDEC' TO calendar
STORE T TO baddate
ERASE
@ 7,0

DO WHILE baddate
   @ 7,1 SAY 'ENTER THE DATE AS MM/DD/YY' GET mdate PICTURE '99/99/99'
   READ
   @ 8,0
   SET DATE TO &mdate
   STORE DATE() TO mdate

   IF $(mdate,1,2)$monthmask
      STORE  $(daymask,@($(mdate,1,2),monthmask),2) TO days

      IF $(mdate,1,2)='02' .AND. $(mdate,7,2)$'84,88'
         STORE '29' TO days
      ENDIF

      IF $(mdate,4,2)>='01'.AND. $(mdate,4,2)<=days
         STORE F TO baddate
      ELSE
         @ 8,20 SAY 'INVALID DAY'
      ENDIF
   ELSE
      @ 8,1 SAY 'INVALID MONTH'
   ENDIF
ENDDO

@ 8,0
SET DATE TO &mdate
STORE DATE() TO mdate
STORE  $(calendar,@($(mdate,1,2),monthmask),3) TO cdate
STORE $(mdate,4,2)+' '+cdate+' 19'+$(mdate,7,2) TO cdate
SAVE ALL LIKE ?date TO Date
RELEASE month,day,monthmask,daymask,calendar,days,baddate
RETURN
```

Program 5. MENU1.CMD/.PRG Program to change and verify system date.

Unless we intend never to do anything with dates, we must establish some consistent method of dealing with them. At the very least, we need to exclude the possibility of storing dates in the form of the E and F examples. Until we do, we cannot reliably perform any real operations involving the date.

Insuring that the data is consistently stored in the form of example D is easy. We can use the SET DATE TO command to insure the structure of the date format. An example of a subroutine to do this is shown as **Program 6**. Note that we STORE the system date to a safe place and then RESTORE it before we do the REPLACE. Actually, you need only RESTORE the system date before you close the file. The header date is rewritten with the system date when the file is closed. Note also that we STOREd each field to a variable prior to using SET DATE TO. (We must use the ampersand before the variable name; you cannot use an ampersand with a field name.)

The technique of using the system date to format a date, and then using the system date to replace the content of a field, can be used profitably whenever a field is to be replaced with the current date. This saves the operator time and effort and reduces the chance of error. It also insures uniformity in the structure of the contents of the date field.

Even by providing a consistent structure, we face Hobson's choice. We cannot obtain a meaningful sort on a date field. We can index by using the artifice:

```
INDEX ON $(DATEFIELD,7,2)
■ + $(DATEFIELD,1,6) TO dates
```

This will arrange the database in date order. However, to do a FIND we must use FIND <yy/mm/dd>.

Using any logical operation except DATE= '<date>' can get messy. As an example, if we want to display records where a date is earlier than a test date we get:

```
DISPLAY FOR $(DATE,7,2) + $(DATE,1,6)
■< $(mdate,7,2) + $(mdate,1,6)
```

We can save ourselves a lot of trouble by adopting the Japanese style for dates — YY/MM/DD. This allows us to SORT and to use direct indexing, and it may simplify the logic.

Other Ways of Storing Dates

Another method of storing the date is taken from the Julian Day. Julian Day is a scheme used by astronomers whereby each day is assigned a serial number. The astronomers begin with January 1, 4713 B.C. January 1, 1965 is Julian Day (J.D.) 2,438,762. Variations on the idea (proposed by Joseph Scalizer in 1582) are often used in digital clocks and calculators. A six-digit counter can act as a calendar with a 2737+ year cycle (divide 999,999 by 365.25). Julian Day also allows us to determine the day of the week for any date within the scope of the calendar. This is particularly convenient if one is attempting to develop a program for any kind of scheduling system. (Using the six data digits of a normal date representation provides for only a 99- year calendar without ambiguity.)

Developing a Julian Day system is complicated somewhat by our particular calendar system, the Gregorian, which is derived from the Julian calendar. The Julian calendar has no relation to Julian Day; it was established by Julius Caesar in 46 B.C. It fixed the year at 365 days with a 366-day leap year occurring every fourth year.

Unfortunately, fixing a calendar isn't quite that simple: a year is actually a little shorter than 365¼ days. When it was determined in 1582 that the

```
.........
@ 7,1 SAY 'ENTER BIRTH DATE ' GET bdate PICTURE '99/99/99'
@ 8,1 SAY 'ENTER STARTING DATE ' GET sdate PICTURE '99/99/99'
READ
STORE DATE() TO safety
STORE bdate TO mbdate
SET DATE TO &mbdate
STORE DATE() TO mbdate
STORE sdate TO msdate
SET DATE TO &msdate
STORE DATE() TO msdate
SET DATE TO &safety
REPLACE bdate WITH mbdate, sdate WITH msdate
........
```

Program 6. Subroutine for insuring uniformity in date entry

```
* program to calculate 'Julian Date' from calendar date

SET TALK OFF
ERASE
STORE '  /  /    ' TO date
@ 1,1 SAY 'ENTER DATE ' GET date PICTURE '99/99/9999'
READ
SET DATE TO &date

STORE VAL($(date,7,4)) TO year
STORE 0 TO baseyear
STORE year-baseyear TO year

* first we test to see if the year is a leapyear

DO CASE
  CASE year-INT(year/400)*400=0
   STORE T TO leapyear
  CASE year-INT(year/100)*100=0
   STORE F TO leapyear
  CASE YEAR-INT(YEAR/4)*4 = 0
   STORE T TO leapyear
  OTHERWISE
   STORE F TO leapyear
ENDCASE

* calculate the day of the year

  STORE '01 02 03 04 05  06  07  08  09  10  11  12' TO months
IF leapyear
  STORE '    31  60 91 121 152 182 213 244 274 305 335  366'  TO daybase
  STORE 0 TO adjust
ELSE
  STORE 1 TO adjust
  STORE '    31 59 90 120 151 181 212 243 273 304  334  365'  TO daybase
ENDIF
  STORE VAL($DATE(),4,2)) TO day
  STORE VAL($(daybase,@($(DATE(),1,2),months),3))+day  TO dayofyear

* determine the number of leapyears since the base year

  STORE INT(year/4)-INT(year/100)+INT(year/400)+adjust  TO leapyears

* now calculate the julian date

  STORE 365*(year) +leapyears + dayofyear TO juliandate
```

Program 7. Program to convert a date to a Julian Day

Continued on next page

Continued from the previous page

```
? 'JULIAN DATE = '.juliandate

 RETURN
```

Program 7. Program to convert a date to a Julian Day

date corresponding to the Spring Equinox was off by 10 days, Pope Gregory XIII deleted 10 days from the Julian calendar to correct the date and established the Gregorian calendar which we use today.

Though the Gregorian calendar was almost immediately adopted by Roman Catholic countries, Protestant Europe, and especially England, was somewhat less prompt in accepting the new calendar. In fact, England and the American colonies did not adopt the Gregorian calendar until 1752, and then amidst great protest. After all, people were being cheated out of 11 days of their lives (the delay between 1582 and 1752 was long enough to add another day). The growing season was going to be shorter, and people would be earning less money during the year.

The Gregorian calendar has a leap year every fourth year except on century years. Every fourth century year is a leap year. Those century years that are exactly divisible by 400 are leap years. Thus 1600 and 2000 are leap years but 1700, 1800, and 1900 are not. This is messy enough to provide some interesting programming examples (Programs 7, 8, and 9).

Program 7 takes a standard calendar date and converts it to a "Julian Date" based on January 1, 0. There is no such actual date, but it gives a serial number to each day in the Christian Era. In this program we have imposed no limit on the date, nor are we checking for valid date entry.

Program 7 is also an example of programming in dBASE II without using a database. The program uses a combination of string searches and arithmetic to arrive at the result — a serial number for a date.

Note that the date entry variable allows four digits for the year. Once we have entered the date we insure that the digits are properly aligned by storing it to the system date. Next we store the "year" to a numeric variable. We are going to do a lot of arithmetic using the year. The *baseyear* is entered for your convenience with the included subprogram. It will work with any baseyear that is exactly divisible by 400.

Again, note that we have "commented" the program. Though lines beginning with an "*" are ignored by dBASE II, comments do slow the execution of a program somewhat. Comments can be a great help in reading a tricky program later on. When you've done something slick you really ought to comment the program. (You can always make a "working" copy without the comments if speed is important to you.)

To calculate the Julian Day, we need to determine if the year is a leap year. This is a good use for DO CASE. This command executes only the first CASE that is met. In our program the order that we enter the cases becomes important. For example, if we had put Case 3 first, the century years would be declared as leap years. If we had placed Case 2 first, the leap century years would be declared as non-leap years. The INT function discards the decimal places in a number or expression. When we have the opportunity to use CASE for its intended purpose — as opposed to use as a shorthand substitute for IF — we often need to plan. With CASE, OTHERWISE is the case for "everything else" and is similar to the ELSE in IF/ELSE.

We calculate the day of the year by adding the day to the cumulative number of days through the end of the previous month. The cumulative days are contained in *daybase*. We choose between two possible *daybases* by using the leap year.

Next, we need to calculate the number of leap years since the base date. Again we use the INT function, as in DO CASE.

Finally, we arrive at the actual calculation. The whole problem lies in determining the number of leap years to use in the final calculation. This is a good program example in that it forces one to pay attention to details, and solves a straightforward problem.

Program 8 converts back to a calendar date; it is the same problem in reverse. To speed the process we estimate the year by dividing the Julian Day by 365. This give us an estimated year that is greater than or equal to the actual year. The error grows with the size of the year. This is because the estimated year doesn't take the leap years into account. The logic states that we calculate the estimated year and then calculate the necessary corrections.

Note that the code is nearly identical to that used in Program 7. We use exactly the same tests for leap year and the same calculation to determine the number of leap years.

Once we have an estimated date, we refine the date in the DO loop. It is only necessary to process those dates where the remainder is less than or equal to zero. Those few positive dates were handled directly and completely during our first pass at a result.

Note the way in which we calculate the day and month. This is a technique that is similar to that used to manage data using conventional programming languages. Here we index our way through a dataset, one item at a time, until we reach our intended result.

The execution speed of this program is respectable. However, if one has a need to do this sort of calculation frequently (several times in a database record or in a database search), this is the sort of program that should be implemented in assembly language and used with dBASE via the dBASE II commands LOAD and CALL.

Program 9 illustrates the ease with which we can determine the day of the week for any date from the Julian Day. The program will give the correct result for our base year of zero. If another base year is chosen one would need to adjust the *weekcode* to provide the correct result.

All that we need to do is determine the remainder when we divide the Julian Day by seven. This is what we are doing in the single calculation involving Julian Day.

```
* program to convert from 'Julian Date' to calendar date

SET TALK OFF
INPUT 'ENTER JULIAN DATE ' TO juliandate
STORE 0 TO baseyear
STORE baseyear TO year

* first we need to estimate the year (estimate is >= actual year)

STORE INT(juliandate/365) TO estyear
STORE INT(estyear/4)-INT(estyear/100)+INT(estyear/400)  TO leapyears
DO CASE
  CASE estyear-INT(estyear/400)*400=0
   STORE T TO leapyear
  CASE estyear-INT(estyear/100)*100=0
   STORE F TO leapyear
  CASE estyear-INT(estyear/4)*4 = 0
   STORE T TO leapyear
  OTHERWISE
   STORE F TO leapyear
ENDCASE
IF leapyear
STORE juliandate - leapyears - estyear*365 TO remdays
ELSE
STORE juliandate - leapyears -1 - estyear*365 TO remdays
ENDIF

* remaining days can be +,-, or 0

DO WHILE remdays<0
STORE estyear-1 TO estyear
STORE INT(estyear/4)-INT(estyear/100)+INT(estyear/400) TO leapyears
DO CASE
  CASE estyear-INT(estyear/400)*400=0
   STORE T TO leapyear
  CASE estyear-INT(estyear/100)*100=0
   STORE F TO leapyear
  CASE estyear-INT(estyear/4)*4 = 0
   STORE T TO leapyear
  OTHERWISE
   STORE F TO leapyear
ENDCASE
```

Program 8. Conversion from Julian Day to a calendar date *Continued on next page*

Continued from the previous page

```
IF leapyear
STORE juliandate - leapyears - estyear*365 TO remdays
ELSE
STORE juliandate - leapyears - 1 - estyear*365 TO remdays
ENDIF
ENDDO


STORE '01  02  03  04  05  06  07  08  09  10  11  12' TO months
IF leapyear
STORE  '31   29   31   30  31  30  31  31  30   31   30   31'  TO daysinmon
STORE  '31   60   91   121 152 182 213 244 274 305  335  366'  TO daybase
ELSE
STORE  '31   28   31   30  31  30  31  31  30   31   30   31'  TO daysinmon
STORE  '31   59   90  120 151 181 212 243 273  304  334  365'  TO daybase
ENDIF

STORE 1 TO index,month
DO WHILE index<=45
  IF remdays>VAL($(daysinmon,index,3))
    STORE month + 1 TO month
    STORE remdays-VAL($(daysinmon.index,2)) TO remdays
  ENDIF
    STORE index+4 TO index
ENDDO

STORE STR(month,2)+'/'+STR(remdays,2) TO date
SET DATE TO &date
STORE $(DATE(),1,6)+STR(estyear,4) TO date
? date
RETURN
```

Program 8. Conversion from Julian Day to a calendar date

```
SET TALK OFF
INPUT 'ENTER JULIAN DATE' TO juliandate
STORE '0   1    2    3    4    5    6 ' TO weekcode
STORE 'Fri Sat  Sun  Mon  Tue  Wed  Thu' TO weekdays

STORE STR (juliandate- (INT(juliandate/7))*7,1) TO daytest
? $(weekdays,@(daytest.weekcode),3)

RETURN
```

Program 9. Calculating the day of the week from Julian Day

Chapter Thirteen

DATA ENTRY TECHNIQUES

Data entry is the most time-consuming aspect of working with a database, as it is primarily a manual process. Fortunately, dBASE II provides a variety of tools to assist the user with data entry.

The basic query language commands for keyboard data entry are:

APPEND
INSERT
BROWSE
EDIT

APPEND and INSERT create new data records and provide the means for entering data into those records. BROWSE and EDIT provide a means for changing the contents of existing records.

These are very powerful commands. Each employs a "full screen form" where the cursor is under the user's control, giving the user the same data entry freedom to back up and change entries as with paper business forms.

As powerful as these commands are, there are a number of things that can be done from a dBASE II program to enhance and even improve these standard capabilities. Data entry can be enhanced through:

Custom screen forms
Indirect data entry
Entry into two databases at a time
Error checking
Editing through a menu

The basic dBASE II commands used for data entry programming are:

APPEND BLANK	SET FORMAT TO
@ x,y SAY ... USING	ACCEPT
@ x,y GET ... PICTURE	INPUT
CLEAR GETS	REPLACE
READ	

```
RECORD #00001

PARTNAME  :^                    :
QTY       :   :
MINSTOCK  :   :
PRICE     :       :
DATE      :         :
```

Screen 1. Example of standard entry screen for APPEND and EDIT

Custom Screen Forms

A typical data entry screen provided by the APPEND and EDIT commands is shown as **Screen 1**. This screen uses the fieldname as the prompt for each field "blank." The fieldnames and the "blank" for the content of each field are in a column. If you have more than 22 fields, all of the fields will not be displayed at the same time. The screen will scroll up after the twenty- second field has been entered.

We can easily create customized, full-screen forms using the @ x,y SAY and @ x,y GET commands. The @ x,y simply means "at line x, beginning with column y." A "custom" version of a standard screen is shown as **Screen 2**, and is created by the format file shown as **Screen 3**.

Our custom form will be used by dBASE II with the EDIT, APPEND, and INSERT commands.

In setting up this custom screen, we first SET the format. If the sample format file is named EXAMPLE.FMT we:

```
SET FORMAT TO EXAMPLE
APPEND
```

FORMAT files must have the file identifier .FMT, or the filename and the identifier must be used when you SET the format. You create a format file using either MODIFY COMMAND or a word processing program.

EDIT, APPEND, and INSERT all operate normally, except that they now use the special screen "form." Clearly, you can only use a format file with the database that it was created for. When you finish using a format file, return screen control to dBASE II with SET FORMAT TO SCREEN.

The READ command can be used with format files. If the format has been SET to produce a special screen "form," the screen will be created and the current record can be edited with READ.

There are several features of a format file worth noting.

1. We are not restricted to the order in which we created the fields; they can be displayed in any order. We can tailor the screen so that the particular items we want to change appear first.

2. We don't have to display all of the fields. This means that we only have to name the items we want to "edit."

3. We can "edit" any variable named with a GET. We can enter and edit memory variables as well as fields.

4. We can put any descriptive text we want on the screen.

We use only two dBASE II commands in a FORMAT file: @ x,y SAY and @ x,y GET. The GET command can be augmented with PICTURE; SAY can be augmented with USING. PICTURE and USING "mask" character fields and variables. Care should be taken when they are used with numeric fields or variables.

SAY is intended to display such character data as descriptive text, field contents, memory variables and combinations of these. When more than one item is displayed with SAY, the items must be concatenated with + signs.

```
@ 3,4 SAY 'PART DESCRIPTION:
■' + PARTNAME
```

You can directly display the content of a numeric field or variable if it is the *only* item for a SAY command.

```
@ 8,1 SAY COST
```

```
                    INVENTORY  RECORD  11281

PART DESCRIPTION :                    :

QUANTITY ON HAND :    :        MIMIMUM STOCK LEVEL :  :

CURRENT PRICE :       :        DATE OF LAST CHANGE:  /  /  :
```

Screen 2. Custom screen format of Screen 1

```
* this format file is used with INV.DBF
@ 2,36 say 'INVENTORY  RECORD: '+STR(#,5)
@ 5,2 say 'PART NAME ' get PARTNAME PICTURE "!!!!!!!!!!"
@ 7,2 say 'QUANTITY ON HAND ' get QTY
@ 7,37 say 'MIMIMUM STOCK LEVEL' get MINSTOCK
@ 9,2 say 'CURRENT PRICE ' get PRICE
@ 9,37 say 'DATE OF LAST CHANGE ' get DATE PICTURE "99/99/99"
```

Screen 3. Format file to create Screen 2 format

Otherwise, you will need to use the STR function to display the numeric item.

```
@ 8,1 SAY 'WHOLESALE COST
■' + STR(COST,7,2)
```

GET displays the content of a field or a memory variable. Only one item can be named with each GET. When a data item is displayed by a GET, we can move the cursor to the displayed field and change the current content by typing in new information.

As shown in Screen 1, the SAY and GET commands can be combined on a single command line. The PICTURE and USING clauses can also be combined with SAY and GET on the same line.

```
@ x,y SAY ..... USING "...  " GET .....
■PICTURE "...."
```

Here, PICTURE provides a "mask" to help with data entry. For example, in the format file in Screen 3 we use:

```
PICTURE "!!!!!!!!!!!!!!!!"
```

This insures that only upper case characters are entered into the field. If we were to type in lower case letters, this "mask" would convert the lower case letters to upper case.

PICTURE "999999" prevents us from entering anything but a number into the named character field. Only numbers can be entered into spaces protected by nines. This is a good way of screening phone number entries.

PICTURE "99/99/99" provides a structure for dates. The "/" is entered for us. When we enter the date, dBASE II "skips over" the slashes.

USING is similar to PICTURE except that it is used to "mask" the items displayed by SAY.

The IBM PC, as well as many other computers, displays items named with a GET in reverse video. Items named by a SAY are displayed normally. Some other systems display GET normally and SAY at half intensity. To defeat the reverse video or the half intensity feature of dBASE II we can use the command SET INTENSITY OFF. To return to the normal video display, use SET INTENSITY ON.

dBASE II uses colons ":" to bracket the items named with a GET. This allows you to "see" a field even when it contains only blank space. You can get rid of the colons with SET COLON OFF, as well as create special effects. For example, if a field area is underlined, you will most likely want to "turn off" the colons. The colons are restored with SET COLON ON.

Most CRT screens have 24 lines, each with 80 character spaces. In dBASE II, these lines are numbered 0 to 23 and the columns are numbered 0 to 79. It is not a good idea to use Line 0 (the top line) or Column 0 (the leftmost screen position).

You can also use the NOTE (or *) command in a format file to document the file. For example, you can use the note to identify which database file the format file is used with. (In Screen 3, our note identified INV as the relevant database file).

Format files can be invoked either from a program or from the keyboard. When they are used in conjunction with a program (as in the programs to add, edit, and delete records in Chapter Five), they are most profitable during the program development phase, or when the same screen format is to be used by several programs. This minimizes the program code during the development process, since it is easier to see what you're doing while developing the program if it is not cluttered with AT's and SAY's.

FORMAT files are separate files. Opening a file takes a fraction of a second — noticeably longer on MS-DOS systems with floppy disk drives. On some systems when you SET the format you will perceive a noticeable hesitation. If this is the case you will probably want to move the FORMAT into your program once the program has been developed.

Indirect Data Entry

When updating an inventory, the user has to add the quantity received to the quantity on hand, and then enter the result of the addition to the database. We want the user to simply enter the quantity received into the computer and have the computer make the addition and change the database. This is an example of indirect data entry.

We used this technique extensively in the examples in Section Two. A simple example of this technique is shown by these four lines of dBASE II code:

```
ACCEPT "ENTER PART NUMBER" TO pn
LOCATE FOR PARTNUMBER = pn
INPUT "QUANTITY RECEIVED" TO qtyrcvd
REPLACE QTY WITH QTY + qtyrcvd
```

Indirect entry reduces the effort required of the user, and in so doing, reduces the chance of error.

Entering Data into Two Databases at a Time

Data can be entered into two different database files at the same time. To do this we must be using both a primary and a secondary file, with the two files each positioned to the record we want to edit. From a program or format file, the fields to be edited in both files are displayed using the GET command. Technically, only the selected file can be changed, although it will appear that each field displayed can be edited.

On the screen, there is no indication that the records are in different files. Since dBASE II only acknowledges changes to selected files, we have to trick dBASE II into writing onto the unselected file. To do this, we select the other database and replace *any* item in the current record in that database with itself. This will cause the screen-edited data to be written to this secondary file. dBASE II has already taken care of the first file. This technique is much easier than trying fancy tricks with screens, and it provides for real full-screen editing of the two files. You are, however, limited to 64 items for any full-screen editing.

This technique is also directly applicable to databases where one record is continued across two files because it is too large for one. Let's suppose we have an elementary school. Each student's record requires 60 fields. To accommodate the record we use two files, SCHOOL1 and SCHOOL2. The records are added evenly, so that Record 100 in SCHOOL2 is the continuation of Record 100 in SCHOOL1. The 60 fields and their accompanying descriptive text all fit nicely on one screen. The screen is created by the format file SCHOOL.FMT.

A program segment that illustrates the operation is shown below.

```
SELECT PRIMARY
GO 100
SELECT SECONDARY
GO 100
SET FORMAT TO SCHOOL
READ
SELECT PRIMARY
REPLACE NAME WITH NAME
```

Error Checking

Data entry offers the user the greatest opportunity of making errors in the database. In a large number of cases, protection against entry error can be provided. We *cannot* protect against the user entering a legitimate — but wrong — value.

The PICTURE clause can be used to provide some limited protection against errors. As described above, PICTURE can be used to check each character entered, and to force a character to be upper case or a number. This feature can be used to prevent a telephone number from being entered as 555-12A1. The masking aspect of PICTURE can be used to "fill in" parts of an entry — such as the slashes (/) in a date entry. PICTURE can be used as a "first line of defense" against errors.

To illustrate error checking in a program, consider the entering of students into a school roster. The items to be entered are NAME, ROOM, GRADE, and RETAINED (the latter indicates whether or not the student was failed the past year). All four fields are character fields. We can validate that the last three items are, at least, legitimate values. One program to validate these entries is shown as **Program 1**. A preferable alternative is shown as **Program 2**.

Though serviceable, Program 1 eliminates the major advantage of full screen entry: the freedom to change your mind, to back up an item and change the entry. This is due to the CLEAR GETS command within each checking loop. You need these CLEAR GETS — you are only allowed 64 GETS between either an ERASE or a CLEAR GETS. At more than 64 GETS, dBASE II will go on strike.

The best way to handle error checking for this kind of entry problem is shown by Program 2. Note that there really isn't a lot of difference except that, after the initial entry to "batch test" the entered data, we enter the data in true full-screen form.

Though Program 2 has more lines of code, it is preferable to the original program.

Dynamic Entry Screens

In-line checking of data entry, like that shown in Program 1, should be limited to situations where the "form" presented to the user varies with the answer to a specific question. In this case we are not so much checking the validity of a response, but looking for a cue as to what to do next.

To illustrate this point, let's consider a problem facing many American school districts these days. An increasing number of students are from non-English speaking families. Schools are required to classify students from non-English speaking families by the student's proficiency in English. If the student's home language is a part of the student's database record, we can ignore English proficiency questions for students whose home language is English. The program segment below illustrates how data entry can be facilitated.

```
@ 3,1 SAY "STUDENT'S NAME" GET NAME
@ 5,1 SAY 'ROOM' GET ROOM
@ 5,20 SAY 'GRADE' GET GRADE
@ 5,40 SAY 'RETAINED (Y/N)?' GET retained
@ 7,1 say 'IS THE HOME LANGUAGE
■ENGLISH (Y/N)?' GET query
READ
IF query $ 'Nn'
  @ 7,0
  @ 7,1 say 'HOME LANGUAGE'
  ■GET LANGUAGE
  @ 9,1 SAY 'ENGLISH PROFICIENCY
  ■LEVEL' GET PROFICIENT
ELSE
  REPLACE LANGUAGE WITH 'ENGLISH'
ENDIF
```

In this simple example, the user is presented with the opportunity to enter the home language and English proficiency only if the response to the

```
@ 3,1 SAY "STUDENT'S NAME" GET NAME
READ

DO WHILE .NOT. ROOM $ '1, 3,15,22,31,4A'
@ 5,1 SAY 'ROOM' GET ROOM
READ
CLEAR GETS
ENDDO

DO WHILE .NOT. GRADE $ '1,2,3,4,5,6,K'
@ 5,20 SAY 'GRADE' GET GRADE
READ
CLEAR GETS
ENDDO

DO WHILE .NOT. RETAINED $ 'YnNn'
@ 5,40 SAY 'RETAINED (Y/N)?' GET RETAINED
READ
CLEAR GETS
ENDDO
```

Program 1. Sample program with error checking

```
@ 3,1 SAY "STUDENT'S NAME" GET NAME
@ 5,1 SAY 'ROOM' GET ROOM
@ 5,20 SAY 'GRADE' GET GRADE
@ 5,40 SAY 'RETAINED (Y/N)?' GET RETAINED
READ

DO WHILE .NOT. ROOM $ '1, 3,15,22,31,4A'
@ 5,1 SAY 'ROOM' GET ROOM
READ
CLEAR GETS
ENDDO

DO WHILE .NOT. GRADE $ '1,2,3,4,5,6,K'
@ 5,20 SAY 'GRADE' GET GRADE
READ
CLEAR GETS
ENDDO

DO WHILE .NOT. RETAINED $ 'YnNn'
@ 5,40 SAY 'RETAINED (Y/N)?' GET RETAINED
READ
CLEAR GETS
ENDDO
```

Program 2. Improved program with error checking

question "Is the home language English?" is negative.

There are a number of cases where the response to a screen entry can alter a "form" for a user. Another example of tailoring screen entry to relevance of data would be asking single persons for their spouses' names.

Editing Through a Menu

We can make a menu of the items displayed for editing. This can be convenient when the display consists of a large number of items, and the items to be changed vary considerably from record to record. The technique also allows us to make a greater use of codes since we work with only a single item with each READ. (Note that this is markedly different from putting a READ with each "in-line" entry).

Program 3, which is based on our school example, illustrates the use of a menu for editing. One of the advantages of a menu selection approach to editing is that the "editing" software for each entry can be very elaborate. We can actually search other files and make very extensive uses of "coding" with this approach. This is an extremely powerful technique that is rarely used.

Browsing

BROWSE is not a good command to use when you are writing a program for someone else. To effectively use it you need to be familiar with the control keys. In all other situations the use of control keys on the screen can be described when necessary. You can't do this with BROWSE, unless the computer terminal has a status line that can be replaced with a user line (see Chapter Fourteen).

Another drawback to BROWSE is that the extent of the database being "browsed" cannot be as easily controlled as with other editing techniques. Also, the field titles used in BROWSE are not adequate for small fields.

BROWSE can, however, obviate writing detailed instructions in dBASE II and many lines of code. **Program 4** illustrates updating reading scores for selected classes in a SCHOOL database. This database is indexed by class (GRADE + ROOM + NAME). Providing an equivalent entry capability by writing the detailed instructions in dBASE II would require a great many more lines of code.

All of the topics covered in this chapter can be useful adjuncts to the basic data entry commands APPEND, INSERT, BROWSE and EDIT. All merit experimentation. The ultimate success of a program, however, lies with the ease of use for the person who is actually entering the data. The needs of the person who enters the data must be thoughtfully considered.

```
STORE T TO entryloop
DO WHILE entryloop
STORE '  ' TO item
@ 3,1  SAY " 1 - STUDENT'S NAME" GET NAME
@ 5,1  SAY ' 2 - ROOM' GET ROOM
@ 5,20 SAY ' 3 - GRADE' GET GRADE
@ 5,40 SAY ' 4 - RETAINED (Y/N)?' GET RETAINED
CLEAR GETS
@ 20,1 SAY 'Enter the Item Number to be edited' GET ITEM
READ

DO CASE
   CASE item='  '
     STORE F TO entryloop
   CASE item='1 '
     @3,5 SAY "STUDENT'S NAME" GET NAME
     READ
   CASE item='2 '
          @ 5,5 SAY 'ROOM' GET ROOM
          READ
     DO WHILE .NOT. ROOM $ '1, 3,15,22,31,4A'
          @ 18,1 SAY 'Non-existent room number'
          @ 5,5 SAY 'ROOM' GET ROOM
          READ
          CLEAR GETS
     ENDDO
   CASE item='3 '
          @ 5,24 SAY 'GRADE' GET GRADE
          READ
     DO WHILE .NOT. GRADE $ '1,2,3,4,5,6,K'
          @ 18,1 SAY 'Illegal grade number'
          @ 5,24 SAY 'GRADE' GET GRADE
          READ
          CLEAR GETS
     ENDDO
   CASE item='4 '
          @ 5,44 SAY 'RETAINED (Y/N)?' GET RETAINED
          READ
```

Program 3. "Menu editing" *Continued on next page*

Continued from the previous page

```
        DO WHILE .NOT. RETAINED $ 'YyNn'
             @ 18,1 'Please answer Yes or No'
             @ 5,44 SAY 'RETAINED (Y/N)?' GET RETAINED
             READ
             CLEAR GETS
        ENDDO
   ENDCASE
   @ 18,0
   CLEAR GETS
   ENDDO
```

Program 3. "Menu editing"

```
USE School INDEX Class
STORE T TO entryloop
DO WHILE entryloop

      ERASE
      STORE '   ' TO room
      STORE ' ' TO grade
      @ 1.1 SAY 'ENTER ROOM NUMBER' GET m.room
      READ NOUPDATE
      IF m.room='   '
         STORE F TO entryloop
         LOOP
      ELSE
         @ 2,1 SAY 'ENTER GRADE' GET m.grade
         READ NOUPDATE
      ENDIF
      STORE m.grade+m.room TO class
      FIND &class
      COPY FIELDS NAME,ROOM,GRADE,READSCORE TO Temp WHILE grade+room=class
      SELECT SECONDARY
      USE Temp
      BROWSE FIELDS NAME,READSCORE
      USE
      SELECT PRIMARY
      UPDATE FROM Temp ON GRADE+ROOM+NAME RANDOM;
REPLACE READSCORE WITH READSCORE
      DELETE FILE Temp
 ENDDO
```

Program 4. Use of BROWSE

Chapter Fourteen

DEBUGGING AND SPECIAL EFFECTS

Debugging is the process of getting a program to work the way you want it to work. Whatever your level of programming skill, debugging varies between the trivial and the impossible. It is always frustrating.

There are two basic kinds of errors that you can make when writing a program: *mechanical errors* and *design errors*. Of the two, mechanical errors are preferable. Usually the program won't "run" until you have found and fixed all of the mechanical errors. Design errors are more insidious — your program can "run" but gives you wrong results. Even worse is the case where you get an incorrect answer only some of the time.

Mechanical Errors

Examples of mechanical errors are misspelled commands, a mistake in the command structure, and a non-allowed operation. The first two are usually called syntax errors.

dBASE II will detect and partially diagnose most of the possible mechanical errors. It's up to you to complete the diagnosis and correct the error. That is debugging.

One example of a mechanical error is to enter DISPLAY as DISPAY. dBASE II's reaction would be to halt your program's execution and display:

```
 . DISPAY
**** UNKNOWN COMMAND
DISPAY
CALLED FROM B:EXAMPLE.PRG
CORRECT AND RETRY (Y/N)?
```

dBASE II neither aborts the program nor attempts to second-guess your error. It simply halts the program and gives you the opportunity to correct the error from the keyboard. This allows the program to continue until the next error. Keyboard "fixes" are not permanent; you need to go back in and correct the program.

Debugging most of these kinds of errors is a

nuisance — a "time fine" we pay for being careless. Occasionally we need to do slightly more work to debug an error.

```
*** SYNTAX ERROR ***
              ?
DISPLAY FOR ROOM = "6" .AND.
■ GRADE = 5
CALLED FROM B:EXAMPLE1.PRG
CALLED FROM B:EXAMPLE.PRG
CORRECT AND RETRY Y/N?
```

In the sample error above, it isn't quite so clear what's wrong. dBASE II has told us which program the error is in. It has also told us that the error is to the right of the ? placed over the R in ROOM. What is the problem? Are there fields or memory variables named ROOM and GRADE? Did we misspell one of them? Do the field types match the comparisons? In this example we can track down the problem with the ? command and the TYPE function.

The type function returns a letter indicating the kind of field or variable (C, N, or L) or a "U" if the variable does not exist.

```
? TYPE(ROOM),TYPE(GRADE)
 C C
```

Our test tells us that both fields exist and that both fields are character fields. The syntax used in the command for the contents of the grade field indicates a numeric field — there are no delimiters. Missing delimiters (or mismatched delimiters) are a common cause of syntax errors. We can "fix" this problem by putting delimiters around the "5" of GRADE.

Not all dBASE II error messages provide as much help as the two examples above. For example, let's attempt to run the following section of dBASE II code:

```
SELECT PRIMARY
USE EXAMPLE
SELECT SECONDARY
USE EXAMPLE
```

dBASE II does not permit you to have the same file open as both the primary and the secondary file. (This is too bad, since one can think of some very good uses for it — unfortunately, there are a number of very bad side effects also.) If you try the above routine from a program you will be told

```
FILE IS CURRENTLY OPEN
```

and you will be ejected from the program. Notice that you are not informed as to the names of the programs in use nor are you given the opportunity to correct the error. This particular error is the reason for carefully closing out all secondary files — and sometimes even primary files — at the end of each program. At least tracking down the error is relatively easy: you know what to look for.

There are other mechanical errors that can also result in your being kicked out of the program and returned to the keyboard or even to the operating system. Some of these errors may not — at least not consistently — give you any clue at all as to what has happened. All you know is that the program didn't finish, and sometimes you might not even know *that*, if the program was designed to return to the keyboard and did not provide status displays.

One of the most common causes of bizarre computer behavior is forgetting the second half of a paired command: an ENDDO, ENDIF or ENDCASE. When this happens, the logic of the program can become "screwed up." This sort of error will rarely result in an error message that is helpful.

Another situation that can cause dBASE II to go

off the deep end without alerting you occurs when you misuse memory variables. dBASE II has error messages to cover the cases of *too many* memory variables and *out of memory* for memory variables.

Nevertheless, there are situations when the use of too many memory variable bytes will send the system over the edge, especially if you have not structured the creation and release of variables so that all of the available memory space is in a block. Even though dBASE II may tell us there is adequate space, there may not be enough contiguous space for the variable you are trying to store.

The first things to try when you are summarily ejected from a program:

- Check the memory variable status.
- Verify that each IF has an ENDIF.
- Verify that each DO WHILE ... has an ENDDO.
- Verify that each DO CASE has an ENDCASE.

An interesting phenomenon can occur when you are thrown out of a program while in a DO CASE. It may seem as though you have lost control of the keyboard — dBASE II does not respond to keyboard commands. When this happens, try the command ENDCASE.

Design Errors

Design errors in your program occur when you have given dBASE II a series of perfectly valid commands with no mechanical errors involved. Nevertheless, the program does not produce the intended result.

Let's look at the simple program below. This is the skeleton of a program to print class rosters from a school database of STUDENTS, GRADE, ROOM, etc.

```
USE SCHOOL
INDEX ON GRADE + ROOM + NAME TO
■ ROSTER
DO WHILE .NOT. EOF
  DO HEADING
  STORE GRADE + ROOM TO class
  SET MARGIN TO 30
  DISPLAY OFF NAME WHILE
    GRADE + ROOM = class
  SET MARGIN TO 0
ENDDO
```

When we run this program we get nothing. Just a dot prompt. No class rosters. There are *no* mechanical errors. dBASE II has done exactly what we told it to do. When dBASE II finishes with the INDEX command, the database is at the last record *and* the end-of-file flag has been set. The DO WHILE .NOT. EOF statement does exactly what we told it to do, and there are no rosters printed. In this case we need to GO TOP before entering the DO loop.

For the most part, debugging amounts to observing carefully what is happening to your program and applying a bit of common sense. Most errors are simple and straightforward. When things get messier, there are a number of remedies that you can try.

Things to Try

Make your own diagnostic messages. In this case you can display the content of a memory variable or a series of text strings on the screen. Here you temporarily modify your program to provide for this kind of screen output — which is particularly advantageous when you are being ejected without notice.

This can be used to monitor the contents of an accumulator in a DO loop. Suppose you are not getting the correct subtotals during a process. Presumably the subtotal is to print at the end of a loop. You can monitor the process as it goes through the loop and attempt to see where it goes wrong by displaying the accumulator at every step.

Add a RETURN. The RETURN command is used to terminate a program. You can have all of the text you like after the RETURN. The RETURN command will allow you to stop the program at the point you choose. Now you can examine the state of the databases and memory variables. You might add a RETURN, run the program, examine the result, and MOVE the RETURN until you locate the problem.

Use the standard debugging tools. dBASE II provides a set of tools (besides the error messages) that you can use to help track down your problem. These are:

```
SET STEP ON
SET ECHO ON
SET TALK ON
SET DEBUG ON
```

SET STEP ON/OFF allows you to step manually through your program one command line at a time. You can interject commands from the keyboard at each step, and terminate (SET STEP OFF) at any step.

SET ECHO ON/OFF displays the command line on the CRT. SET TALK ON/OFF displays the dBASE II response to most commands. These commands are most effective for debugging when used together. They allow you to step through the program and view each command and its response one at a time. Obviously, if you attempt to carry the STEP process through a counting loop it will become very tedious. Remember, you can insert these items as command lines in your program during a debugging process.

SET DEBUG ON/OFF is provided to help you in debugging processes that involve full screen operations. SET DEBUG ON routes ECHO and STEP output to the printer instead of to the screen, which keeps the screen from becoming cluttered.

All in all, debugging is an overrated process. Most of your problems will be mechanical. Of these, the majority result from typing errors, misspellings, and missing delimiters.

Time spent in debugging can be greatly reduced by developing your programs a little at a time, using small modules. Try using a top-level program that looks something like:

```
DO PART1
DO PART2
DO PART3
DO PART4
  etc.
```

If you take this approach of using small modules and developing your program in stages, you are far less likely to end up with a serious debugging problem. It isn't at all a bad idea to hold program modules to one screen. This can cause your program to run slower initially since you will be opening and closing a number of program files. But once you have everything working and put it all back together, you will have a fast and smoothly working program.

Making the Hardware Help You

All database systems are inherently disk-based systems — the data files are stored on disk. When you access data from these disk files, the disk head moves to where the data is located on the disk.

dBASE II database records are stored in disk records. The size of the disk record is set by the operating system. The size of the dBASE II record is set when the database is created. There can be many database records per disk record, or more than one disk record for each database record.

The two major operating systems used with dBASE II, MS-DOS (PC-DOS) and CP/M, use slightly different disk storage schemes. Each, however, assigns disk space to a file in fixed chunks. The "chunk" size is relatively small. Thus, we have on the disk a few records from database A followed by a few from database B, etc. This situation is shown in **Figure 1**.

When we "read" the database, in order to avoid skipping around on the disk we want to "group" all of the database records into a set of contiguous disk records. This provides for the least possible disk head movement. To group records, put your most frequently used database on the outer tracks when you set up a new database system. Then append as many blank dBASE II records as you will be using in the completed database. If you will be using indexes with this database, create them now. Don't worry that they will be meaningless.

At this point there is a dummy database on the outer tracks. Since all dBASE II records are contiguous, the dummy index files are contiguous in chunks moving inward toward the center of the disk. Now we use MODIFY STRUCTURE to "clear out" all of these blank records and REINDEX. Although we now have a database with no records and empty index files, the operating system thinks dBASE II is actually using all of those empty records. dBASE II does *not* release the disk space back to the operating system. When we begin adding our real database records they will go into the space formerly occupied by the blank records.

This scheme confines the range of the disk head movement and gives us the "best" disk head use. This attention to disk detail can make enormous differences in processing speed.

To illustrate the point, we constructed a scheme where we appended a database to itself. The first half of the database was located at the outer edge of the disk. The second half was located at the inner edge. Then we indexed the database (the index was in a previously blocked area in the center of the disk). To "read" the file — used with the index — took nearly an hour. On every other record the disk head had to be repositioned the width of the disk. This is about as bad a situation as you can imagine. Reading this same database without the index took only three minutes. Physically arranging the database as described above allowed us to read the indexed database in a little over four minutes.

If the database is to be used normally with one or more indexes, we can "speed up" the disk reads by first sorting the file on the most frequently used index. This matches the physical and logical record positions. If we combine our file "grouping" operation and the sorting operation we have done about as well as we can for disk operations.

By the way, the same concept should hold for dBASE II itself. dBASE II (version 2.4) is composed of three files: dBASE.COM, dBASEOVR.COM, and dBASEMSG.TXT. If possible, place dBASE.COM at the inside of the disk. When we use dBASE II, we load it and then are done with it, which is not true with the other two files. A large number of commands, such as SUM and DO CASE, are "called" from dBASEOVR.COM. This means we want this file to be as accessible as possible on the system disk, but not as accessible as any database files.

dBASE II allows you to work without any knowledge of how the disk system operates. Although this is good, understanding how the disk system stores and retrieves data can provide you the opportunity to "speed up" dBASE II processing substantially without any clever coding tricks and without spending a nickel for "fast" disks or RAM

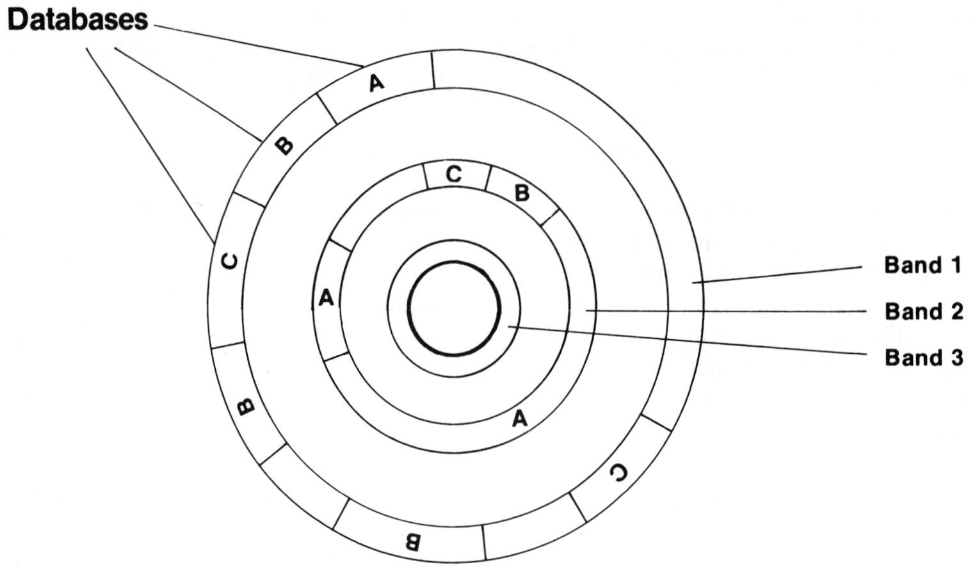

Figure 1. Disk storage of files

disks. Take a little time to understand the disk handling system — it will be well worth your while.

Special Effects

CRT displays and printed reports are what others see as the product of our coding efforts. dBASE II does not use any special characteristics of the printer and only a few of the capabilities of the CRT. On the IBM Personal Computer, it uses normal and reverse video. If you have a color monitor, you can have dBASE II in color.

We can extend our control over the peripheral devices enormously and with little effort with the CHR function, which is roughly analogous to the CHR$ function from BASIC. dBASE II normally filters out any control characters (the non-printable ASCII characters) that we might try to enter into fields or memory variables. The CHR function allows us to incorporate control characters into variables.

Control of the screen is very different in IBM Personal Computers and most 8-bit CP/M computers. On the PC, screen attributes can be controlled by the SET COLOR TO command; with most 8-bit computers, you need to use the CHR function. On both the IBM PC and 8-bit CP/M computers, you can use the CHR function to control special *printer* attributes.

The Printer

Many printers have a large number of special attributes that can be invoked either by setting switches on the printer or by the use of special control codes in your software. Typical of these are:

- horizontal tabs
- vertical tabs
- line spacing
- print density
- font selection
- color selection
- underlining

The equivalent of horizontal and vertical tabs can be accomplished with the dBASE II @ x,y SAY. Sometimes, in using these "tabs" in headings, you might want to switch fonts or print sizes on the fly. This can provide a printed output that is out of the norm. And it can give ordinary computer print output a lot of added pizzazz.

For example, suppose that we would like to have our company name printed in larger type than the remainder of the text. A good number of printers offer software of 10, 12 and 16 characters per inch. Many of these offer an enhanced print mode where each character is printed double width: in effect, 5, 6, 8, 10, 12, and 16 cpi.

We want our printer to produce a page heading that looks like

BOB'S BETTER BOOKS
10150 JEFFERSON BLVD
CULVER CITY, CA
90230

Most printers use control sequences of two or three bytes. These usually start with the <ESCAPE> key. The IDS 560 printer, for example, uses <ESCAPE> + Control A to select the enhanced print mode, and <ESCAPE> + Control B to select the normal print mode. The 16 cpi mode is selected by <ESCAPE> + Control ___ and the 12 cpi mode by <ESCAPE> + Control |.

To print the first line of the heading at eight characters per inch, we first select 16 cpi print density. Then we select the enhanced mode. Once the line has been printed we need to select back to normal mode and select 12 cpi print density. ASCII code tables to relate the ASCII symbols to decimal, binary, and hex codes are found in Appendix D. For our particular example, the CHR functions are shown in the table below. Referring to Appendix D, we see that the ASCII escape is decimal value 27. To issue the <ESCAPE> from dBASE II we put the decimal value for <ESCAPE> into the CHR function. To issue the Control A we put the decimal value for a Control A (01) into a CHR function.

enhanced mode	ESCAPE + ^ A	chr(27) + chr(01)
normal mode	ESCAPE + ^ B	chr(27) + chr(02)
16 cpi	ESCAPE + ^ _	chr(27) + chr(31)
12 cpi	ESCAPE + ^ |	chr(27) + chr(30)

We can write the code to print out our heading as:

```
@5,25 SAY CHR(27)+CHR(31)+CHR(27)
■ +CHR(01) +"BOB'S BETTER BOOKS"
@ 6,23 SAY CHR(27)+CHR(30)+CHR(27)
■ +CHR(02) +'10150 JEFFERSON BLVD'
@ 7,27 SAY 'CULVER CITY, CA'
@ 8,32 SAY '90230'
```

Each use of the CHR function sends one byte to the printer. Our special title required eight more bytes than just printing it the normal way. You might need to experiment a bit to get the feel of how to set the line start positions.

Another approach to this same problem would be:

```
STORE CHR(27) TO esc
STORE esc+CHR(31) TO p16cpi
STORE esc+CHR(30) TO p12cpi
STORE esc+CHR(01) TO enhance
STORE esc+CHR(02) TO normal
@ 5,25 SAY p16cpi+enhance+"BOB'S
■ BETTER BOOKS"
@ 6,23 SAY p12cpi+NORMAL+'10150
■ JEFFERSON BLVD'
@ 7,27 SAY 'CULVER CITY, CA'
@ 8,32 SAY '90230'
```

This command excerpt takes more code but it's much clearer. If we were to use a lot of special function printing it would be better to take this approach, particularly since it allows us to know what is going on without a manual.

Our particular printer will allow you to send control codes in BASIC, and therefore in dBASE II. For example, to set the horizontal tabs (in BASIC) to two, four and six inches we use:

```
10 PRINT CHR$(27);"F,240,480,720,$"
```

In dBASE II, this BASIC command becomes

```
? CHR(27) +'F,240,480,720,$'
```

The "F" is the printer's control code to set horizontal tabs. The $ is a terminator. The printer will look for this character to end the sequence. The F is only recognized as a control character when it is the first character after an ESCAPE CHR(27).

Not all printers will allow you to send control sequences in ASCII as in the above example. Those that do not will require you to send the entire sequence as a sequence of CHR functions.

The CHR function is the key to getting the most from your printer. It allows you to customize and personalize your printed output. The new printers come with a wide range of attractive capabilities that will remain largely unused until you become familiar with the use of CHR.

Fancy Screens

Most computer terminals use control codes similar to those used by printers. The IBM PC uses a monitor with the monitor control as a part of the PC. We will discuss the terminal first and then the monitor because of the similarity between the terminal and the printer.

As with the printer, the CHR function is the key to special effects on your terminal. Among the special effects available on most terminals are:

- Normal video
- Half intensity video
- Reverse video
- Underlining
- Blinking
- Line drawing
- Graphics

You can invoke these special effects with the CHR function in exactly the same way as with the printer. dBASE II allows you to use some of these in a limited way without using the CHR function. The CHR function, however, allows you complete freedom in using these attributes, within the capabilities of your terminal.

As with printers, the equipment manuals that explain how to use these effects are somewhat uneven. A couple of years ago many were barely usable by anyone. That's no longer true. Most equipment manuals have improved by a remarkable degree. Still, if you've never tried to set the attributes, it may take a little experimentation on your part.

To demonstrate the use of screen attributes (special effects), we will use the Televideo 950 Terminal. This is a widely used terminal that's been around for a while. Many of the Televideo screen attributes require a screen space. Some of the newer terminals handle screen attributes in a separate memory in the terminal and do not require screen space.

As an illustration, we will modify the program to create our business system main menu — Program 1 from Chapter Four. We want the screen display to look like that shown in **Screen 1**.

In this example we want BOB'S BETTER BOOKS to be highlighted by reverse video, the date and "Pick One" to be underlined, and the area containing the menu to be in a box. The box is created from smooth lines; the Televideo 950 can do line drawing of this type. In addition to being underlined, we want "Pick One" to be blinking.

Our modified program — the part of it of interest — is shown as **Program 1**. For clarity we have stored the appropriate CHR functions to memory variables *reverse*, *normal*, *underline*. We can use the CHR functions directly as in the first printing example.

Before we entered the DO loop in this program, we stored the appropriate control sequences to memory variables with descriptive names. The normal variable is the standard display characteristic of the Televideo terminal. *grafon* is graphics mode on. (Note that we use the dBASE II command SET INTENSITY OFF. We are trying to control the screen and don't want to conflict with dBASE II's own controls. Televideo graphics don't appear to work as intended when INTENSITY is ON. If you have any trouble with screen controls, SET INTENSITY OFF and try again.)

On many terminals such as the Televideo 950, a

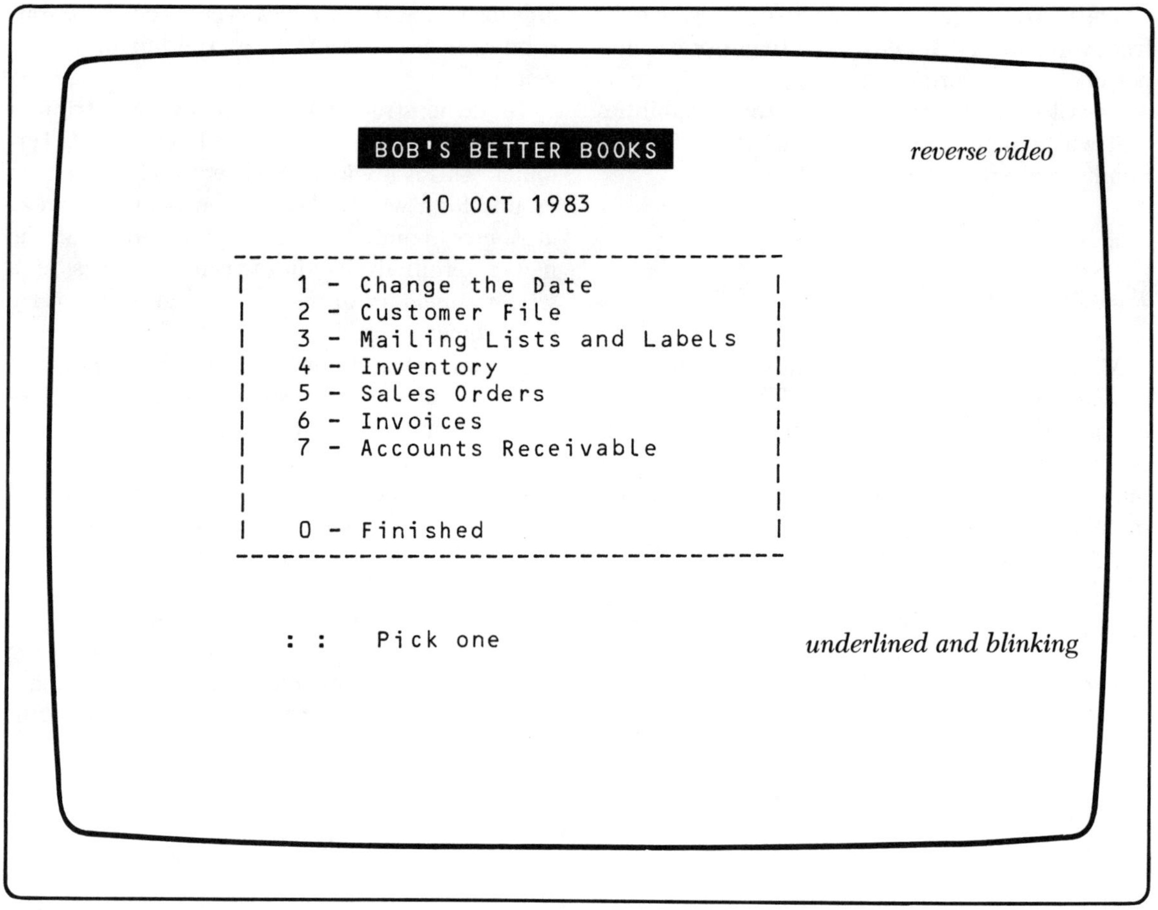

Screen 1. The main menu screen display with special effects

```
STORE CHR(27) TO esc
STORE esc+'G0' TO normal
STORE esc+'G4' TO reverse
STORE esc+'G8' TO underline
STORE esc+'G:' TO underblink
STORE esc+'$' TO grafon
STORE esc+'%' TO grafoff

DO WHILE T
ERASE
 SET INTENSITY OFF
@ 5,30 say "BOB'S BETTER BOOKS"+ normal
@ 5,29 SAY reverse
@ 7,33 SAY '10 OCT 1983'+ normal
@ 7,32 SAY underline
@ 10,25 SAY '1 - Change the Date'
@ 11.25 SAY '2 - Customer File'
@ 12,25 SAY '3 - Mailing Lists and Labels'
@ 13.25 SAY '4 - Inventory'
@ 14,25 SAY '5 - Sales Orders'
@ 15,25 SAY '6 - Invoices'
@ 16,25 SAY '7 - Accounts Receivable'
@ 19,25 SAY '0 - Finished '
@ 21,29 SAY 'Pick One'+ normal
@ 21,28 SAY underblink


@  9,21 say grafon+'FKKKKKKKKKKKKKKKKKKKKKKKKKKKKKKKKKG'
@ 20,21 say 'EKKKKKKKKKKKKKKKKKKKKKKKKKKKKKKKKKH'
STORE 10 TO line
DO WHILE line <= 20
@ line,21 SAY 'J'
@ line,55 SAY 'J'
STORE line+1 TO line
ENDDO
?? grafoff

STORE ' ' TO choice
@ 21,24 GET choice
READ NOUPDATE

 SET INTENSITY ON
```

Program 1. Modification to menu screen display showing special effects

screen attribute is valid from the current location to the end of the screen, or until another attribute is encountered. If we were to turn reverse video on, print the title, and then turn reverse video off with *normal*, we would see a big flash as reverse video continued to the end of the screen before being truncated by the *normal* at the end of the text string. To prevent this flash, we set normal at the end of the text string before we invoke the special screen attribute.

Please note that these attributes take up screen space. They require that we "give up" one character space at each end of the special attribute. On some of the newer terminals, screen attributes are handled in a special memory in the terminal. When this is the case it is not necessary to give up screen space for special effects. In addition, you often don't need to set the end of the effect "off" before you turn it "on." On many of these terminals the effect is handled in a smoother manner.

Televideo graphics use a scheme of substituting a graphics character for a keyboard character. A vertical bar is entered as a J, an upper right corner bracket as an F, and so on. When the graphics mode is turned on, the terminal interprets the alphanumeric characters as graphics characters. When you finish drawing the box, you turn the graphics off in order to communicate normally with the terminal.

The Status Line

Many terminals have a "status line" where information regarding terminal status is displayed as the twenty-fifth line. Since the terminal status line can be annoying or distracting, particularly while performing standard data entry, most terminals allow you to replace the status line with a "user line" of your choice. On the Televideo, for example, we can do this with:

```
? CHR(27) + 'f' + " BOB'S BETTER
■ BOOKS" + CHR(13)
```

which would replace the Televideo standard status line with a user line, BOB'S BETTER BOOKS. This user line will remain there until we either change it or turn off the terminal. It is fixed on the screen independent of other screen operations, including ERASE.

We can take advantage of this to print column titles in the status line when doing listings. In this way we need not worry about remembering what the columns are or reprinting the column title at the top of the screen periodically. The information will appear to "come out of" the column titles.

Special Function Keys

Many terminals come with programmable function keys. The IBM PC and many others like it have the special function keys loaded automatically when dBASE II is loaded. The function assigned to each key can be changed easily with SET Fx TO <command>. Unfortunately, all terminals are not identical in the way that the function keys are handled. You can use the CHR function to "load" programmable special function keys on many terminals.

The Televideo 950, for example, has 11 special function keys that are programmable. Each key can be programmed to two special functions (e.g. F1 and shift F1).

To illustrate the point, let's program the function key F1 to issue a Control W when unshifted and a Control C when shifted. The "address" of key F1 is 1 unshifted and < shifted.

The form of the control command is:

```
ESC| p1 p2 message ^ Y
```

^ Y is the terminator — needed because of variable length message.

p1 is the key address
p2 is a code 1, 2 or 3 where 1 is send to computer
2 is send to screen
3 is send to both

We will be sending the code to the computer p2 = 1.

A Control W is ASCII 23 in decimal
A Control Q is ASCII 17 in decimal

The unshifted control key is loaded by:

```
? CHR(27) +'|1 ' + CHR(23) + CHR(25)
```

The shifted control key is loaded by:

```
? CHR(27) +'|< ' + CHR(17) + CHR(25)
```

As you can see, control can be exerted over a number of terminal functions using the CHR function. The "difficult" part is usually translating the terminal manual into terms that you can work with. Sometimes you will need to go through a trial and error process; you can't harm anything — at least not permanently. Turning the terminal off will always erase whatever mistakes you made.

The IBM Personal Computer Monitor and Keyboard

Here we can do many of the same things that we have been doing with the CHR function by using the SET commands. The function keys on the PC are automatically loaded when dBASE II is loaded. If you don't like the standard selection you can change it. For example, if you want F1 to issue the DISPLAY command, you can:

```
SET F1 TO "DISPLAY;"
```

The item being added must be in quotes. The semicolon issues a line feed and a carriage return. You cannot (at least as of this edition) use CHR to embed control characters within the IBM function keys. This isn't particularly serious since the arrow keys work the way arrow keys are supposed to, which isn't always true of many computer terminals.

The monitor can be made to produce the same kinds of effects that we performed using the Televideo. With the PC we do *not* use the CHR function. We use the SET COLOR TO command. This command controls the screen attributes for both the color *and* the monochrome monitor. On the PC two bytes are actually used for each screen character position. One byte is the attribute, the other is the character.

There are quite a few monitors and color boards available for the PC. They don't appear to be exactly identical in the bit assignments for special effects attributes. This means that you should experiment to determine screen control values.

The form of the SET COLOR command is:

```
SET COLOR TO <foreground,background>
```

where foreground and background are numbers.

```
* determine screen attributes

SET TALK OFF
SET INTENSITY OFF
STORE 0 TO x,y,color
ERASE
DO WHILE y<76
  DO WHILE x<16
   SET color TO color
    @ x,y SAY ' '+STR(color,3)+' '
    STORE color + 1 TO color
    STORE x + 1 TO x
  ENDDO
   STORE 0 TO x
   STORE y+5 TO y
ENDDO
SET INTENSITY ON
RETURN
```

Program 2. Program to determine screen attributes for monitor

The background color value can be omitted. A sample program to determine the color (or monochrome) screen attributes is shown as **Program 2**.

This is a relatively simple program which will draw vertical bars on the screen. Each bar contains 16 "color" values. The color combination (or the monochrome effect) will be produced on the screen. The number will be the SET COLOR number you want for the particular effect. You will notice that for numbers above 127 the numbers themselves will be blinking.

The color pattern produced by this program on an Amdek color terminal is shown as **Figure 2**. The pattern produced on a monochrome monitor is shown as **Figure 3. Program 3** is a program to create a color version of our Main Menu program from Chapter Four.

In this program we first create a flat blue background. This is created by the loop which erases the screen a line at a time. With the color set to 1,23 (white on blue) the @ x,0 command paints a blue background. The next step is to print the page heading and the date (white letters on a blue background). Now we change the color setting to 1,159 — still white letters on blue, but the white letters will blink.

Next we change the color setting to 1,112: black on white. Note that all spaces will produce the background effect of a solid white square in the center of the screen. Finally we print the menu selection in black letters in this square.

The CHR function can be used here to evoke the special graphics symbols. You need to experiment since there are differences between systems. As an example, with the Princeton Graphics System, storing a CHR(4) to D will produce a diamond every time we display the D.

A little effort to learn the capabilities of your equipment can produce dramatic and dazzling effects on almost any computer system. The CHR function is used with the printer and non-PC terminals. It can also be used to produce graphics symbols on IBM PC monitors. SET COLOR can be used on the PC in exactly the same manner for the PC as the CHR function was used for special terminal displays.

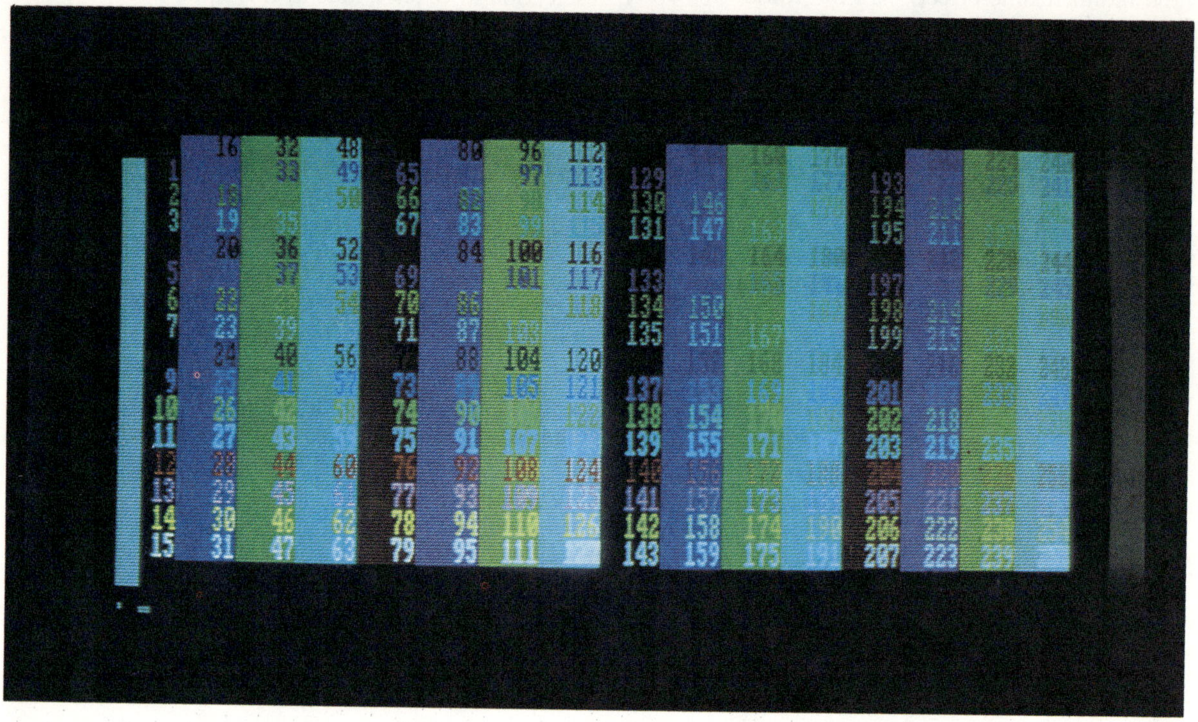

Figure 2. Color pattern produced by Program 2

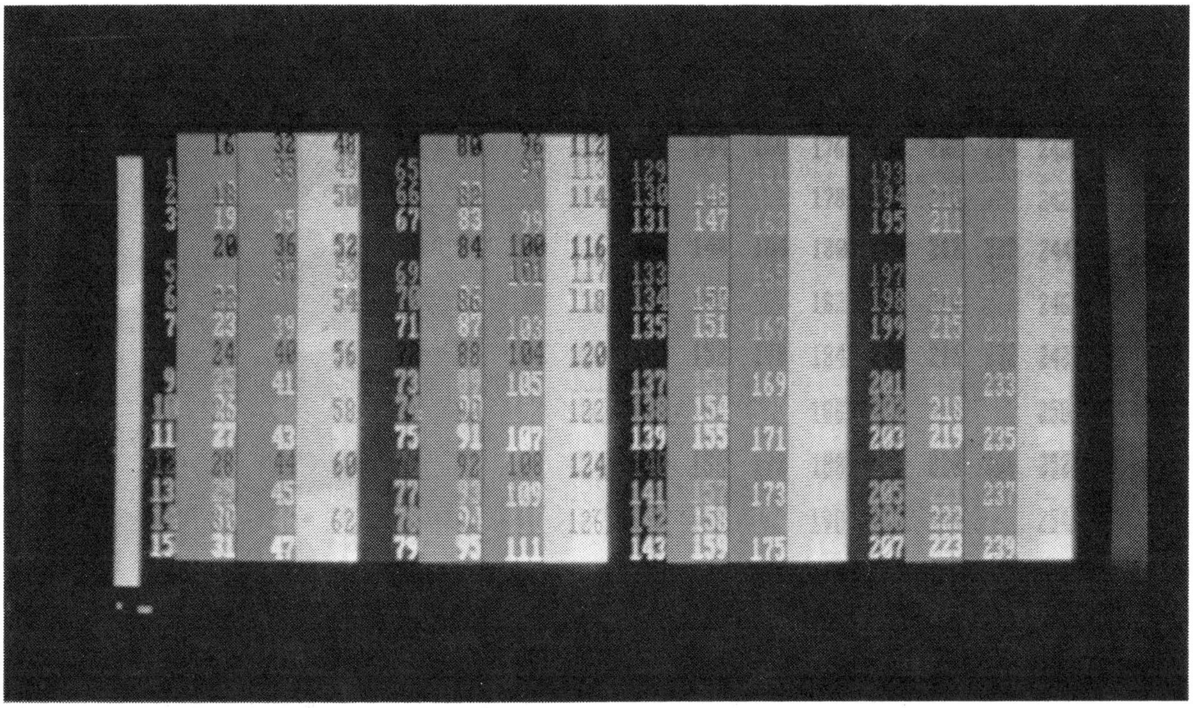

Figure 3. Monochrome effect produced by Program 2

```
DO WHILE T
SET INTENSITY ON
SET TALK OFF
STORE 0 TO x
SET COLOR TO 1,23
DO WHILE x<24
@ x,0
STORE x+1 TO x
ENDDO

@ 5,30 say "BOB'S BETTER BOOKS"
@ 7,33 SAY '10 OCT 1983'
SET COLOR TO 1,159
@ 21,29 SAY 'Pick One'
SET COLOR TO 1,112
STORE 10 TO x
DO WHILE x<20
 @ x,20 SAY '
 STORE x+1 TO x
ENDDO

@ 10,25 SAY '1 - Change the Date'
@ 11,25 SAY '2 - Customer File'
@ 12,25 SAY '3 - Mailing Lists and Labels'
@ 13,25 SAY '4 - Inventory'
@ 14,25 SAY '5 - Sales Orders'
@ 15,25 SAY '6 - Invoices'
@ 16.25 SAY '7 - Accounts Receivable'
@ 19,25 SAY '0 - Finished '

STORE ' ' TO choice
@ 21,24 GET choice
READ NOUPDATE
```

Program 3. Modification to menu screen display showing special effects in color for the IBM PC

ASHTON·TATE

ASHTON·TATE

APPENDIX A*

List of Commands

? <exp> [,<exp>]
@ <coordinates> [SAY <exp> [USING'<picture>']]
[GET <variable> [PICTURE '<picture>']]
ACCEPT ["<cstring>"] TO <memvar>
APPEND [FROM <file> [SDF] [DELIMITED] [FOR <exp>]] or [BLANK]
BROWSE [FIELDS <field list>]
CANCEL
CHANGE FIELD <list> [<scope>] [FOR <exp>]
CLEAR [GETS]
CONTINUE
COPY TO <file> [<scope>] [FIELD <list>] [FOR <exp>] [SDF]
[DELIMITED [WITH <delimiter>]] or [STRUCTURE]
COUNT [<scope>] [FOR <exp>] [TO <memvar>]
CREATE [<filename>]
DELETE [<scope>] [FOR <exp>]
DELETE FILE <file>
DISPLAY [<scope>] [FOR <exp>] [<exp list>] [OFF] [FIELDS <field list>]
DISPLAY STRUCTURE

*Source: *dBASE II®* *Product Manual* (version 2.4, pages 151-153).

ASHTON·TATE

DISPLAY MEMORY
DISPLAY FILES [ON <disk drive>] [LIKE <skeleton>]
DO <file>
DO WHILE <exp>
EDIT
EJECT
ELSE
ENDDO
ENDIF
ENDTEXT
ERASE
FIND <key>
GO or GOTO [RECORD], or [TOP], or [BOTTOM], <n>
HELP [command]
IF <exp>
INDEX
INDEX ON <char string expression> TO <index file name>
INPUT ["<cstring>"] TO <memvar>
INSERT [BEFORE] [BLANK]
JOIN TO <file> FOR <expression> [FIELDS <field list>]
LIST
LOCATE [<scope>] [FOR <exp>]
LOOP
MODIFY STRUCTURE
MODIFY COMMAND <command file>
NOTE or *
PACK
QUIT [TO <list of CP/M level commands or .COM files>]
READ [NO UPDATE]
RECALL [<scope>] [FOR <exp>]
REINDEX
RELEASE [<memvar list>] [ALL [LIKE <skeleton>]]
REMARK
RENAME <current file name> TO <new file name>
REPLACE [<scope>] <field> WITH <exp> [AND <field> WITH <exp>]
REPORT [<scope>] [FORM <form file>] [TO PRINT] [FOR <exp>]
RESET
RESTORE FROM <memfile> [ADDITIVE]
RETURN
SAVE TO <file> [ALL LIKE <skeleton>]
SELECT [PRIMARY or SECONDARY]

SET <parm> [ON] [OFF]
SET ALTERNATE TO <file>
SET DEFAULT TO <drive>
SET DATE TO <string>
SET FORMAT TO <format file name>
SET HEADING TO <string>
SET INDEX TO <index file list>
SET MARGIN TO <n>
SKIP < +/-> [<n>]
SORT ON <field> TO <file> [ASCENDING] or [DESCENDING]
STORE <exp> TO <memvar>
SUM <field> [<scope>] [TO <memvar list>] [FOR <exp>]
TEXT
TOTAL TO <file> ON <key variable> [FIELDS <field list>]
UPDATE FROM <file> ON <key variable> [ADD <field list>][REPLACE <field list>]
USE <file> [INDEX <index file name>]
WAIT [TO <memvar>]

Functions:

@(<string1>,<string2>)	AT function
*	deleted record function
#	record number function
!(<char string>)	upper case function
$(<char string>,<start>,<length>)	substring function
CHR(<numeric expression>)	numeric to ASCII
DATE( )	system date function
EOF	end-of-file function
FILE(<file>)	existence function
INT(<numeric expression>)	integer function

LEN(<char string>)	length function
RANK(<string>)	ASCII value function
STR(<numeric expression>,<width> [,<decimals>])	string function
VAL(<char string>)	value function
TRIM(<char string>)	trims strings
TYPE(<exp>)	supplies data type

APPENDIX B*

Limitations and Constraints

number of fields per record	32 max
number of characters per record	1000 max
number of records per database	65535 max
number of characters per character string	254 max
accuracy of numeric fields	10 digits
largest number	1.8×10^{63} approx
smallest number	1.0×10^{-63} approx
number of memory variables	64 max
number of characters per command line	254 max

*Source: *dBASE II® Product Manual* (version 2.4, page 154).

ASHTON·TATE

number of expressions in SUM command	5 max
number of characters in REPORT header	254 max
number of characters in index key	99 max
number of pending GETS	64 max
number of files open at one time	16 max

APPENDIX C*

Error Messages

BAD DECIMAL WIDTH FIELD
Redefine Decimal.

BAD FILE NAME
Syntax error in filename.

BAD NAME FIELD
Redefine Name.

BAD TYPE FIELD
Must be C, N, or L.

BAD WIDTH FIELD
Redefine size of data field.

CANNOT INSERT — THERE ARE NO RECORDS IN DATABASE FILE
Use the APPEND command instead.

*Source: *dBASE II® Product Manual* (version 2.4, pages 155-158).

ASHTON·TATE

CANNOT OPEN FILE
Internal error, contact dealer for support.

COMMAND FILE CANNOT BE FOUND
Check spelling.

DATA ITEM NOT FOUND

DATABASE IN USE IS NOT INDEXED
FIND is only permitted on indexed databases.

DIRECTORY IS FULL
The CP/M disk directory cannot hold anymore files.

DISK IS FULL
No space left on disk.

END OF FILE FOUND UNEXPECTEDLY
The database in USE is not in the correct format. If all records are correct and present, then PACK and re-INDEX the database.

"FIELD" PHRASE NOT FOUND
Rewrite command line.

FILE ALREADY EXISTS

FILE DOES NOT EXIST

FILE IS CURRENTLY OPEN
Type a USE or CLEAR command to close the file.

FORMAT FILE CANNOT BE OPENED

FORMAT FILE HAS NOT SET
SET the appropriate format file.

ILLEGAL DATA TYPE

ILLEGAL GOTO VALUE
Must be > 0 and < 65535

ILLEGAL VARIABLE NAME
Only alphanumerics and colons are allowed in variable and field names.

INDEX DOES NOT MATCH DATABASE
dBASE II cannot match the key with the database. Try another index file.

INDEX FILE CANNOT BE OPENED
Check spelling or INDEX the database.

JOIN ATTEMPTED TO GENERATE MORE THAN 65,534 RECORDS
The FOR clause allows too many joined output records, make it more stringent.

KEYS ARE NOT THE SAME LENGTH

MACRO IS NOT A CHARACTER STRING
&macros must be character strings.

MORE THAN 5 FIELDS TO SUM
Sum is limited to 5 fields.

NESTING LIMIT VIOLATION EXCEEDED

NO EXPRESSION TO SUM

NO "FOR" PHRASE
Rewrite command with correct syntax.

NO "FROM" PHRASE
Rewrite command with correct syntax.

NO FIND
More a diagnostic type message than an error message. dBASE couldn't find the key. Record # has been set to 0.

NON-NUMERIC EXPRESSION

NONEXISTENT FILE

"ON" PHRASE NOT FOUND
Rewrite command with correct syntax.

OUT OF MEMORY FOR MEMORY VARIABLES
Reduce the number or size of memory variables.

RECORD LENGTH EXCEEDS MAXIMUM SIZE (OF 1000)
Reduce size of some fields or create a second database on a common key.

RECORD NOT IN INDEX
Index file was not updated after a record was added.
Reindex.

RECORD OUT OF RANGE
Record number greater than number of records in database. The Record doesn't exist.

SORTER INTERNAL ERROR, NOTIFY SCDP
Internal error, contact dealer for support.

SOURCE AND DESTINATION DATA TYPES ARE DIFFERENT
Check that both datatypes are numeric or both character.

SYNTAX ERROR

SYNTAX ERROR FORMAT SPECIFICATION

SYNTAX ERROR, RE-ENTER

"TO" PHRASE NOT FOUND
Rewrite command with correct syntax.

TOO MANY CHARACTERS
Shorten the command line.

TOO MANY FILES ARE OPEN
There is a maximum of 16 files allowed to be open at one time.

TOO MANY MEMORY VARIABLES
There is a maximum of 64 memory variables.

TOO MANY RETURNS ENCOUNTERED
Probably an error in the structure of a command file.

"WITH" PHRASE NOT FOUND
Rewrite command with correct syntax.

UNASSIGNED FILE NUMBER
Internal error, contact dealer for support

***UNKNOWN COMMAND
Check spelling.

VARIABLE CANNOT BE FOUND
Need to create the variable, or check the spelling.

ASHTON·TATE

APPENDIX D

ASCII CODE TABLE
CONTROL CHARACTERS

BINARY	HEX	DECIMAL	SYMBOL	CODE	DESCRIPTION

ASCII CODE TABLE

CONTROL CHARACTERS

BINARY	HEX	DECIMAL	SYMBOL	CODE	DESCRIPTION
0000000	00	0	NUL	^@	Null
0000001	01	1	SOH	^A	Start of Heading
0000010	02	2	STX	^B	Start of Text
0000011	03	3	ETX	^C	End of Text
0000100	04	4	EOT	^D	End of Transmission
0000101	05	5	ENQ	^E	Enquiry
0000110	06	6	ACK	^F	Acknowledge
0000111	07	7	BEL	^G	Bell
0001000	08	8	BS	^H	Backspace
0001001	09	9	SH	^I	Horizontal Tabulation
0001010	0A	10	LF	^J	Line feed
0001011	0B	11	VT	^K	Vertical Tabulation
0001100	0C	12	FF	^L	Form feed
0001101	0D	13	CR	^M	Carriage Return
0001110	0E	14	SO	^N	Shift Out
0001111	0F	15	SI	^O	Shift In
0010000	10	16	DLE	^P	Data Link Escape
0010001	11	17	DC1	^Q	Device Control 1
0010010	12	18	DC2	^R	Device Control 2
0010011	13	19	DC3	^S	Device Control 3
0010100	14	20	DC4	^T	Device Control 4
0010101	15	21	NAK	^U	Negative Acknowledge
0010110	16	22	SYN	^V	Synchronous Idle
0010111	17	23	ETB	^W	End of Transmission Block
0011000	18	24	CAN	^X	Cancel
0011001	19	25	EM	^Y	End of Medium
0011010	1A	26	SUB	^Z	Substitute
0011011	1B	27	ESC	^[	Escape
0011100	1C	28	FS	^§	File Separator
0011101	1D	29	GS	^]	Group Separator
0011110	1E	30	RS	^^	Record Separator
0011111	1F	31	US	^	Unit Separator
1111111	7F	127	DEL	DEL	Delete

ASCII CODE TABLE

PRINTABLE CHARACTERS

BINARY	HEX	DECIMAL	SYMBOL	BINARY	HEX	DECIMAL	SYMBOL
0100000	20	32	SPACE	1010000	50	80	P
0100001	21	33	!	1010001	51	81	Q
0100010	22	34	"	1010010	52	82	R
0100011	23	35	#	1010011	53	83	S
0100100	24	36	$	1010100	54	84	T
0100101	25	37	%	1010101	55	85	U
0100110	26	38	&	1010110	56	86	V
0100111	27	39	'	1010111	57	87	W
0101000	28	40	(	1011000	58	88	X
0101001	29	41	)	1011001	59	89	Y
0101010	2A	42	*	1011010	5A	90	Z
0101011	2B	43	+	1011011	5B	91	[
0101100	2C	44	,	1011100	5C	92	§
0101101	2D	45	-	1011101	5D	93	]
0101110	2E	46	.	1011110	5E	94	^
0101111	2F	47	/	1011111	5F	95	_
0110000	30	48	0	1100000	60	96	`
0110001	31	49	1	1100001	61	97	a
0110010	32	50	2	1100010	62	98	b
0110011	33	51	3	1100011	63	99	c
0110100	34	52	4	1100100	64	100	d
0110101	35	53	5	1100101	65	101	e
0110110	36	54	6	1100110	66	102	f
0110111	37	55	7	1100111	67	103	g
0111000	38	56	8	1101000	68	104	h
0111001	39	57	9	1101001	69	105	i
0111010	3A	58	:	1101010	6A	106	j
0111011	3B	59	;	1101011	6B	107	k
0111100	3C	60	<	1101100	6C	108	l
0111101	3D	61	=	1101101	6D	109	m
0111110	3E	62	>	1101110	6E	110	n
0111111	3F	63	?	1101111	6F	111	o
1000000	40	64	@	1110000	70	112	p
1000001	41	65	A	1110001	71	113	q
1000010	42	66	B	1110010	72	114	r
1000011	43	67	C	1110011	73	115	s
1000100	44	68	D	1110100	74	116	t
1000101	45	69	E	1110101	75	117	u
1000110	46	70	F	1110110	76	118	v
1000111	47	71	G	1110111	77	119	w
1001000	48	72	H	1111000	78	120	x

Continued from the previous page

ASCII CODE TABLE

PRINTABLE CHARACTERS

BINARY	HEX	DECIMAL	SYMBOL	BINARY	HEX	DECIMAL	SYMBOL
1001001	49	73	I	1111001	79	121	y
1001010	4A	74	J	1111010	7A	122	z
1001011	4B	75	K	1111011	7B	123	{
1001100	4C	76	L	1111100	7C	124	|
1001101	4D	77	M	1111101	7D	125	}
1001110	4E	78	N	1111110	7E	126	~
1001111	4F	79	O	1111111	7F	127	DEL

APPENDIX E

SUPPLEMENTARY PROGRAMS

```
* menu4-2  edits inventory file records

SET INDEX TO Isbn,Author,Title,Pubcode,Subject
SELECT SECO
USE Publish INDEX Pubid
STORE T TO editrec
ERASE
DO WHILE editrec
SELECT PRIM

 STORE '              ' TO misbn
 @ 21,1 SAY 'ENTER THE ISBN NUMBER' GET misbn PICTURE '9999999999-!'
 READ NOUPDATE
 @ 20,0

 IF MISBN='    '
    STORE F TO editrec
    LOOP
 ENDIF

 FIND &misbn
 IF #=0
   DO Isbntest
   IF .NOT. validtest
     @ 20,1 SAY misbn+'  IS AN INVALID ISBN NUMBER'
   ELSE
     @ 20,1 SAY misbn+'  IS NOT IN THE DATABASE'
   ENDIF
  LOOP
 ENDIF
 STORE PUBCODE TO mpub
 SELE SECO
 FIND &mpub
 SELE PRIMARY
 SET FORMAT TO Menu4-1
 READ
 SET FORMAT TO SCREEN
 CLEAR GETS
ENDDO
RELEASE misbn, validtest, editrec,mpub
RETURN
```

MENU4-2 EDIT INVENTORY RECORDS

```
* menu4-3  DELETES inventory file records

SET INDEX TO Isbn,Author.Title.Pubcode,Subject
ERASE
STORE T TO delerec
DO WHILE delerec


 STORE '                 ' TO misbn
 @ 21,1 SAY 'ENTER THE ISBN NUMBER' GET misbn PICTURE '9999999999-!'
 READ NOUPDATE
 @ 20,0

 IF misbn='    '
    STORE F TO delerec
    LOOP
 ENDIF

 FIND &misbn
 IF #=0
   DO Isbntest
   IF .NOT. validtest
     @ 20,1 SAY misbn+'  IS AN INVALID ISBN NUMBER'
   ELSE
     @ 20,1 SAY misbn+'  IS NOT IN THE DATABASE'
   ENDIF
  LOOP
 ENDIF

@ 1.1  SAY TITLE
@ 2,1  SAY AUTHOR
@ 3.1  SAY SUBJECT

STORE ' ' TO query
DO WHILE .NOT. query$'YN'
  @ 5,1 SAY 'DELETE THIS BOOK (Y/N)?' GET query PICTURE '!'
  READ
  CLEAR GETS
ENDDO
IF QUERY='Y'
  DELETE
ENDIF
ENDDO
RELEASE misbn. validtest. delerec,query
PACK
RETURN
```

MENU4-3 DELETE INVENTORY RECORDS

```
* Program .....:MENU5-2.CMD (or MENU5-2.PRG)

USE Sales
STORE T TO editrec
ERASE
DO WHILE editrec
STORE '      ' TO mso
@ 1,1 SAY 'SALES ORDER NUMBER TO BE EDITED' GET mso PICT '999999'
READ

IF mso='      '
 STORE F TO editrec
 LOOP
ENDIF

GO BOTTOM
DO WHILE SONUMBER>mso .AND. #>0
 SKIP -1
ENDD
IF #=0 .OR. SONUMBER#mso
 @ 3,1 SAY mso+' WAS NOT IN THE DATABASE'
 LOOP
ENDIF
@ 3,0
STORE CUSTID TO mcustid
SELE SECO
USE Openord
LOCATE FOR SONUMBER=mso
IF EOF
  @ 3,1 SAY 'SALES ORDER HAS BEEN FILLED - YOU MAY NOT EDIT'
  LOOP
ENDIF
CLEAR GETS

@ 3,0
STORE T TO editloop
USE Customer INDEX Custid
FIND &mcustid
@ 3,30 SAY NAME
DO WHILE editloop
SELECT PRIMARY

@ 3,1 SAY 'CUSTOMER ID NUMBER' GET mcustid
@ 5,1 SAY 'CUSTOMER PO NUMBER' GET PONUMBER
READ
```

MENU5-2 EDIT A SALES ORDER

Continued on next page

Continued from the previous page

```
IF CUSTID#mcustid
 SELE SECO
 USE Customer INDEX Custid
 FIND &mcustid
 IF #=0
   @ 3,30 SAY 'INVALID CUSTOMER ID'
   LOOP
 ELSE
   @ 3,30 SAY NAME
   SELECT PRIMARY
   REPLACE CUSTID WITH mcustid
 ENDIF
ENDIF
STORE F TO editloop
ENDDO ----- for custid checking loop

SELECT PRIM
USE Salesdet
DO Search
STORE # TO placemark

COPY FIELD ISBN,QTY TO Tempfile WHILE SONUMBER=mso
GO placemark
STORE placemark-1 TO recno
SELE SECO
USE Tempfile
BROWSE
GO TOP


DO WHILE .NOT. EOF
 STORE recno+1 TO recno
 SELECT PRIMARY
 GO recno
 REPLACE P.ISBN WITH S.ISBN, P.QTY WITH S.QTY
 SELECT SECONDARY
 SKIP
ENDDO

ERASE
@ 1,1 SAY 'VERIFYING ISBN NUMBERS'
USE Inv INDEX Isbn
SELECT PRIMARY
GO placemark
```


Continued on next page

Continued from the previous page

```
DO WHILE mso=SONUMBER .AND..NOT.EOF
 STORE ISBN TO misbn
 SELECT SECO
 FIND &misbn
 IF #=0
  @ 3,1 SAY misbn+' IS INVALID ' GET misbn
  READ NOUPDATE
 ENDIF
 SELECT PRIMARY
 IF misbn#ISBN
  REPLACE ISBN WITH misbn
  LOOP
 ENDIF
 SKIP
ENDDO
SELE PRIMARY
 USE Sales
ERASE
ENDDO -- for main loop
RELEASE editrec,placemark,mso,misbn,recno
SELECT SECONDARY
USE
SELECT PRIMARY
RETURN
```

MENU5-2. Edit a sales order

```
* Program .....:MENU5-3.CMD (or MENU5-3.PRG)
* Notes .......:This program voids a Sales Order.

USE Sales
STORE T TO editrec
ERASE
DO WHILE editrec
  STORE '      ' TO mso
  @ 1,1 SAY 'SALES ORDER TO BE VOIDED' GET mso PICT '999999'
  READ

  IF mso='      '
    STORE F TO editrec
    LOOP
  ENDIF
  @ 3,0
  @ 5,0
  GO BOTTOM
  DO WHILE SONUMBER>mso .AND. #>0
    SKIP -1
  ENDDO
  IF SONUMBER#mso
    @ 3,1 SAY mso+' NOT FOUND '
    LOOP
  ENDIF

  @ 3,1 SAY 'CUSTOMER ID CODE: ' + CUSTID
  @ 3,30 SAY 'CUSTOMER P.O. NUMBER: ' + PONUMBER

  STORE ' ' TO query
  DO WHILE .NOT. QUERY $'YynN'
   @ 5,1 SAY 'VOID ORDER (Y/N)? ' GET query
   READ
  ENDDO

  IF query$'nN'
    LOOP
  ENDIF
    @ 5,0

  SELECT SECONDARY
  USE Openord
  LOCATE FOR mso=SONUMBER
```

MENU5-3 VOID A SALES ORDER

Continued on next page

Continued from the previous page

```
    IF EOF
     @ 5,1 SAY mso+' ALREADY FILLED '
    ELSE
     DELETE
     PACK
    ENDIF

    SELECT SECONDARY
    USE Salesdet
    DO Search
    REPL QTY WITH 0 WHILE mso=SONUMBER

ENDDO  --- for editrec
RELEASE editrec,findstart.mso
SELE SECO
USE
SELE PRIM
RETURN
```

MENU5-3. Void a sales order

```
* menu6-2 display back orders
ERASE
USE Backord
STORE 20 TO PAGESIZE
INPUT 'DO YOU WANT A PRINTED COPY' TO QUERY
IF QUERY
  SET PRINT ON
  SET FORMAT TO PRINT
  STORE 55 TO PAGESIZE
ENDIF
  SET MARGIN TO 15
DO WHILE .NOT. EOF
  STORE 'CUSTOMER NAME         ISBN NUMBER     DATE     QTY' TO HEADING
  @ 6,1 SAY HEADING
  ?
  STORE 8 TO LINE
DO WHILE .NOT.EOF .AND. LINE < PAGESIZE
 STORE LINE+1 TO LINE
 STORE SONUMBER TO MSO
 SELE SECO
 USE SALES
 DO SEARCH
 STORE DATE TO ORDDATE
 STORE CUSTID TO MCUSTID
 USE CUSTOMER INDEX CUSTID
 FIND &MCUSTID
 ? NAME.ISBN,ORDDATE,QTY-QTYDEL
 SELE PRIM
 SKIP
ENDDO
  EJECT
ENDDO
SET PRINT OFF
SET FORMAT TO SCREEN

RELEASE MCUSTID,MSO,QUERY,ORDDATE,PAGESIZE.LINE.FINDSTART.HEADING
```

MENU6-2 DISPLAY BACK ORDERS

ASHTON·TATE

GLOSSARY

.AND.

A Boolean operator that is used to join two logic expressions so that the resulting expression applies to the shared characteristics of the expression. For example: GRADE="3".AND.ROOM="122" restricts the expression to third graders who are assigned to room 122.

.NOT.

A Boolean operator which is used to invoke the opposite of the expression. For example: .NOT.GRADE = "3" means all grades except the third.

.OR.

A Boolean operator which is used to join two groups within a logical expression. For example, the third and fourth grades can be joined within the logical expression GRADE="3".OR.GRADE="4".

?

A dBASE II command for displaying selected items.

??

A command for displaying data. This command is similar to the ? except that it does not issue a carriage return and line feed.

@

An operator used in conjunction with the SAY and GET commands to generate displays on either the CRT or the printer. Also used as a function to locate the position of a substring within a character string.

*

Normally used to indicate multiplication. In dBASE II it is also used to indicate database records marked for deletion and as a command to insert comments in programs.

#

The "pound sign" is used as a multipurpose function. It is normally used as a shorthand for "not equal to." In dBASE II it is also used as a symbol for "record number." For example: DISPLAY FOR # = 3 would display the third data record.

!

A symbol which, in dBASE II, tells the computer to not distinguish between upper and lower case characters.

$

A dBASE II operator that allows you to search for a sequence of characters contained in a field or a memory variable. It is often called either a substring or string operator. It can be interpreted as meaning "contained in." For example: "Robert"$NAME would allow you to search the field NAME for the character string ROBERT.

ACCEPT TO [memory variable name]

A dBASE II command which allows the input of character strings into designated memory variables without need for delimiters. Normally used within procedures (dBASE II command files).

ADL

Applications Development Language — the computer language used with dBASE II.

APPEND

The dBASE II command to add records to a database.

APPEND BLANK

A variation of APPEND which adds blank records to a database. Normally used within procedures.

APPEND FROM<filename>

Used to append data from the named file to the file in use.

BACKUP
The process of copying a disk or diskfile to another disk for protection against possible future failure. Also the backup copy of the file or disk.

BASIC
A computer language. An acronym standing for Beginners All Purpose Symbolic Instruction Code.

BOOLEAN
A method of computer logic based on the work of George Boole, who developed a certain type of algebra.

BOOTING
The process of starting up the computer.

BROWSE
A dBASE II command used for editing. Several records are displayed simultaneously for full screen editing.

BYTE
The amount of memory required to store a character such as an "A"or "#"or "9."

CALL
To cause the execution of a program by means of a command in another program. Also a dBASE II command to invoke an assembly language program.

CANCEL
A command used to terminate a procedure and return control of the computer to the keyboard.

CASE
A variation of the IF statement. Case can only be used within DO CASE/ENDCASE.

CHANGE
A dBASE II command used for editing.

CHARACTER
Any keyboard symbol that can be printed such as an "A"or "$"or "1"or "a"(includes blank spaces).

CHARACTER FIELD
A database field that is intended to contain characters.

CHARACTER STRING
A continuous sequence of characters such as "John Doe."

CHR( )
A function which allows you direct control of the special functions of a printer or a CRT.

CLEAR
This command resets dBASE II. All databases in USE are closed, all memory variables are released, and the system is just as it would be when you initially enter dBASE II.

CLEAR GETS
A command which removes all pending GETS internally without altering the screen (as the ERASE command would). This will limit the domain of a READ to only those GETS issued after the CLEAR GETS command.

COBOL
A computer language used extensively in mainframe business application. The first English-like computer language. An acronym for Common Business Oriented Language.

COMMAND
dBASE II terminology for a computer instruction.

COMMAND FILE
A set of computer instructions stored or saved on a disk for repetitive use. dBASE II terminology for a computer procedure.

CONCATENATION
The joining of two character strings to form a third character string.

CONDITION
A logical expression that can be used to more explicitly define a command such as DISPLAY. DISPLAY FOR NAME = "JOHN DOE" modifies the command DISPLAY so that it applies only for records meeting the condition NAME = "JOHN DOE".

CONDITIONAL REPLACEMENT
A technique for changing the contents of a database where the REPLACE command is modified by a condition. REPLACE TEACHER WITH "ADAMS" FOR ROOM = "171" will replace the contents of the field TEACHER with "ADAMS" for only those records meeting the condition ROOM = "171".

CONTINUE
A command which positions to next record with conditions specified in the LOCATE command.

CONTROL KEY
A key which potentially gives a third value to all of the keys of the keyboard. Similar to the shift key, which gives a second meaning to each of the keys of the keyboard.

COPY TO <filename>
A dBASE II command which copies the database in use to the named database. Used to create a copy of the database for backup. Variations exist which will allow you to copy only selected parts of the database in use to the named database.

COUNT
A data displaying command which counts the number of records that meet some conditional expression.

CP/M®

Control Program/Microcomputer. A popular operating system for microcomputers. CP/M® is a registered trademark of Digital Research Corporation.

CPU
Central Processing Unit — the central processor of the computer system. It contains the main storage, arithmetic unit and special register groups.

CREATE
The dBASE II command to allow you to establish the structure of a new database file.

CRT
Cathode Ray Tube. Popularly used to denote the video display device used in conjunction with computers.

CTRL KEY
Control Key — used in combination with various keys to give them a second meaning and function.

DASD
Direct Access Storage Device such as a disk.

DATA

A piece of information. Normally useless as an independent item. Can convey information when used with another item of data. For example, the phone number 555-3213 is relatively useless by itself. It conveys information when used in conjunction with another data item, Butch Johnson.

DATABASE

A repository of stored information organized in such a way that data is easily retrieved. Normally associated with an organized base of data stored within a computer that is usable by multiple applications. An everyday example of a non-computer database is the telephone directory.

DBMS

Database Management System.

DEBUG

The process of removing errors from a program.

DEFAULT

When the computer receives a command it must take some action. Unless otherwise instructed it will take a pre-programmed action. That pre-programmed action is called the default.

DELETE

A dBASE II command which marks records for deletion (see also PACK).

DELETE FILE

Command to delete a file. The file cannot be in use.

DELIMITERS

A way of identifying character strings to the computer. For example, it allows the computer to distinguish between the field NAME and the word "NAME".

DISK

A circular plate, coated with magnetic material, for storing data. The medium on which a computer may permanently or temporarily store information to be used or read at a later date.

DISK DRIVE

A mechanical device used to read and write information onto a disk.

DISPLAY

A dBASE II command to display the contents of a data record.

DISPLAY ALL
A variation of the DISPLAY command. This variation will display all records of the database in use — pausing every 15 records.

DISPLAY FILES ON<drive id>
A dBASE II command which displays the filename, number of records, and date of last change of all database files on the named disk.

DISPLAY FOR<condition>
A variation of the DISPLAY command. The FOR <condition> clause modifies the DISPLAY command so that all records meeting the condition will be displayed 15 at a time.

DISPLAY MEMORY
A variation of the DISPLAY command which will display the name, type, size, and content of all memory variables.

DISPLAY OFF
A variation of DISPLAY which displays the database record without the record number.

DISPLAY STRUCTURE
A variation of the DISPLAY command which is used to display the structure of the database currently in use.

DO<filename>
A dBASE II command which is used as an alternative to multiple nested IF, ENDIF statements. It must be accompanied by an ENDCASE command. Normally used in procedures.

DO WHILE<condition>
A dBASE II command which tells the computer to repeatedly execute the sequence of commands between the DO WHILE statement and its concluding ENDDO statement as long as the condition is satisfied. Used in dBASE II command files (procedures).

DOS
Disk Operating System — software.

EDIT<record number>
A command which allows changing of a data field's contents. In dBASE II it invokes a full screen operation which allows you to change the contents of desired fields by moving the cursor to the appropriate location and typing in the new data.

EJECT
A dBASE II command which ejects a page on the printer.

ELSE
A command file alternate path of command execution within IF.

ENDCASE
A command file command that terminates DO CASE.

ENDDO
A command file terminator for DO WHILE command.

ENDIF
A command file terminator for IF command.

EOF
End Of File — a dBASE II function; also a special ASCII file character.

ERASE
A command which clears the CRT.

ESCAPE
A key on many computer terminals, ESCAPE has the ASCII value of 27. On terminals without ESCAPE you can use CONTROL [. ESCAPE will allow you to interrupt a program or a long running command.

FIELD
In systems such as dBASE II, a field contains an item of information. It corresponds to a column of information on a paper database.

FIELD DESCRIPTION
A field description consists of three parts: the field name, field type, and the field width including decimal places (if any).

FIELDNAME
The field "title." Containing ten or fewer characters, must begin with a letter, and may not contain blank spaces.

FIELD SIZE
The number of character positions needed to contain the data to be placed in the field.

FIELDTYPE
The kind of data that may be stored in a field. The three fieldtypes are character, numeric, and logical.

FIELDWIDTH
The number of spaces needed in the field to contain the data.

FILE
A collection of information such as a database file or a command file stored as an identifiable unit on a disk.

FILE<"filename">
A function used to test for the existence of a file.

FILENAME
Used to identify the file to the computer. Must contain eight or fewer characters, must begin with a letter, and may not contain any blank spaces.

FILETYPE
A three-character extension on the filename following the filename and a period. Used to distinguish among different file types with the same name and to identify to the computer certain kinds of files which it has been programmed to deal with in a specific way. As an example, .DBF file is recognized by dBASE II as a database file.

FIND<key>
A dBASE II command to find the record with the key. May be used only with indexed files.

FLOPPIES
Floppy disks.

FLOPPY DISK
A storage medium commonly used on microcomputers. Information is stored on a thin flexible mylar disk.

FLOPPY DISK SYSTEM
A computer system which uses floppy disks.

FORMAT FILE
Special file used to produce video "forms".

FORTRAN

A traditional computer language used mainly in scientific application. Acronym for Formula Translator.

GET

A dBASE II command which is used in conjunction with the @ command to display the contents of a field or a memory variable. When used in conjunction with the READ command, the contents of the field or memory variable may be changed by simply typing in the new information.

GO BOTTOM

A command which makes dBASE II go to the last record in the database being used.

GO TOP

A command which makes dBASE II go to the first record in the database being used.

GOTO <record number>

This command is used to reposition the record pointer of the database to the named record number.

HARD DISK

A disk which is a rigid metal plate covered with magnetic film; capable of storing large amounts of data.

HARD DISK SYSTEM

A computer system which uses hard disks.

I/O

A mechanism by which the commputer accepts and distributes the information among the peripheral devices. An acronym for Input/Output.

IF <condition>

A statement that tells the computer to execute a set of commands provided that a condition is satisfied.

INDEX ON <fieldlist> TO <filename>

A dBASE II command which creates an index file with the named filename. The index file causes the contents of the database file to appear to be arranged in the logical order of the contents of the listed fields.

INPUT TO <memory variable name>

A dBASE II command which allows keyboard input of numeric data to a memory variable. Only numeric data will be accepted. Normally used within procedures.

INSERT
A dBASE II command which inserts a new data record into the middle of a database file.

INT( )
A function which will round off a number which has a decimal by throwing away everything to the right of the decimal point. Short for integer.

JOIN
A command which outputs the JOIN of two relational databases.

KEYBOARD
A device similar to a typewriter keyboard by which a user may "talk" to a computer.

LEN (memory variable name)
A dBASE II function that tells you how many characters are in the named string memory variable.

LIST
A dBASE II command to display all data records in a database continuously.

LOCATE FOR<condition>
A dBASE II command used to find a record that satisfies the condition.

LOGICAL FIELDS
Fields with only two possible contents. Used when there will only be two possible mutually exclusive entries such as "T" and "F" or "Y" and "N".

LOGICAL RECORDS
Records in an index file or another similar file which are "images" of part of the actual data. Normally used as an aid to using the actual data.

LOOP
A command which causes execution of a command file to skip back to the beginning of DO WHILE. It is used as an escape when some undesired condition is encountered.

MASS MEMORY
Peripheral storage devices such as disk drives and tape drives.

MEMORY VARIABLE
Allows you to store information in the computer's main memory for your temporary use. Similar in concept to memory on an electronic calculator. All information is lost when machine is turned off.

MENU
A computer procedure that displays a set of choices for action.

MENU SYSTEM
A computer procedure that uses a menu selection to choose a course of action for the computer to follow.

MICROCOMPUTER
A small computer designed principally for use by a single user.

MILLISECOND
1/1000th of a second.

MINICOMPUTER
A small computer that is generally configured for simultaneous use by a small number of people. Slightly larger and more powerful than a microcomputer.

MODIFY COMMAND
A dBASE II command that allows you to create and/or edit the contents of a procedure (command file).

MODIFY STRUCTURE
A dBASE II command that allows you to change the structure of a database. Changing the structure will usually destroy the database contents. The command should be used with care.

MS-DOS
Microsoft Disk Operating System. MS-DOS is a registered trademark of Microsoft.

NOTE <text material>
A dBASE II command (normally used in procedures) which causes the computer to ignore the text that is written on the line. Used to describe the procedure for future reference.

NUMERIC FIELDS
Fields that contain numbers that are meant to be used in numeric calculation.

OPERATING SYSTEM
Software that makes your computer hardware system into a computer.

PACK
A command which physically DELETEs all records marked for deletion.

PASCAL
A computer language having some of the features of dBASE II.

PC
Personal Computer — this has recently become synonymous with the IBM PC and other similar computers.

PERIPHERALS
Devices used with the computer such as a printer and disk drives.

PHYSICAL RECORDS
The actual data records.

PIP
A CP/M® command that allows you to copy computer files from one disk to another.

PL/1
A modern computer language. PL/1 stands for Programming Language One.

POINTER
A software mechanism that directs the computer to the database record of interest.

PRIMARY KEY
A unique way of identifying the record that is directly usable by the computer system. In dBASE II, the PRIMARY KEY is the record number.

PRINTER
A peripheral device which outputs data from the computer onto paper.

PROGRAM
A series of commands to be executed by the computer as a unit. A procedure is a program. In dBASE II a command file is a program.

PROGRAMMER
Any person who writes programs.

PROMPT
An indication from the computer that it is ready to accept keyboard commands. Also a request for specific information to be input from the keyboard.

QUERY

A user request for information from the computer. Normally a keyboard request.

QUIT

A command that causes dBASE II to close all files currently being used and exit to the operating system.

RAM

An acronym for Random Access Memory. This is normally the computer's main memory. Random access memory is really computer memory that is directly addressable and can be written to as well as read from.

RANK( )

Function to return the ASCII value (in decimal) of a printable character.

READ

A dBASE II command which is used in conjunction with the GET command to perform full screen (cursor) editing of the contents of memory variables and data fields.

RECALL

A dBASE II command which "undeletes" records previously marked for deletion.

RECORD

An integral unit of data items. In dBASE II, it is that information which is contained on a row in a rectangular table of rows and columns.

RECORD LOCKOUT

An artifice to protect against possible simultaneous editing of a single data item in systems where there may be more than one user at a time.

RECORD NUMBER

An identifying number assigned to each data record by the database management system. The record number is unique for each record (no two records have the same record number).

RELATIONAL DATABASE SYSTEM

A type of database management system based on the use of rectangular tables of rows and columns. Different database files are linked (related) by the contents of a data field where the field contents may be common to both database files.

RELEASE <memory variable names>

A dBASE II command which "erases" the named memory variables.

RENAME <filename1> TO <filename2>
A dBASE II command to rename a file. The file cannot be currently in use.

REPLACE <fieldname> WITH <new contents>
A dBASE II command which replaces the contents of the named data field with the desired new contents. Most often used within procedures. May be effectively used from the keyboard in conjunction with FOR <condition>.

REPORT
A dBASE II command which prepares a report based on the contents of a database and your answers to a series of simple questions. The report is displayed on the CRT. The answers to the questions are entered from the keyboard for the first use of a specific report. The answers are saved in a .FRM file and the report will thereafter be generated automatically. There may be many reports available at any one time.

REPORT TO PRINT
A variation of REPORT that causes the report to be printed.

RETURN
A command which ends a command file and returns to the next higher procedure. Control returns to the keyboard if there is no higher procedure.

RETURN KEY
Similar to the carriage return key on a typewriter. Should probably be labeled as ENTER on a computer terminal.

ROM
An acronym for Read Only Memory.

RUB
A key which deletes the character to the left of the cursor.

SAVE
A command which copies the currently defined memory variables to mass storage.

SAY
A dBASE II command used in conjunction with the @ operator to display the information on the CRT or the printer.

SCREEN ATTRIBUTE
Special video characteristics such as reverse video.

SELECT PRIMARY
A command that selects the PRIMARY database.

SELECT SECONDARY
A command that selects the SECONDARY database.

SEQUENTIAL ACCESS
An access method for data records whereby the computer examines each record sequentially — beginning with the first record — until the desired record(s) are located.

SET ECHO ON/OFF
All commands which come from a command file are echoed on the screen as if they had been entered from the keyboard. ECHO is normally off and must be turned on if needed.

SET PRINT ON/OFF
Routes the computer output to the printer. Normally output is not directed to the printer.

SET TALK ON/OFF
The results from commands are normally displayed on the CRT. This is often undesirable when using command files.

SKIP[n]
A command which positions the database forward or backward a number of records.

SORT
A command which will cause the database to be physically rearranged into some desired order — normally by the numerical value of some field(s) or alphabetically according to the contents of a character field.

STORE
A command which stores data into memory variables.

STR( )
Function that treats a numeric variable as if it were a character string.

STRING
Shorthand for a character string such as "John Doe".

STRUCTURE
The predefined organization of your database. It is established by the fieldname, fieldtype, and fieldwidth.

SUB STRING
A part of a character string. For example, "John" is a substring of the variable "John Doe."

SUM<fieldname>
A command that adds the contents of the named fields.

TERMINAL
The means by which you communicate with your computer and it communicates with you. The most popular terminal devices with microcomputers are video display terminals.

TEXT
dBASE II command to display text without the need to use delimiters to identify the text.

TYPE
This function is the data type function and yields a "C", "N", or "L" depending on whether the one-character string is, respectively, Character, Numeric, Logical or "U" (undefined).

UPDATE
A command which merges records from two databases.

USE<filename>
A command which tells dBASE II which database you want to work with.

VAL(x)
Allows the contents of a character data field or memory variable to be used in arithmetic calculations.

VIDEO SCREEN
The video display device associated with your computer.

WAIT
A command file command that interrupts command file processing and waits for a single character input from the keyboard with a WAITING prompt.

WAIT TO<memory variable name>
The same as WAIT except that the TO clause causes the keyboard character to be stored in the named memory variable.

ASHTON·TATE

INDEX

A

B

C

D

E

F

G

H

I

J

K

L

M

N

O

P

Q

R

S

T

U

V

W

SURVEY

Thank you for purchasing dBASE II for Every Business.

Our readers are important to us. Please take a few moments to provide us with some information, so we can better serve you.

Once we receive your reader survey card, your name will be kept on file for information regarding program disks to accompany the book.

Name: ____________________

Company Name: ____________________

Address: ____________________

City/State: ____________________ Zip Code: __________

Country: ____________________ Date: __________

1) How did you first learn about this publication?

21-1 ( ) Someone who saw or bought it
-2 ( ) Software dealer or salesperson
-3 ( ) Hardware dealer or salesperson
-4 ( ) Advertising
-5 ( ) Published review
-6 ( ) Computer store display
-7 ( ) Computer show
-8 ( ) Book store
-9 ( ) Directly from Ashton-Tate

2) Where did you purchase this publication?

22-1 ( ) Directly from Ashton-Tate™
-2 ( ) From my dBASE II® Dealer
-3 ( ) Computer show
-4 ( ) Book store

3) Have you purchased other Ashton-Tate products?

23-1 ( ) Yes -23-2 ( ) No

If Yes, please check which ones:

23-3 ( ) dBASE II®
-4 ( ) Friday!™
-5 ( ) dBASE II RunTime™
-6 ( ) dNEWS™
-7 ( ) *Through the MicroMaze*
-8 ( ) *Everyman's Database Primer*
-9 ( ) *Reference Encyclopedia for the IBM® Personal Computer*

4) What type of software programs are you using now?

24-1 ( ) Accounting
-2 ( ) Sales
-3 ( ) Word Processing
-4 ( ) Other (Please specify) __________

5) What type of information-management software programs are you interested in?

25-1 ( ) Academic/Scientific
-2 ( ) Agriculture
-3 ( ) Building
-4 ( ) Business
-5 ( ) Financial
-6 ( ) Health Care
-7 ( ) Home/Hobby
-8 ( ) Insurance
-9 ( ) Membership/Registry
-10 ( ) Professional
-11 ( ) Real Property
-12 ( ) Software Utilities

6) What software do you expect to purchase from this catalog?

26-1 __________

7) Who are you purchasing the software for?

27-1 ( ) Business
-2 ( ) Self

8a) Who will be the actual user of the software?

28-1 ( ) I will be
-2 ( ) Someone else will be

Title: __________

8b) What make and model computer do you use?

28-3 __________

9) Do you expect to purchase any other software programs during the next 12 months?
If so, what type?

29-1 ( ) Accounting
-2 ( ) Sales
-3 ( ) Inventory
-4 ( ) Other (Please specify) __________

10) What software programs would you like to see developed?

30-1 __________

11) How can we improve this catalog?

31-1 __________

12) What is your primary business?

A. Computer Industry

32-1 ( ) Manufacturing
-2 ( ) Systems house
-3 ( ) DP supply house
-4 ( ) Software
-5 ( ) Retailing
-6 ( ) Other __________

B. Non-Computer Business

33-1 ( ) Manufacturing
-2 ( ) Retail trade
-3 ( ) Wholesale trade
-4 ( ) Financial, banking
-5 ( ) Real estate, insurance
-6 ( ) Engineering
-7 ( ) Government
-8 ( ) Education
34-1 ( ) Military
-2 ( ) Health services
-3 ( ) Legal services
-4 ( ) Transportation
-5 ( ) Utilities
-6 ( ) Communications
-7 ( ) Arts, music, film
-8 ( ) Other __________

13) What is your position and title?
Please check one in each list.

POSITION

35-1 ( ) Data processing
-2 ( ) Engineering
-3 ( ) Marketing/Advertising
-4 ( ) Sales
-5 ( ) Financial
-6 ( ) Legal
-7 ( ) Administration
-8 ( ) Research
-9 ( ) Operations/production
-10 ( ) Distribution
-11 ( ) Education
-12 ( ) Other __________

TITLE

35-13 ( ) Owner
-14 ( ) Chairperson
-15 ( ) President
-16 ( ) Vice President
-17 ( ) Director
-18 ( ) Manager
-19 ( ) Dept. head
-20 ( ) Independent contractor
-21 ( ) Scientist
-22 ( ) Programmer
-23 ( ) Assistant
-24 ( ) Other __________

14) How many employees are in your company?

36-1 ( ) Less than 10
-2 ( ) 10 to 25
-3 ( ) 26 to 100
-4 ( ) 101 to 300
-5 ( ) 301 to 1,000
-6 ( ) over 1,000

15) I would like to remain on your mailing list.

37-1 ( ) Yes 37-2 ( ) No

38-1 I'd like to purchase additional copies of the current edition of *Application Junction* at $19.95.

☐ My check is enclosed.

My MasterCard/Visa card number is:

____

Expiration date __________

Signature of cardholder __________

NO POSTAGE
NECESSARY
IF MAILED
IN THE
UNITED STATES

BUSINESS REPLY MAIL

FIRST CLASS PERMIT NO. 959 CULVER CITY, CA

POSTAGE WILL BE PAID BY ADDRESSEE

ASHTON·TATE™

10150 WEST JEFFERSON BOULEVARD
CULVER CITY, CALIFORNIA 90230